THE MAYA

MICHAEL D. COE
STEPHEN HOUSTON

THE MAYA

NINTH EDITION

WITH 213 ILLUSTRATIONS,
28 IN COLOUR

Thames & Hudson

Ancient Peoples and Places
FOUNDING EDITOR: GLYN DANIEL

FRONTISPIECE Figure of a dancing king from
a wall panel in Structure I3R-5, La Corona,
Guatemala. Dedicated 28 October AD 677, this
image shows a local ruler, vassal of the powerful
dynasty of Calakmul. He wears an elaborate back
ornament, labeled *paat pihk*, "back-skirt." Such
ornaments often appear with depictions of the
dancing Maize God, perhaps alluding to cosmic
and geographical motifs. In this "back-skirt,"
the Principal Bird Deity perches on a symbol for
"sky," from underneath which emerges a snake,
an emblem of Calakmul.

First published in the United Kingdom in 1966 by Thames & Hudson Ltd,
181A High Holborn, London WC1V 7QX

Ninth edition 2015

British Library Cataloguing-in-Publication Data
A catalogue record for this book is available from the British Library

ISBN 978-0-500-29188-7

Printed and bound in China by Toppan Leefung Printing Limited

To find out about all our publications, please visit **www.thamesandhudson.com**.
There you can subscribe to our e-newsletter, browse or download our current
catalogue, and buy any titles that are in print.

CONTENTS

PREFACE

It has been almost fifty years since the first edition of *The Maya* appeared. Michael Coe wrote the book in the belief that the time was ripe for a concise and accurate, yet reasonably complete, account of these people that would be of interest to students, travelers, and the general public – one, preferably, that could be carried in the pocket while visiting the stupendous ruins of this great civilization. In all subsequent editions, he has tried to keep to these goals. As the decipherment of the hieroglyphs proceeded, it became possible to let the Maya express themselves in their own voice, as the previously mute inscriptions began to speak. With that aim in mind, and to represent a younger generation, Coe has brought on board a co-author, Stephen Houston, his student at Yale and another authority on Maya writing and civilization.

In the last decade, the pace of Maya research has quickened to an extraordinary extent. Hardly a week goes by without the announcement of a new royal tomb or discovery, especially at the close of the dry season, when such finds tend to be made. Based upon new research exploring Maya glyphs and iconography, as well as upon technological advances in fields such as remote sensing and paleonutrition, major archaeological advances have been made in Mexico, Guatemala, Belize, and Honduras. We now know a great deal about how to conceptualize Maya societies as the seats of royal courts. Coming into view, too, are the "founding fathers" of such ancient cities as Copan and El Zotz, and the places from which they came. The historical role of Calakmul looms far larger than imagined by earlier researchers, as does the relative independence of zones like coastal Belize, or the varying nature of societies in areas less endowed with inscriptions. Palenque, which has a history of archaeological investigation reaching back into the eighteenth century, now seems to have had a mighty king (Ahkal Mo' Nahb); nothing more to us than a name a decade ago, this ruler was responsible for some of the greatest sculptural art ever produced by the Maya. Perhaps the most exciting new developments in scholarship center upon San Bartolo, in the forests of northeastern Guatemala, where amazing murals dating back two millennia have been discovered – the oldest Maya paintings yet known – or in sites nearby, such as Holmul and Xultun, celebrated in recent years for their glyphic texts, paintings, and monumental stuccos; Calakmul, with its unique murals of everyday life in a large market; and Ek' Balam, an extraordinary site in Yucatan with long painted texts and some of the most astonishing stucco reliefs ever found. These elite remains are matched by an ever more sophisticated understanding of environmental change and modest settlement at places around Xunantunich, Belize, Chunchucmil in Yucatan, or the ancient kingdom of Palenque and its neighbors. Yet some puzzles still remain to be solved: above all, the nature of Preclassic civilization, the features of Maya society in Highland Guatemala, and what really happened during the transition between the Classic and Postclassic periods. Was there truly a "Toltec-Maya" occupation of the huge site of Chichen Itza? Unfortunately, until the day that Chichen becomes treated more as a major site crying out for broad-scale excavation, and less as a venue for mass tourism, those questions will not be answered.

Here we have relied on the advice and learning of numerous colleagues, including those who have recently passed away, especially Pat Culbert, Peter Harrison, Barbara Kerr, Juan Pedro Laporte, Enrique Nalda, Juan Antonio Valdés, and Houston's first professor of all things Maya, Robert Sharer. We are particularly indebted to Thomas Garrison, Takeshi Inomata, and Scott Simmons, who gave useful comments on many points in the manuscript. Others on whom we have relied for new information (but they may not always know this!) are Jaime Awe, Tim and Sheryl Beach, Marcello Canuto, Arlen and Diane Chase, Ramón Carrasco, Oswaldo Chinchilla Mazariegos, John Clark, George Cowgill, Francisco Estrada-Belli, Claudia García-Des Lauriers, Charles Golden, Heather Hurst, Scott Hutson, David Joralemon, Justin Kerr, Brigitte Kovacevich, Rodrigo Liendo Stuardo, Simon Martin, Sam Merrin, Mary Miller, Sofia Paredes Maury, Jorge Pérez de Lara, Michelle Rich, Rob Rosenswig, Frauke Sachse, Catharina Santasilia, William Saturno, Andrew Scherer, David Stuart, Karl Taube, Alex Tokovinine, Ben Watkins, David Webster, Brent Woodfill, Marc Zender, and Jarosław Źrałka. However, if there are mistakes in this book, they are ours alone.

A word about words: here, glottalized consonants are indicated by a following apostrophe (as in *k'ahk'*, "fire"). The only exceptions to these new rules will be the names of sites so well known in the literature, and to students and tourists, that it would be confusing to change their spelling (such as Tikal, which logically ought to be Tik'al). Throughout, vowels have about the same pronunciation that they have in Spanish; long vowels are indicated by doubling, as in *muut*, "bird," a feature that has, with other sounds, been detected over the last decade or two in Maya writing. Unglottalized consonants are pronounced approximately as in English, with these exceptions:

'	the glottal stop (in initial position, or between two vowels); it most closely resembles the tt in the Cockney English pronunciation of bottle
h	a glottal fricative, as in German *ach* or *Bach*
q	a postvelar stop, like a guttural k, restricted to highland Mayan languages
tz	a voiceless sibilant consonant, with the tip of the tongue held against the back of the teeth
x	like English sh

Certain of the words that the reader will encounter here are in Nahuatl, the national tongue of the Aztec state, which was a great trading lingua franca at the time of the Spanish Conquest (recent research also points to the influence of its linguistic cousin, Pipil). Nahuatl names were transcribed in Roman letters in terms of the language spoken by the *conquistadores* of the sixteenth century. Neither they nor Maya names have been accented here, since both are regularly stressed: Maya ones almost always on the final syllable, and Nahuatl ones on the penultimate. Note, too, that the names of Mayan languages have recently changed, often after consultation with local speakers [6, 7]. Yet this can also lead to confusion: "Yukatekan" refers to a set of related languages, "Yucatecan" to an area.

Readers may well wonder about the sources of the exotic-sounding names for ancient cities and archaeological sites that appear in these pages. Some of these are in bona fide Yukateko Maya, and were in use in early Colonial-period Yucatan, such as Uxmal, Chichen Itza, Coba, and Tulum; but these may or may not have been the original names of these places. Acanceh, Ek' Balam, and Mayapan in Yucatan definitely were so. Others are patently Hispanic, for example Piedras Negras ("black rocks"), Ceibal ("place of ceiba trees"), Palenque ("fortified place"), Naranjo ("orange tree"), and El Mirador ("the overlook"). Not a few have been bestowed by the archaeologists themselves, drawing upon one or another Mayan language, not always accurately; among these are Bonampak, Uaxactun, Xunantunich, Kaminaljuyu, and Takalik Abaj. Recent epigraphic work has shown that the Peten site of Yaxha was really called exactly that in Classic times; but also that the true Classic name for Tikal was *Mut*, and that for Palenque, *Lakamha*. Other ancient city names are sure to emerge as hieroglyphic research progresses.

There have been important advances in the accurate correlation of dates derived from radiocarbon determinations with those of the Christian calendar. Dendrochronological studies of the bristlecone pine show that before about 700–800 BC there is an increasing deviation from "true" dates back to a maximum of some 800 years at radiocarbon 4500 BC. The last few years have also seen great progress in Mayanist calibration of radiocarbon dates, especially through Bayesian statistics, a means of weighting and excluding radiocarbon data. Such methods, applied persuasively by Takeshi Inomata among others, help to exclude improbable samples and link diverse sets of evidence, such as ceramics. For this reason, in something of a departure from past editions, we have elected to use calendar years (BC and AD) throughout much of the book. That said, radiocarbon dating has no real bearing on the chronology of the Classic Maya period (*c.* AD 250–900), which depends upon the accuracy of the correlation between the Long Count calendar and the European Christian calendar. The correlation favored here is by Simon Martin and Joel Skidmore (the 584286 constant, for specialists). All Christian equivalents are given in terms of the Gregorian Calendar. Finally, to figures: readers will see numbers in square brackets in the text, each of which corresponds to an in-text figure or one of the grouped plate images.

DATES	PERIODS	SOUTHERN AREA		CENTRAL AREA	NORTHERN AREA	SIGNIFICANT DEVELOPMENTS
Calibrated		Pacific Coast	Highlands			
1530	**Late Postclassic**	Aztec Xoconocho	Mixco Viejo	Tayasal ↑	Independent states	*Spanish Conquest* *Highland city-states*
1200					Mayapan	*League of Mayapan*
	Early Postclassic	Tohil Plumbate	Ayampuk		Toltec Chichen	*Toltec hegemony in Yucatan*
925	**Terminal Classic**	Cotzumalhuapa	Quen Santo	Bayal/ Tepeu 3	Puuc, Maya Chichen	*Toltec arrive in Yucatan* *Classic Maya collapse, Putun ascendancy*
800	**Late Classic**		Amatle- Pamplona	Tepeu 2 1	Early Coba	*Bonampak murals* *Height of Maya civilization* *Reign of Janahb Pakal at Palenque*
600	**Early Classic**	Tiquisate	Esperanza	Tzakol 3 2 1	Regional styles, Acanceh	*Teotihuacan interference and influence*
250	**Late Preclassic**	Izapan styles ↑ Crucero	Aurora Santa Clara Miraflores	Matzanel Holmul I Chicanel	Late Preclassic	*First lowland Maya dated stela at Tikal* *Massive pyramid-building in lowlands, San Bartolo* *Spread of Izapan civilization, calendar, writing*
AD BC						
300	**Middle Preclassic**	Conchas Jocotal	Las Charcas Arévalo	Mamom Cunil Horizon	Middle Preclassic	*Earliest lowland Maya villages, temple centers*
1000	**Early Preclassic**	Cuadros Cherla Ocós Locona Barra				*Early Olmec influence on Pacific Coast* *Beginnings of social stratification* *Origins of village life, pottery, figurines*
1800	**Archaic**	Chantuto		Belize Archaic		*Some maize horticulture* *Hunting, fishing, gathering*
3000						

CHRONOLOGICAL TABLE

1

▼▼▼▼▼▼▼▼▼▼

INTRODUCTION

The Maya are hardly a vanished people, for they number around five million souls, the largest single block of American Indians north of Peru. Most have adjusted with remarkable tenacity to the encroachments of Spanish American civilization, although over the past few decades these have taken an increasingly violent and repressive form, characterized of late by drug trafficking, displacement, migration abroad, and, in places, gang activity. Yet the Maya endure with dignity, and a growing sense of joint purpose; if in the past they did not view themselves as one group, a pan-Maya identity is stronger now than ever before.

Besides their numbers and cultural integrity, the Maya are remarkable for an extraordinary geographic cohesion. Unlike other more scattered indigenous peoples within Mexico and Central America, at the time of the Spanish Conquest the Maya were confined (with the exception of the Wastek) to a single, unbroken area that includes all of the Yucatan Peninsula, Guatemala, Belize, parts of the Mexican states of Tabasco and Chiapas, and the western portion of Honduras and El Salvador [1]. There are few parts of the world where there is such a good "fit" between language and culture: a line drawn around the Mayan-speaking peoples would contain all those archaeological remains and hieroglyphic texts assigned to the ancient Maya civilization. Such homogeneity in the midst of a miscellany of tongues and peoples testifies to their relative security from invasions by other native groups – the Aztecs, for instance, never extended their empire to include any part of Maya territory, although they had important trading relationships with them.

It would be an error, though, to think of these peoples as existing in some kind of vacuum. An earlier generation of archaeologists, which included the late Sylvanus Morley of the Carnegie Institution of Washington, thought of the Maya as great innovators, and in fact culture-givers to the rest of the peoples of Mexico and Central America. A later generation came to view this fundamentally "Mayacentric" outlook as wrong, believing that the ancient Maya had received much more from the non-Maya Mexican civilizations than they had given. We must now admit that Morley may have been more right than wrong, for reasons that will be made clear in this book. The point to remember is that the Maya were probably always in contact with their sister civilizations in this part of the New World, and that these peoples all profoundly influenced each other throughout their

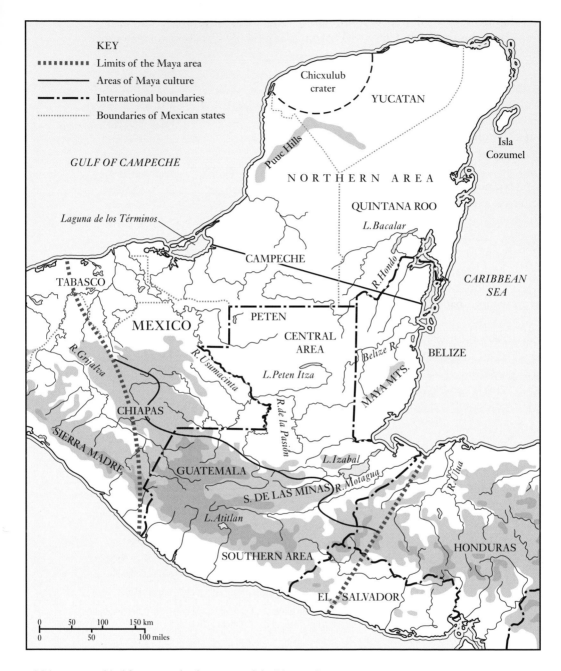

KEY
▪▪▪▪▪▪▪▪▪ Limits of the Maya area
────── Areas of Maya culture
━·━·━·━ International boundaries
·············· Boundaries of Mexican states

Chicxulub crater

YUCATAN

Isla Cozumel

GULF OF CAMPECHE

Puuc Hills

N O R T H E R N   A R E A

QUINTANA ROO

L. Bacalar

Laguna de los Términos

CAMPECHE

R. Hondo

CARIBBEAN SEA

TABASCO

PETEN

MEXICO

CENTRAL AREA

R. Usumacinta

L. Peten Itza

Belize R.

BELIZE

MAYA MTS.

R. Grijalva

CHIAPAS

R. de la Pasión

L. Izabal

SIERRA MADRE

GUATEMALA

S. DE LAS MINAS *R. Motagua*

R. Ulua

L. Atitlan

HONDURAS

SOUTHERN AREA

EL SALVADOR

0   50   100   150 km
0   50   100 miles

1 Major topographical features and culture areas of the Maya region.

development; this will become abundantly clear when we examine the relations between the Early Classic Maya and the great city of Teotihuacan in the Valley of Mexico.

In pre-Spanish times the Maya belonged to the geographical area christened "Mesoamerica" by anthropologist Paul Kirchhoff. The northern frontier coincided approximately with the limits of aboriginal farming in Mexico, the desiccated plateau beyond holding only the possibility of humble collecting and hunting. To the southeast, the Mesoamerican border ran from the Caribbean to the Pacific across what is now Honduras and El Salvador, although in late pre-Conquest times it is apparent that north-westernmost Costa Rica was Mesoamerican in culture. This southeastern frontier generally divided the Maya from peoples of foreign tongue who had different kinds of settlement and material culture. All the Mesoamerican Indians shared a number of traits which were more or less peculiar to them and absent or rare elsewhere in the New World: hieroglyphic writing, books of fig-bark paper or deerskin that were folded like screens, a complex calendar, knowledge of the movements of the planets (especially Venus) against the dynamic background of the stars, a game played with a rubber ball in a special court, highly specialized markets, human sacrifice by head or heart removal, an emphasis upon self-sacrifice by blood drawn from the ears, tongue, or penis, and a highly complex, pantheistic religion which included nature divinities as well as deities emblematic of royal descent. All Mesoamerican religions imagined a cosmic cycle of creation and destruction, and a universe with specific colors and gods assigned to the four cardinal points and to the center. This was an area with close interaction and settled life going back for millennia, and remaining vibrant up to the Conquest and later.

While there are profound differences between the subsistence base of the lowlands and that of the highlands, the ancient foursome of maize, beans, chile peppers, and squash formed then, as it still does, the basis of the Mesoamerican diet. Of course these foods were widely spread elsewhere, from the southwestern United States to Peru and Argentina in pre-Conquest times; wherever native cultures had moved beyond a level of seminomadic lifeways. In Mesoamerica, nonetheless, the preparation of maize is highly distinctive: the hard, ripe kernels are boiled in a mixture of water and white lime, producing a kind of hominy (*nixtamal*) which is then ground into unleavened dough on a quern (*metate*) with a handstone (*mano*), later to be fashioned into steamed *tamales* or into the flat cakes known by the Spanish term *tortillas*. The latter, perhaps introduced into the Maya area in late pre-Conquest times from Mexico, are characteristically toasted on a clay griddle (*comal*) which rests upon a three-stone hearth.

The importance of the *nixtamal* process cannot be overstressed. Maize is naturally deficient in essential amino acids and in niacin (a member of the vitamin B complex). A population whose diet consisted solely of untreated maize would be malnourished and particularly prone to developing pellagra, a vitamin deficiency disease which can cause dementia and even death. Cooking with lime (in Mesoamerica and the American Southwest) or with ashes (in North America) enhances the balance of essential amino acids and frees the otherwise unavailable niacin. Without the invention of this technique, no settled life in Mesoamerica would have been possible. The development of more productive varieties of maize seems also to have triggered large-scale increases in population, a topic to be explored in Chapters 2 and 3.

Given the similarities among the diverse cultures of Mesoamerica, one can only conclude that its peoples must share a common origin, so far back in time that it may never be brought to light by archaeology. Yet there is some consensus among archaeologists that the Olmecs of southern Mexico had elaborated many of these traits beginning over 3,000 years ago, and that much of complex culture in Mesoamerica has an Olmec origin. It is also reasonable to assume that there must have been an active interchange of ideas and things among the Mesoamerican elite over many centuries, a state of affairs which can be documented in the Terminal Classic epoch thanks to recent research; this in itself would tend to bring about cultural homogeneity. It was out of such a matrix of cultural innovation and contact that Maya civilization was born.

THE SETTING

There can be few parts of the globe as geographically diverse as Meso-america, which includes almost every ecological extreme from the snow-swept heights of volcanoes to parched deserts and to rain-drenched jungle [2]. The Maya area is situated in the southeastern corner of this topsy-turvy land, and is somewhat less varied than the larger unit of which it is a part. High-altitude tundra is not found, and deserts are confined to narrow stretches along the upper Río Negro and middle Río Motagua. Tropical forest is – or was – more extensive here than in Mexico outside the Maya area.

There are really two natural settings in the land of the Maya: highlands and lowlands. In their geology, their animal and plant life, and the form that human cultures took within them, these are well set off from each other. The Maya highlands by definition lie above 1,000 ft (305 m) and are dominated by a great backbone of both extinct and active volcanoes, some over 13,000 ft (3,960 m) in altitude, which curves down from southeastern Chiapas toward lower Central America. This mighty cordillera has been formed principally by massive explosions of pumice and ash, of Tertiary and Pleistocene age, that have built up a mantle many hundreds of feet thick overlain by a thin cover of rich soil. Millennia of rain and erosion have produced a highly dissected landscape, studded with deep ravines between steep hogback ridges, but there are a few relatively broader valleys, such as those of Guatemala City, Quetzaltenango, and Comitán, which have long been important centers of Maya life. To the north of the volcanic cordil-lera is a band of even more ancient igneous and metamorphic rocks, and

2 Lake Atitlan in the Maya highlands. This view, photographed by Eadweard Muybridge in the 1880s, shows native traders carrying loads of pottery to market.

beyond this a zone of Tertiary and Cretaceous limestones which, in the more humid country bordering the lowlands, takes the fantastically eroded appearance of a Chinese landscape. Isolated to the northeast are the Maya Mountains, a formation of similar antiquity.

Highland rainfall is dependent, as in the rest of the New World tropics to the north of the equator, upon a rainy season which lasts roughly from May through early November. Trade winds bring storms from the Atlantic and Caribbean, the areas most intensely heated by the sun during this time of year. The rainy season follows a double-peaked distribution in both the highlands and lowlands, with the heaviest falls in June and October. For the highlands, the greatest rainfall is registered along the Pacific slopes of Chiapas and Guatemala, a zone noted in pre-Conquest days for its cacao production, which flourishes under moist conditions. In general, however, the precipitation for the Maya highlands is no greater than for the temperate countries of northern Europe.

The highland flora varies according to soil and topography; on the dry tops of slopes and ridges, pines and grasses dominate, while further down in the wetter ravines, oaks flourish. Compared with that of the lowlands, the wild fauna is not especially abundant, but this may be due to the far denser human occupation.

Native farming practices in the highlands are quite different from those of the lowlands, although inhabitants of both regions depend upon the burning of unwanted vegetation and upon rest periods for farm plots. The moderate fallowing practiced in the highlands depends upon the position of the field on the slope, with only about ten years of continuous cultivation possible in higher fields, after which the plot must be abandoned for as many as fifteen years, while at lower altitudes up to fifteen years continuous use with only a five-year rest is practicable. In densely populated areas of Highland Guatemala, almost all the available land may be cleared or in second-growth; today, commercial agriculture, including cattle-ranching and the cultivation of fruit, flowers, vegetables, and coffee sent to North America, crowds out more traditional agriculture. Several kinds of maize are planted over the year; tilling is by furrowing and, after the sprouts have appeared, by making hillocks. In these maize fields, or *milpas*, secondary crops like beans and squashes, or sweet manioc, are interplanted, as well as chile peppers of many sizes, colors, and degrees of "hotness." In summary, while it utilizes the same kinds of plants as the lowlands, the highland system of agriculture seems to be well-adapted to an area of high population with good, deep soils where the competition posed by heavy forests and weeds is not a major problem.

But it is the lowlands lying to the north which are most central to the story of Maya civilization. A greater contrast with the highland environment can hardly be imagined, as every tourist flying to visit the ruins of Tikal from Guatemala City must have realized. The Peten-Yucatan Peninsula is a single, great limestone shelf about 9,840 ft (3,000 m) thick. It juts up into the blue waters of the Gulf of Mexico, which borders it on the west and north; its reef-girt eastern shores face the Caribbean. These limestones have risen from the sea over a period of some 30 million years. The uplift has been greatest in the older Peten and Belize region of the south; the topography here is more rugged, with broken karst hills rising above the plain. As one moves north to Yucatan itself, the country becomes flatter – it looks like a featureless, green carpet from the air, but this is deceptive, for on foot the pitting of the porous limestone is all too apparent. In the northern reaches of the peninsula, the only notable topographical variation is the Puuc range, a chain of low hills no more than a few hundred feet high strung out like an inverted "V" across northern Campeche and southwestern Yucatan. In this general region a 6-mile wide meteor collided with Earth 66 million years ago, creating the Chicxulub crater and, in its margins, an area abounding in sinkholes today. Its impact was global, causing the mass-extinction of all dinosaurs other than the ancestors of birds.

Unlike the sierra to the south, there are few permanently flowing rivers in the lowlands, except in the west and in the southeast, where extensive alluvial bottomlands have been formed. The great Usumacinta with its numerous tributaries is the most important system, draining the northern highlands of Guatemala and the Lakandon country of Chiapas, twisting to the northwest past many a ruined Maya city before depositing its yellow silts in the Gulf of Mexico. Sizeable rivers flowing into the Caribbean are: the Motagua, which on its path to the sea cuts successively through pine and oak-clad hills, cactus-strewn desert, and tropical forest; the Belize River; the New River; and the Río Hondo, which separates Belize from Mexico.

The lowland climate is hot; uncomfortably so toward the close of the dry season. In May come the rains, which last until December, but compared with other tropical regions of the world these are not especially abundant. In much of the Peten, for instance, only about 70–90 inches (178–229 cm) fall each year, and moving north to Yucatan there is a steady decrease from even this level. Nor are these rains reliable; in bad years there may be severe droughts. Really heavy precipitation is, however, found in the far south of the Peten and Belize; in the Lakandon country of Chiapas [3]; and in the Tabasco plains, which are covered with great sheets of water during much of the summer. For this reason they were largely shunned by the pre-Conquest Maya.

Lakes are rare in the lowlands, especially in the Yucatan Peninsula. The absence of ground water in many regions makes thirst a serious problem. In the Peten of northern Guatemala, there are broad, wetland depressions, or *bajos*, which fill during the summer but are often dry in the rainless winter season. Smaller and similarly seasonal waterholes called *aguadas* are found in some places in Yucatan, but there the major source of drinking (and bathing) water for the inhabitants is the *cenote*, a word corrupted by the

3 Lakandon Maya in the Chiapas rainforest.

Spaniards from the Yukateko term *tz'onot*. These are circular sinkholes, some of great size, formed by the collapse of underground caves and, ultimately, by the effects of the Chicxulub crater. Because the deeper parts of *cenotes* are perennially filled with water percolating through the limestone, these have necessarily served as focal points for native settlement since the first occupation of the land. Along the coast of the Mexican state of Quintana Roo are yet larger caverns, including Ox Bel Ha, likely the longest underwater cave in the world.

The relative aridity of the northern half of the peninsula presented especially grave problems to the inhabitants of the Puuc area, where *cenotes* are largely nonexistent. According to geographer Nicholas Dunning and art historian Jeff Kowalski, the water table lies at least 210 ft (65 m) below the surface, and even deep caves could never have supplied the needs of the dense populations of the Puuc. As a response, the Maya excavated and constructed thousands of underground bottle-shaped cisterns called *chultunob* (sing. *chultun*), the entrances of which were surrounded by broad, plastered aprons to catch the water which fell during the rainy season.

A high monsoon forest (now largely destroyed by unrestrained lumbering, farming, and above all cattle-ranching) once covered the southern lowlands, dominated by mahogany trees towering up to 150 ft (45 m) above the jungle floor, sapodillas, which gave wood to the ancients and chewing-gum to ourselves, and the breadnut tree. Many fruit trees important to the Maya grew here, such as the avocado. The forest was only partly evergreen; in the dry season many species dropped their leaves. But in a few places favored by higher rainfall, there was real, nondeciduous rainforest. The diversity of species here is among the highest in the world. According to the naturalist David Wallace, Central America – which encompasses much of the Maya region – hosts 7% of the planet's life, squeezed into under 0.5% of its land.

Interspersed in the monsoon forest, particularly in the Peten and southern Campeche, are open savannahs covered with coarse grasses and dotted with stunted, flat-topped trees. There is no real agreement on the origin of these savannahs, but modern opinion has turned away from the idea that they were created by the ancient Maya through over-cultivation of the land. On the other hand, they were certainly maintained, for while they were avoided by farmers, they were periodically burned off by hunters so as to attract game to new grasses which sprouted in the ashes. When Cortés and his army crossed these grasslands on their way to the Itza capital of Tayasal, they came upon a herd of sacred deer that had no fear of humans, and thus allowed themselves to be easily slaughtered by the *conquistadores*. To the north and west, where there is a profound drop in annual rainfall, the forest turns into a low, thorny jungle, finally reaching the state of scrub (especially adapted for dry conditions) along the northern shore of the Yucatan Peninsula.

For the ancient Maya, there was a rich fauna in the lowlands. Deer and peccary abounded, especially in Yucatan, which the Maya called "The Land of the Turkey and Deer." Spider monkeys and the diminutive but noisy howler monkeys were easy to hunt and well-favored in the native cuisine. Among the larger birds were the ocellated turkey, with its golden-green plumage, the curassow, and the guan. More dangerous beasts were the jaguar, largest of the world's spotted cats, which was pursued for its resplendent pelt as well as for sacrificial offerings, and the water-loving tapir, killed for both its meat and its incredibly tough hide, employed in making shields and armor for Maya warriors. Also lurking in *milpa* and jungle, and to be avoided at all costs, were vipers such as the dreaded *barba amarilla*, or "yellow jaw" (*Bothrops asper*), among the most aggressive snakes in the world.

Of more importance to the development of Maya civilization was the agricultural potential of the lowlands, which was by no means uniform. Some of the soils of the Peten and the Puuc range of southwestern Yucatan are deep and fertile, but these are restricted to a mosaic pattern of various-sized pockets, as Scott Fedick of the University of California, Riverside, has shown. The larger the area covered by such soils, the larger the Classic populations and the centers which they supported. As for northern Yucatan, the sixteenth-century Franciscan bishop, Diego de Landa, our great authority on all aspects of Maya life, tells us that "Yucatan is the country with least earth that I have seen, since all of it is one living rock and has wonderfully little earth." It is small wonder that the early Colonial chronicles speak much of famines in Yucatan before the arrival of the Spaniards, and it might be that the province relied less upon plant husbandry than upon its famed production of honey, salt, and slaves.

It is now almost universally recognized, albeit unwillingly, that many tropical soils which are permanently deprived of their forest cover quickly decline in fertility and become quite unworkable as a layer of brick-like laterite develops on the surface. Tropical rainfall and a fierce sun, along with erosion, do their destructive work in a surprisingly brief span, and agricultural disaster results. On such soils about the only kind of farming possible is that practiced by the present-day lowland Maya – a shifting, slash-and-burn system under which the forest is permitted to regenerate at intervals. While seemingly simple, it requires great experience on the farmer's part. A patch of forest on well-drained land is chosen and cut down in late fall or early winter; the larger trees are usually left, for shade and to prevent erosion. The felled wood and brush are fired at the end of the dry season, and all over the Maya lowlands the sun becomes obscured by the smoke and haze which cover the sky at that time [4]. The maize seed is planted in holes poked through the ash with a dibble stick. Then the farmer must pray to the gods to bring the rain.

A cleared plot or *milpa* usually has a life of only two years, by which time decreasing yields no longer make it worthwhile to plant a third year. The Maya farmer must then shift to a new section of forest and begin again, leaving his old *milpa* fallow for periods which may be from four to seven years in the Peten, and from fifteen to twenty years in Yucatan. Before recent forest destruction, when seen from the air the landscape looked like

4 Burning a lowland *milpa* or maize field at Uaxactun, Peten, Guatemala.

some great patchwork quilt of varying shades of green, a veritable mosaic of regenerating plots and new clearings.

Was shifting cultivation the only system of food production practiced by the ancient Maya? In 1972, the geographer Alfred Siemens and the late Dennis Puleston reported their discovery from the air of extensive areas of raised fields in southern Campeche. These are narrow, rectangular plots elevated above the low-lying, seasonally inundated land bordering rivers or *bajos*, and are remarkably similar to the chinampas on which Aztec agriculture was based in central Mexico. Sporadic evidence for ancient raised fields has since been found in northern Belize [5] and in adjacent Quintana Roo, where water levels vary little through the annual cycle of dry and wet seasons. Radiocarbon analysis suggests that most of them date to the Late Preclassic (prior to AD 250) and Classic (AD 250–800), and thus could have provided the subsistence base for the increase in population which we know for that period. Timothy Beach and Sheryl Luzzadder-Beach of the University of Texas at Austin have proposed that these fields were probably a creative response to rising water levels, a worrisome shift in the environment.

Some Mayanists, such as the late Patrick Culbert of the University of Arizona, have proposed that the immense, swampy *bajos* that cover about 40% of the central and northeast Peten could have been cultivated by ancient farmers. It is certainly true that in this region, and away from the river systems, most Classic sites are situated on higher ground within or contiguous to these interior wetlands. It is possible that farmers planted their maize on the rich soils that border the *bajos*. Maize does very poorly in wet ground, but, as archaeologist Vernon Scarborough has pointed out, the *bajos* progressively dry out during the winter months, and some kind of flood-recession farming may have been practiced. Linear features crossing the *bajos* may have doubled as roads or dams. All this, however, remains speculation, and many of the *bajos* are very likely to have been watery places in the Preclassic period. Stone-walled terraces which probably acted as silt traps, most dating to the Classic period, are common in various localities in the lowlands, especially in western and northern Belize and in the Río Bec region of southern Campeche. Some involved laborious construction, as at Caracol, Belize; others, such as those found by Stephen Houston at Tamarindito, Guatemala, were no more than small raised banks to capture eroding soil.

The claims that the Classic Maya were almost totally dependent upon the techniques of intensive maize agriculture are probably exaggerated

5 Prehistoric Maya raised fields in Blue Creek area, northern Belize. Rectangular plots can be seen out on the floodplain.

through the understandable enthusiasm created by new finds. Much of the Maya lowland area is, and was, unsuitable for raised fields or for terracing, and it remains certain that most of the maize eaten by the pre-Conquest lowland Maya was grown in *milpa* plots by the still-used methods of shifting cultivation. Nevertheless, plants other than maize, particularly root crops, may have played an important role in the Maya diet, as first suggested by Bennett Bronson. Sweet manioc, for instance, does very well in the lowlands, is easy to propagate, and requires very little attention. Also important were the house gardens, still ubiquitous in Maya villages and hamlets; these would have fostered avocados, papayas, sweetsops, guavas, and a host of other native fruits.

What all this means is that the lowlands could have been far more densely occupied by the Classic Maya than we would have estimated under the old, monolithic *milpa* hypothesis. This conclusion is reinforced by surveys of ancient ruins in northern Yucatan, which reveal virtually continuous occupation from one end of the survey area to the other, implying a pre-Conquest population far higher than today's. One view perceives as many as eight to ten million people in the lowlands *c.* AD 800; David Webster of Pennsylvania State University would go as low as two to three million. Yet few archaeologists feel especially confident about their estimates. These new facts and hypotheses also bear upon the question of what proportion of this population would have been released from their agricultural pursuits to engage as full-time participants in the making of Maya civilization; they may also bear, if controversially, upon the question of why it collapsed (Chapter 6).

NATURAL RESOURCES

From the time of their initial contact with the Maya, the Spaniards learned (to their bitter disappointment) that there were no sources of gold and silver in the Maya lowlands, and soon came to look upon the region as a hardship post. Yet the native inhabitants, to whom the yellow metal was of little value and in fact almost unknown until *c.* AD 800, had abundant resources which were of far greater importance to them in their daily life, rituals, and trade.

Construction material in the form of limestone occurred almost everywhere; since it only hardens after prolonged exposure to the air, it was easily quarried and worked with their stone-age technology. In some of the limestone beds of the southern lowlands the Maya found deposits of flint and chert, from which they chipped the axes absolutely essential for slash-and-burn farming. Even in very early times, flint-working communities sprang up to exploit this resource, the great workshop at Colha in northern Belize, for example, having been founded far back in the Preclassic period. But rock harder than limestone was necessary for the production of the *manos* and *metates* used in grinding maize dough; trading networks brought vast quantities of these objects down from the volcanic regions of Guatemala and the granitic outcrops of the Maya Mountains in Belize. The volcanic high-lands, above all the great pumice and obsidian exposures at El Chayal and San Martín Jilotepeque, to the northeast and northwest of Guatemala City respectively, also yielded obsidian – a natural volcanic glass. As archaeologist Robert Cobean has noted, obsidian was to ancient Mesoamerica what steel is to modern civilization. It was turned into knives, lance and dart points, prismatic blades for woodworking and shaving, and a host of other tools.

The human body demands a constant concentration of sodium in the blood, as this element is lost by excretion. Meats are rich in sodium, so that a primarily hunting people such as the Inuit (Eskimo) do not need to take in salt, but tropical farmers like the Maya require about 8 g of salt a day to maintain their sodium balance. The archaeologist Anthony Andrews calculates that a great Classic city like Tikal, with, by his reckon-ing, a population conservatively estimated at 45,000, would have had to import over 131 tons of salt each year. Happily, the greatest salt sources in all Mesoamerica lie within the Maya area. The must lucrative were the salt beds along the lagoons of Yucatan's north coast. There, grids of shallow, rectilinear pans (still in use) allowed the lagoon water to evaporate during the dry season. Once a thick layer of salt had hardened, it was raked up and transported in baskets. On the eve of the Conquest, these beds were controlled by Yucatan's most powerful kingdoms, and their product was traded to places as distant as the Río Pánuco in northern Veracruz. Similar conditions existed along the Pacific Coast, but there and at important inland mineral-spring sources, such as Bolontewitz on the Río Chixoy, the brine was cooked down rather than sun-evaporated. Recently, firm evidence for Late Classic salt boiling has been found within the mangrove-lined lagoons of southern Belize by archaeologist Heather McKillop. Regardless of method, access to salt sources or to salt trade networks was critical to the growth and security of Maya states.

The Maya elite had other special needs, above all jade, quetzal feathers, and marine shells. Green jade was obtained along the middle and upper reaches of the Río Motagua, where it occurs as pebbles and boulders in the river deposits; an ancient source of blue-green jade was rediscovered in 1998, when torrents from Hurricane Mitch dislodged overlying soil and rock. The highly prized tail feathers of the quetzal, which flash blue, green, and gold in dazzling iridescence, were obtained from the bird's natural habitat, the cloud forests of Alta Verapaz and the Sierra de las Minas in Guatemala, Chiapas in southeastern Mexico, and Honduras. Many thousands of such feathers saw their way into the gorgeous costumes of Maya rulers and their retinues, so that the quetzal may well have been near extinction by the time Maya civilization collapsed in the ninth century AD. The most prized shell was the beautiful red-and-white thorny oyster (*Spondylus* sp.), obtained by divers from waters off the Caribbean and Pacific coasts. Large numbers of conch shells (*Strombus* sp.) were also imported by the inland Maya, and used as trumpets in ceremonies, in warfare, and in the chase.

AREAS

The Maya occupied three separate areas, each distinct in nature: Southern, Central, and Northern, the latter two entirely within the lowlands.

The Southern Area includes the highlands of Guatemala and adjacent Chiapas, together with the torrid coastal plain along the Pacific and the western half of El Salvador. In general, the Southern Area differs markedly from its counterparts. Some of the most characteristically Maya traits are missing: the corbel vault in architecture and, except in Late Preclassic times, the Maya Long Count and the stela-altar complex. Much of the region, such as the central and western Chiapas highlands, was only occupied by Mayan-speakers at a relatively late date.

It was in the Central Area that Maya civilization crystallized into the form by which it is most widely known today. Focused upon what is now the Department of Peten in northern Guatemala, it reaches from Tabasco, southern Campeche and Quintana Roo across the densely forested southern lowlands to include Belize, the Río Motagua of Guatemala, and a narrow portion of westernmost Honduras. All the most typically Maya traits are present in this region – architectural features such as the corbel vault and roof comb, the fully developed Long Count, hieroglyphic writing, the stela-altar complex, and many others. These triumphs, however, were registered during the Classic period. Since the opening decades of the tenth century AD, much of the area has been a green wilderness with pockets of limited or dispersed population.

As one would expect, the Northern and Central Areas have much in common, since there are virtually no natural barriers to cultural exchange or movements of peoples between the two. But there are clear differences as well. In part this is because the agricultural potential of much of Yucatan is poor. Places where people may live in large concentrations (cities and towns) are often dictated by the distribution of *cenotes* and waterholes. Other differences are cultural, the result of Mexican influences to be discussed in Chapter 7. In contrast to the southern lowlands, there was no mass abandonment of the Northern Area; many of the cities were depopulated, but people dispersed into the countryside. Overall native population figures remain high even today.

PERIODS

The discovery of the ancient Maya civilization was a piecemeal process. Local inhabitants regarded the ancient buildings as the haunted abodes of ancestors and mythic beings. European recognition came later. Following the imposition of Spanish power in the Yucatan Peninsula, various persons, such as the formidable Bishop Landa, or Fray Antonio de Ciudad Real who visited the famous site of Uxmal in 1588, wondered at the age of the mighty ruins which lay scattered across the land, but they could discover little from the natives. Real interest in Maya remains only began after the publication, in a London edition of 1822, of the pioneering explorations and excavations which Antonio del Río, a Spanish captain of dragoons, had made at the site of Palenque in the late eighteenth century. Del Río was accompanied by the Guatemalan artist Ricardo Almendáriz, whose drawings were reasonably accurate. Modern Maya archaeology, however, stems from the epic journeys undertaken between 1839 and 1842 by the American diplomat and lawyer, John Lloyd Stephens, and his companion, the English topographical artist Frederick Catherwood, which revealed the full splendor of a vanished tropical civilization to the world.

Stephens and Catherwood were the first since Bishop Landa to assign the ruined "cities" which they encountered to the actual inhabitants of the country – to the Maya Indians rather than to the peripatetic Israelites, Welshmen, Tartars, and so forth favored by other "authorities" – but they had no way of even roughly guessing at their age. It was not until the Maya calendrical script had been studied by Ernst Förstemann, the State Librarian of Saxony, and others, and the magnificent publication of Maya inscriptions by the Englishman Alfred Maudslay at the close of the nineteenth century, that a real breakthrough was achieved in Maya chronology. In addition, large-scale excavations in Maya sites were begun at this time by the Peabody Museum of Harvard, to be followed by the Carnegie Institution of Washington, Tulane University, the University of Pennsylvania, and the Institute of Anthropology and History in Mexico.

The dating of the ancient Maya civilization now rests on four lines of evidence: "dirt" archaeology itself, particularly the stratification of cultural materials such as pottery; radiocarbon dating, in use since 1950 and since improved by advanced statistical methods; native historical traditions passed on to us by post-Conquest writers but bearing on the late pre-Conquest period; and the correlation of the Maya and Christian calendars. The correlation problem is an unbelievably complex topic which demands a few words of explanation. The Maya Long Count, which will be explained in greater detail in Chapters 3 and 9, is an absolute, day-to-day calendar which has run like some great clock from a point in the mythical past. Long Count dates began to be inscribed in 36 BC on present evidence and subsequently, during the Classic period, all over the ancient cities of the Central and Northern Areas. By the time of the Conquest they were expressed in a very abbreviated and somewhat equivocal form. Now, it is explicitly stated in native chronicles (the Books of Chilam Balam) that the Spanish foundation of Mérida, capital city of Yucatan, which in our calendar took place in January 1542, fell shortly after the close of a specified period of the truncated Long Count. Bishop Landa, an impeccable source, also tells us that New Year's Day in a Maya system, the 52-year Calendar Round, fell on 16 July 1553 in the Julian calendar. All attempts to fit the Maya calendar to the Christian must take these two statements into account.

It so happens that there are only two correlations which meet these requirements as well as those of "dirt" archaeology. These are the 11.16 or Thompson correlation, and the 12.9 or Spinden correlation, which would make all Maya dates 260 years earlier than does the former. Which of these is correct? The ancient Maya spanned the doorways of their temples with sapodilla wood beams, many of which have not only survived but can be radiocarbon dated. A very long series of such samples from Tikal was run by the University of Pennsylvania and again, more recently, with more precise determinations from accelerator mass spectrometry. These studies give overwhelming support to the Thompson correlation. Another study, by Simon Martin and Joel Skidmore, clinches the matter by looking at Maya eclipse records that can be tied to scientific predictions. Most Mayanists are content: any other chronology would have played havoc with what we now think we know about the development of Maya culture over two millennia.

As we now understand it, the cultural sequence in the Maya area runs something like this. The earliest occupation of both highlands and lowlands was during the Early Hunters period, beginning at least 13,000 years ago, and ending with the close of the Pleistocene (Ice Age) *c.* 9500 BC. Before 2000 BC there were simple horticulturalists, hunters, and farmers following the "Archaic" lifestyle, far better known for the upland peoples of Mexico. During the Preclassic (or Formative) period, *c.* 2000 BC – AD 250, village-farming became firmly established in all three Areas; the first really intensive settlement of the Maya land. More advanced cultural traits (pyramid-building, the construction of cities, the inscribing of stone monuments, and the painting of murals) are found by the terminal centuries of the Preclassic, to the extent that some even wonder why this early florescence should not be included in the Classic which it presages. The spectacular Classic period, spanning *c.* AD 250–800, is defined as that interval during which the lowland Maya were erecting stone monuments dated in the Long Count. But a great and as yet unexplained cataclysm shook the lowlands from the late eighth through the ninth century. This is the Terminal Classic period, a complex time varying greatly by region. By the end of this phase the Classic cities had been largely abandoned, while the Northern and Southern Areas seem to have felt the impact of incursions either by Mexicans, or more likely, by Mexicanized Maya. Thus was inaugurated the Postclassic, which endured until the arrival of the bearded adventurers from across the seas.

PEOPLES AND LANGUAGES

While the cohesion of the Mayan-speaking peoples is quite extraordinary for any time or place, the linguistic family called "Mayan" contains a number of closely related but mutually unintelligible languages, the result of a long period of internal divergence [6]. A Maya from Yucatan would have the same trouble understanding an Indian from highland Chiapas as an Englishman would a Romanian. There have been several attempts to

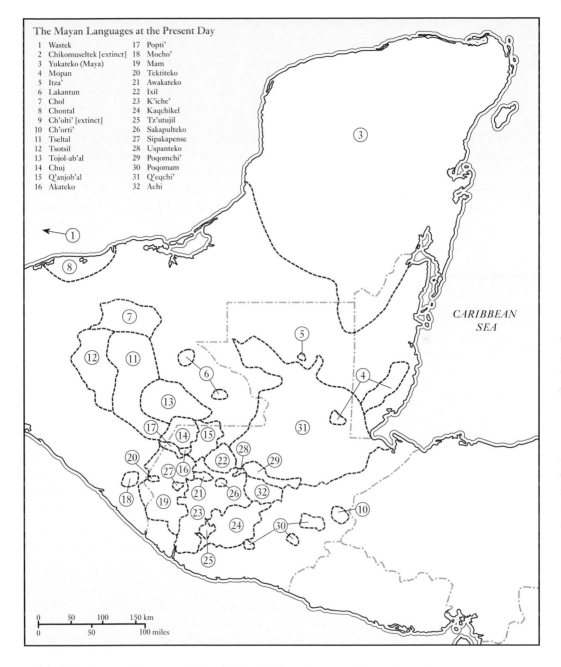

The Mayan Languages at the Present Day

1	Wastek	17	Popti'
2	Chikomuseltek [extinct]	18	Mocho'
3	Yukateko (Maya)	19	Mam
4	Mopan	20	Tektiteko
5	Itza'	21	Awakateko
6	Lakantun	22	Ixil
7	Chol	23	K'iche'
8	Chontal	24	Kaqchikel
9	Ch'olti' [extinct]	25	Tz'utujil
10	Ch'orti'	26	Sakapulteko
11	Tseltal	27	Sipakapense
12	Tsotsil	28	Uspanteko
13	Tojol-ab'al	29	Poqomchi'
14	Chuj	30	Poqomam
15	Q'anjob'al	31	Q'eqchi'
16	Akateko	32	Achi

CARIBBEAN SEA

0   50   100   150 km
0   50   100 miles

6 Colonial and present-day geographic distribution of Mayan languages. The numbers refer to language families in the key.

assemble a "family tree" of Mayan tongues according to their descent from a single language; the chart presented here follows the work of Danny Law of the University of Texas at Austin [7]. An ingenious method of vocabulary comparison developed by the late Maurice Swadesh has led some linguists to suggest approximate dates for the splitting-off of these from the ancestral Mayan language and from each other. It should be stressed, however, that there are many uncertainties built into this methodology; above all, the assumption that the rate of change or divergence in "basic" vocabularies is constant throughout time and space. Some specialists, basing themselves on Classic inscriptions, believe that such proposals are too speculative, in that they give hard dates that seem far too late. Nevertheless, even if this scheme proves to be wrong in absolute terms, it offers useful information about the overall relation of languages.

At some point in the distant past, there was a single Mayan language, Proto-Mayan, perhaps located in the western Guatemalan highlands. According to one linguistic scenario, Wastekan and Yukatekan split off from this parent body, with Wastek migrating up the Gulf Coast to northern Veracruz and Tamaulipas in Mexico, and Yukatekan occupying the Yucatan Peninsula. Of the Yukatekan languages, Yukateko today is the dominant tongue, spoken by townspeople and rural farmers alike, while Lakandon is represented by only a few hundred remaining natives inhabiting the Chiapas rainforest, or what is left of it, southwest of the Usumacinta. Once isolated and reclusive, the Lakandon sometimes wear their hair long and still make bows-and-arrows (now entirely directed at the tourist trade). They appear to be survivors of a larger group which began diverging from Yukateko after the Classic Maya collapse.

The parent body then split into two groups, a Western and an Eastern Division. In the Western group, the ancestral Ch'olan-Tseltalan moved down into the Central Area, where they split into Ch'olan and Tseltalan. The subsequent history of the Tseltalans is fairly well known: in Highland Chiapas, many thousands of their descendants, the Tsotsil and Tseltal, maintain unchanged the old Maya patterns of life. Of the Ch'olans, who played a major role in the Maya story, we will see more later. Other Western language groups include Q'anjob'al, Tojol-ab'al, Mocho', and Chuj, which stayed close to the probable homeland and which seem to have had less to do with the main developmental line of Preclassic and Classic Maya civilization.

The Eastern Division includes the Mamean group of languages. Mam itself spilled down to the Pacific coastal plain at an unknown time. Another Mamean language is spoken by the Ixil, a very conservative Maya group centered on the ancient town of Nebaj; they have been the principal target of a particularly bloody repression in recent times. Much of the late pre-Conquest history of the Southern Area concerns the powerful K'iche' and Kaqchikel of the Eastern Division. They and their relatives, the Tz'utujil, live in villages along the shores of the volcano-girt Lake Atitlan. Since the

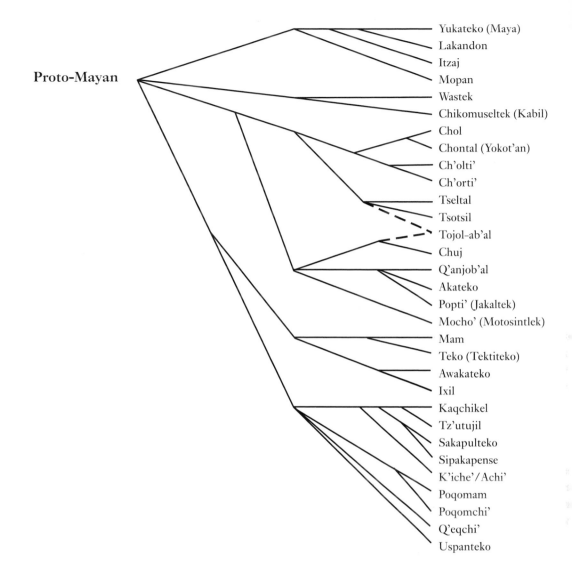

Proto-Mayan

Yukateko (Maya)
Lakandon
Itzaj
Mopan
Wastek
Chikomuseltek (Kabil)
Chol
Chontal (Yokot'an)
Ch'olti'
Ch'orti'
Tseltal
Tsotsil
Tojol-ab'al
Chuj
Q'anjob'al
Akateko
Popti' (Jakaltek)
Mocho' (Motosintlek)
Mam
Teko (Tektiteko)
Awakateko
Ixil
Kaqchikel
Tz'utujil
Sakapulteko
Sipakapense
K'iche'/Achi'
Poqomam
Poqomchi'
Q'eqchi'
Uspanteko

7 Classification and descent of the Mayan languages.

Conquest, a more dominant role has been taken by the Q'eqchi', who have expanded from a center in the Alta Verapaz of Guatemala to colonize southern Belize and the once Ch'olan-speaking lowlands around Lake Izabal, Guatemala, and are now the predominant non-Spanish linguistic group in the Peten. Indeed, they have resided there for less time than speakers of Spanish in historical communities like Dolores and Flores.

What, then, was the language recorded by the ancient Maya inscriptions and books? A glance at the linguistic map will show that the Yucatan Peninsula is occupied by Yukateko to the exclusion of all other languages, and there can be no quibbling that this was the daily speech of the Maya scribes of the Northern Area, including those who produced three of the four surviving codices. But it was not necessarily the language written down in these books. Yukateko is puzzling, as it shows relatively little variation across the peninsula, suggesting to some scholars a relatively late expansion of the language or, alternatively, social conditions that led to linguistic integration over a wide area.

Yukateko was probably spoken over much of Belize during the Classic, for Mopan in the southern part of the country belongs to this group. But much of the Central Area appears as a blank on the map, with the exception of those lands occupied by the Lakandon, by the surely recent Q'eq'chi, and by the Yukatekan Itzaj, who probably moved into the Peten from the north no earlier than the thirteenth century AD. The idea that the language of most of the inscriptions of the Central Area was Yukatekan has little to recommend it.

Some years ago the late Sir Eric Thompson proposed that the Central Area was inhabited by Ch'olan-speakers during the Classic period. From its present distribution alone – with Chontal and Chol in the low hills and plains in the northwest, and Ch'orti' in the southeast – it seems certain that Ch'olan once predominated across a great arc extending right through the Central Area, at least to the Belize border. We have some Spanish documents which confirm this point.

Recent linguistic and epigraphic research has thrown new light on this puzzle: the language of the inscriptions is neither Yukatekan nor even Western Ch'olan (Chontal and Chol proper), but rather an ancestral form of Eastern Ch'olan now called "Classic Ch'olti'an." Its direct descendants are Ch'olti', which was once spoken in the Motagua Valley but eventually became extinct when these people were relocated by the Spaniards to the highlands in the seventeenth century AD; and Ch'orti', still spoken by about 9,000 Maya living in the Department of Chiquimula, eastern Guatemala, directly west of the great Classic city of Copan. Tourists who travel overland from Guatemala to that beautiful site pass through villages where the inhabitants speak in a tongue that was once heard, in earlier form, at Copan, Tikal, and Palenque over a thousand years ago!

Early on, Classic Ch'olti'an became a literary language of high prestige among scribes throughout the Maya lowlands, and even among the

Yukatekan-speakers of the northern peninsula. There is ample evidence that even the inscriptions and Late Postclassic screenfold codices of the Northern Area basically record this same language, rather than Yukateko, although a certain amount of bilingualism is evident in these writings. In this, it played a role for the Maya similar to that of prestige languages in other civilizations. One thinks of Sumerian in Mesopotamia, Middle Egyptian along the Nile, Sanskrit in India and in the Hinduized cultures of Southeast Asia, and Literary Chinese: these, like Classic Ch'olti'an, continued to be the preferred written languages long after the spoken ones had died out or transformed into something else. Languages other than Mayan were found in isolated pockets, indicating either intrusions of peoples from foreign lands or remnant populations engulfed by the expansion of the Mayan tongues.

The somewhat shadowy Pipil (also known as Nawat), whose speech was very close to Nahuatl, the official language of the Aztec Empire, were concentrated in western El Salvador, but there were other Pipil communities on the Pacific Coast and in the Motagua and Salamá valleys of Guatemala. Some authorities think that they invaded the Maya country from Mexico during the Toltec disruptions of the Early Postclassic. Tiny populations of Zoquean speakers near the Pacific Coast in the Chiapas–Guatemala border region were probably vestiges of a once more-widespread distribution of the Mixe-Zoquean language family. Xinkan, with no known affiliations, seems to have extended over all the eastern part of the Pacific coastal plain before the arrival of Mayan and Pipil, but the Xinkan territory is an archaeological and ethnological blank. Nahuatl itself, as a great trading lingua franca, was spoken at the time of the Conquest at the port of Xicallanco on the Laguna de los Términos in southern Campeche. Loan words from other languages do appear in Mayan, testifying to early contacts and their cultural contributions. The Zapotecs of Oaxaca, who possibly invented the essentials of the Mesoamerican calendar and who might have been the first to use hieroglyphic writing, named several of the days in the 260-day count so fundamental to Maya thought. And in late times, during the Postclassic epoch, many words, names, and titles were introduced into the Maya area from Nahua speech by Mexican or Mexicanized warlords.

CLIMATE CHANGE AND ITS CULTURAL IMPACT

We have usually assumed that the climatic conditions which now prevail in the Maya area have always been the same, all through Maya prehistory and history. But recent paleoclimatic research has challenged this assumption, revealing far more climatic fluctuation than previously anticipated. Sediment cores taken in Lake Punta Laguna, not far from the Classic site of Coba in the eastern Yucatan Peninsula, reveal relevant evidence in the form of ostracods (tiny freshwater crustaceans). When incorporated into sediments, these express the relative levels of oxygen-16 and oxygen-18;

in water of enclosed tropical lakes, the abundance of these isotopes is controlled by the ratio of evaporation and precipitation. High concentrations of oxygen-18 mean low rainfall conditions, while oxygen-16 tends to evaporate away. Because samples could be dated with some degree of precision, there is now, thanks to many researchers, a continuous record of climate changes for the Maya lowlands extending over a period of 3,500 years. This has since been supplemented by research on stalagmites in Belizean caves. Growing slowly yet steadily, cave deposits show, with precision of a few dozen years, a similar pattern of droughts that lasted for decades. One episode struck between AD 200 and 300, another from AD 820 to 870, then two more at AD 1020 to 1100 and AD 1530 to 1580. Shorter, severe droughts occurred at AD 420, 930, and 1800. According to archaeologist Douglas Kennett, such cycles arose from the infamous El Niño, a shift in air pressure and water temperature that strongly affects weather in South America and beyond.

These results are striking, with profound implications for the study of the pre-Conquest Maya (and, obviously, for the ancient Maya themselves). During much of the Preclassic period, the climate was wet (low concentrations of oxygen-18); at this time, the now-swampy *bajos* were shallow lakes. But prior to the beginning of the Classic (*c.* AD 250), severe droughts afflicted the Maya region. As we shall see, this transition corresponds to the demise of the extraordinarily large Late Preclassic cities of the northeastern Peten. The most dramatic discovery is the drought from AD 820 to 870. As shown in Chapter 6, this period saw the collapse of Maya civilization in the southern Maya lowlands, to be followed somewhat later by the abandonment of the Puuc cities in the north. Now we have solid evidence from a number of sources that by the ninth century the Classic lowland Maya had severely degraded their environment to the point that high populations could no longer be sustained. There were lesser factors which probably played a part in the Collapse, but conditions of extreme drought, and year after year of crop loss, must have been the "nail in the coffin" that ended this brilliant cultural florescence.

Opposite
I Portion of a building in the Nunnery complex at Uxmal, as seen in a lithograph published in 1844 by the English topographical artist Frederick Catherwood.

II View of the cracked and fallen Stela C at Copan in a storm, from a lithograph of 1844 by Catherwood. Dedicated on 6 December AD 711, the monument depicts the 13th Copan ruler, Waxaklahun Ubaah K'awiil.

I

II

III Reconstruction view of the site of El Mirador, in the northern Peten, Guatemala. This Late Preclassic city was one of the greatest ever built in the Pre-Columbian Americas, and is testimony that Maya civilization flourished here centuries before the opening of the Classic.

IV

IV The stairway of this Early Classic temple-pyramid is flanked by red-painted deity masks, perhaps of solar gods with fire signs on their foreheads; Kohunlich, southeast Quintana Roo, Mexico. Fifth century AD.

V Stucco panel from Temple XIX, Palenque. The striding figure is Upakal K'inich, son and heir apparent of Ahkal Mo' Nahb III. Late Classic, eighth century AD.

VI Detail of mural, Structure B-XIII, Uaxactun. A Maya personage painted in black greets a visitor costumed as a Teotihuacan warrior. To the right is a palace scene with seated noble ladies. Tzakol culture, Early Classic.

VII Palenque's Temple of the Inscriptions, seen from the Palace. This temple-pyramid is the funerary monument of the seventh-century king Pakal the Great, who was laid to rest in a massive sarcophagus deep within its base. The temple superstructure contains a very long hieroglyphic record of his reign. Late Classic.

V

VII

VI

VIII View of the Caracol, Chichen Itza, Mexico. This unique circular building of the Terminal Classic period functioned as an observatory.

IX General view of Uxmal, looking north from the Great Pyramid. In the middle distance is the House of the Turtles, and beyond it the Nunnery Quadrangle (left) and the House of the Magician (right). These structures belong to the Terminal Classic period.

X The four-sided Castillo at Chichen Itza, a Toltec-Maya temple dedicated to the god K'uk'ulkan; the view is from the Temple of the Warriors. In the foreground is a so-called "chacmool," a reclining figure which may have been used for heart sacrifice. Early Postclassic.

VIII

2

▼▼▼▼▼▼▼▼▼▼▼

THE EARLIEST MAYA

The Popol Vuh, the great epic of the K'iche' Maya, recounts that the fore-father gods, Tepew and Q'ukumatz, brought forth the earth from a watery void, and endowed it with animals and plants. Anxious for praise and veneration after the creation, the divine progenitors fashioned human-like creatures from mud, but to mud they returned. Next a race of wooden figures appeared, but these mindless manikins were destroyed by the gods, and replaced by men made from flesh. These, however, turned to wickedness and were in their turn annihilated, as black rains fell and a great flood swept the earth. Finally true men, the ancestors of the K'iche', were created from maize dough. Neither tradition nor archaeology have thrown much light on Maya origins. Tribal memories are weak, and a combination of luxuriant vegetation and ephemeral sites has made the search for really early remains a challenge. Although open sites are extremely difficult to detect in the monsoon forests, because of the karst limestone characteristic of the Maya lowlands there are countless caves, many yet unexplored, which we now realize could have been used by hunters and gatherers.

EARLY HUNTERS

In spite of over eight decades of research, there is little agreement among archaeologists as to when the first settlement of the New World took place. One theory holds that the initial colonization of this hemisphere must have been made by Siberian peoples crossing Beringia, a thousand-mile-wide land bridge exposed during the last maximum of the Pleistocene when the sea level was far lower than it is today, some 14,000 years ago. Yet long before this, boats must have been used by the peoples of Eurasia, for recent evidence shows that isolated Australia was settled as early as 50,000 years ago. The presence or absence of the Bering Strait is thus not necessarily relevant to the problem: the very first Americans may well have taken a maritime route.

Opposite
XI A glory of Maya architecture, Structure 33 at Yaxchilan commemorates the local king, Bird Jaguar IV, although his son, Shield Jaguar III, ordered the construction. The high "roofcomb," a lattice-work of stone and plaster, may copy a perishable feature. Inside the temple sits the effigy of Bird Jaguar, and the front stairway covers a royal tomb, its occupant not yet identified. Late Classic, *c.* AD 780.

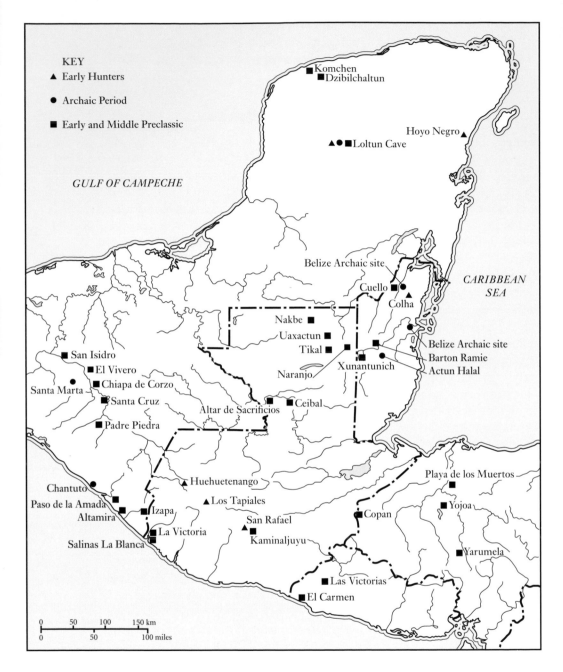

8 Sites of the Early Hunters, Archaic, and Early and Middle Preclassic periods.

While radiocarbon dates from human occupations in Pennsylvania, the Valley of Mexico, the Andean highlands of Peru, and more recently Brazil suggest to some scholars that American Indians had colonized both North and South America by at least 20,000 years ago, some authorities still do not accept these dates as valid, preferring a post-12,000 BC arrival. Nonetheless, the site of Monte Verde in Chile has revealed a very early occupation of southern South America by hunter-gatherers, with radiocarbon dates clustering, when calibrated, to *c.* 12,800 BC. There, excavations by Thomas Dillehay have uncovered a small village with log-built houses; wooden stakes had been driven into the ground to hold down structures. While the tool kit of these people lacks chipped projectile points, unifacial stone tools and pointed weapons of wood and bone were part of the artifact assemblage. By the eleventh millennium BC, the first Indians were already camped on the windswept Straits of Magellan at the southern tip of South America, and so we may assume that hunters had by then occupied all that part of the Americas that was worth inhabiting. Large areas of both continents (including the Maya lowlands) were grassland over which roamed great herds of herbivores – mammoths, horses, camels, and giant bison.

The eastern coastal plain of the Yucatan Peninsula is honeycombed with vast cave systems. Formed *c.* 125,000 years ago, when the sea level was about 200 ft (60 m) lower than it is today, these caverns were inundated from *c.* 10,000 years ago, in the Holocene, when the post-Pleistocene rise in world temperatures melted the great continental ice sheets. Today, exploration of most of them is only possible with scuba gear.

In 2007 a team of divers, led by Alberto Nava, descended into a *cenote* to the north of the small site of Tulum, swam through a kilometer-long passage, and finally reached a gigantic flooded chamber that they dubbed Hoyo Negro ("black hole"). At the bottom of this chamber were the bones of extinct mammalian species, alongside the upside-down cranium and long bones of a human individual [9]. Subsequent investigation proved that the skeleton was that of a teenage girl, who had probably tumbled in the deep chamber while seeking drinking water at a time when the cave was largely dry.

Some time after she died, calcite "florets" formed on her bones from dripping stalactites on the cave's ceiling before the waters rose. These have been radiocarbon dated to *c.* 12,900–12,700 years ago. Multiple lines of evidence make it certain, then, that the Hoyo Negro girl lived *c.* 11,000–10,000 BC. She is thus among the oldest known human inhabitants of the New World. Like other Late Pleistocene "Paleo-Americans" her skull is long and high, rather than broad like those of contemporary Native Americans (including the Maya). In the search for origins, this morphological discrepancy led some scholars to posit that the continent was first populated from Southeast Asia rather than Siberia and Beringia. But molecular evidence proves them wrong. Mitochondrial DNA demonstrates that one haplogroup in this girl's genotype matches that found throughout the native peoples of the New World, and probably evolved in Beringia from an Asian prototype.

9 Discovery of the Hoyo Negro skull, Mexico. The cranium belonged to a girl who died in the cave, then dry, perhaps while seeking deep sources of water, *c.* 11,000–10,000 BC.

The Yucatan Peninsula in these distant times bore little resemblance to today's familiar tropical forest and bush. It was then a broad, grass-covered plain, frequented by "big game" – extinct species like horses, mastodons, camelids, the elephant-like gompothere, giant ground sloths, and the fearsome sabertoothed cats, along with animals familiar today such as pumas, coyotes, and tapirs. These were undoubtedly hunted and trapped by the Hoyo Negro people.

In the western United States, Canada, and Alaska, where a number of camps belonging to this ancient epoch have been located, the earliest culture that has stood up to archaeological scrutiny is called Clovis, well dated to *c.* 13,000 years ago in calibrated radiocarbon dates. If we can rely upon the remains in several slaughtering sites in the American Southwest, the Clovis people lived mainly off mammoth-hunting, although in lean times they must have been content with more humble foods. These great elephants were killed by darts hurled from spear-throwers, fitted with finely chipped and "fluted" points from the bases of which long channel flakes had been removed on one or both faces [10, 11]. Clovis points are widely distributed, from Alaska to Nova Scotia, down through Mexico and into Central America. They have even been found in Costa Rica and Panama.

In 1969 archaeologists Ruth Gruhn and Alan Bryan discovered the highland Guatemalan site of Los Tapiales, which they excavated in 1973. It lies in an open meadow on the Continental Divide, in a cold, rainy, foggy environment, and probably represents a small, temporary camp of hunters located on an important pass. The stone tool industry is mainly basalt, and finds include the base of a fluted point, bifaces, burins, gravers, scrapers, and blades. Unfortunately no bone material has survived, and the site's radiocarbon dates are problematic. Luis Méndez Salinas and Jon Lohse have reported on a similar site, at Chivacabe, near Huehuetenango, Guatemala, with an obsidian point and other tools said to have been associated with the remains of megafauna. These and other sites are much disturbed by slumping soil and washouts, yet enough remains to show a certain parsimony with basic materials. The makers and users of the tools reworked them heavily, suggesting poor access to primary sources of obsidian.

Clovis is not the only kind of projectile point found in the Maya area. "Fishtail" points, named for their triangular shape with fluted and slightly splayed stems, probably evolved in the highlands and lowlands of South America during the terminal Pleistocene, and have occasionally been collected from the surface of sites in Belize. There are also many caves in Belize that hold promise for finding these or Clovis points in situ, one of which – Actun Halal – has produced bones from a spectacled bear and a peccary, as well as a cheek tooth from a horse.

10, 11 (*Left*) A fluted Clovis point of the Early Hunters period from San Rafael, west of Guatemala City. L. 2.5 in. (5.7 cm). (*Right*) Early Hunters-period stone tools from Los Tapiales, Totonicapan, Guatemala. *1*, burin; *2*, scraper; *3*, obsidian uniface.

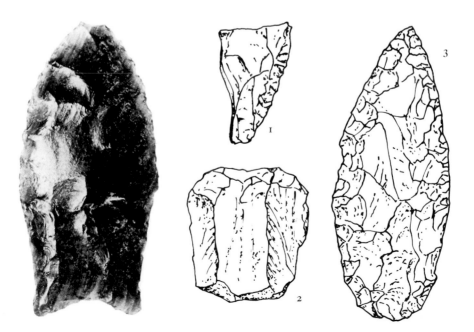

ARCHAIC COLLECTORS AND CULTIVATORS

By *c.* 10,000–9,000 BC, the ice sheets that had covered much of North America in the higher latitudes were in full retreat, and over the next 5,500 years the climate of the world was everywhere warmer than it is today. In Europe, this interval has been called the "Climatic Optimum," but in many parts of the New World conditions were by no means so favorable, least of all for hunters. A combination of hot, dry weather, which turned grasslands into desert, and likely over-hunting by humans finished off the big game. In upland Mexico, the Indians were diverted to another way of life, based on intensified collection of the seeds and roots of wild plants and hunting smaller, more solitary animals. In their economy, in their semi-nomadic pattern of settlement, and even in the details of their tool kits, the Mexican Indians of the Archaic period were part of the "Desert Culture," which extended at that time all the way from southern Oregon, through the Great Basin of the United States (where it survived into the nineteenth century AD), and down into southeastern Mexico.

It was in Mexico, however, in this "Desert Culture" context, that all the important plant foods of Mesoamerica – maize, beans, squashes, chile peppers, and many others – were first domesticated. It seems certain that the practice of plant cultivation reached the Maya area at some time during the Archaic period. An earlier generation of scholars, and particularly Sylvanus Morley, firmly believed that the Maya themselves had been the first to domesticate Indian corn (*Zea mays*). This idea was rooted on the often-revived premise that the wild progenitor of maize was *teosinte*, a common weed in cornfields of the western Guatemalan highlands. This premise used to be a subject of acrimonious dispute among botanists. One school of thought, led by the late Paul Mangelsdorf, contended that *teosinte* was not the ancestor of maize but its offspring through hybridization with another grass, *Tripsacum*, and that the real progenitor was a tiny-cobbed wild species of corn with small, hard kernels that could be popped. Cobs of this sort have been found in dry caves in the Tehuacan Valley of Puebla, Mexico, in levels dating to *c.* 3600 BC. According to Mangelsdorf, they represent ancestral maize; according to his opponents, they are probably *teosinte*. This complex problem has now been resolved. Modern genetic studies have proved beyond a shadow of a doubt that *teosinte* is the long-sought-for progenitor, and that this *ur*-maize first arose from a particular variety still grown in the Balsas River basin of southwestern Mexico.

Nevertheless, Guatemala (which is no larger than the state of Ohio) has more distinct varieties of maize than can be found in all the United States put together, which suggests that this must be a very old center for the evolution of this plant under human tutelage. Quite probably all the uplands, from southern Mexico through Chiapas and highland Guatemala, were involved in the processes leading to the modern races of this most productive of all food plants.

Evidence for the Archaic period is generally poor in the highlands, but it is improving in the Maya lowlands. We have some idea of what the Peten looked like then, based on analysis of windblown pollen recovered from cores in the Central Area. In general, the millennia after the Ice Age was a time of moist and forgiving conditions with a high degree of environmental stability. Tropical forests flourished throughout the zone. Only at the onset of regional drying (*c.* 3000–2000 BC) did this forest surrender to a more open agricultural landscape. Lakes and other lower areas contain deposits known as "Maya clays": thick, inorganic levels resulting from erosion as people began to work the soil. By 2500 BC a little maize was grown in the Peten, again to judge from cores and evidence of charcoal from the burning of forests. This was a good 1,500 years before the first pottery-using farmers are known for the region, raising the question of who these people might have been. If we accept the word of the linguists, they could have been the Yukateko on their trek north to Yucatan from the Maya homeland, but archaeology alone is seldom revealing about language or ethnicity. In any case, this period remains a mystery in the absence of sites across the Maya region.

Northeastern Belize is the exception, providing critical new data for our understanding of this shadowy epoch in the Maya lowlands [12]. The key sites are Colha, occupied right through the Classic period to exploit its high-quality chert, and several lake islands and uplands between Colha and Chetumal Bay, mostly within the drainage of Freshwater Creek. There, investigations by Thomas Hester of the University of Texas and his associates, and by Robert Rosenswig and Marilyn Masson, have shown that there are long periods of Archaic occupation, some at a surprisingly early

12 Chert tools of the Belize Archaic. *a*, hoe; *b*, Lowe point; *c*, scraper; *d*, macroflake.

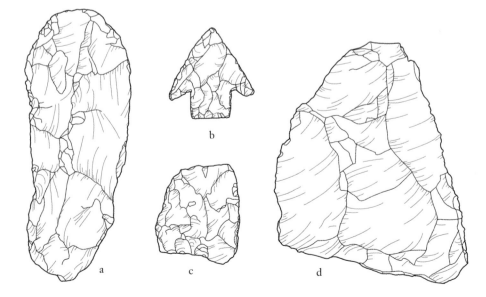

date: one site, Caye Coco, has been found to have maize use by *c.* 4700 BC and perhaps before. Preserved microfossils on tools display clear evidence of chile, beans, manioc, and maize. A kind of "index fossil" for the period is the Lowe Point; this is a stemmed, chert point averaging 3.5 in. (9.5 cm) in length, so large that it was probably used as the "business end" of a spear or harpoon rather than fitted on the end of an atlatl-propelled dart. An alternative hypothesis is that Lowe Points were fitted to short, wooden hafts and used as knives.

The diagnostic chert artifact for northern Belize's Late Archaic occupation (*c.* 4000–1000 BC) is what has been called a "constricted uniface," produced at local workshops in very large numbers along with large blade tools and other chipped artifacts. Microwear and experimental studies indicate that it was hafted and employed both to work wood and as a general-purpose digging tool. Again, large-scale forest clearance continued, and agriculture intensified. Additional data for the Late Archaic has been found in western Belize, at the small cave of Actun Halal. Well-dated to 2400–1200 BC, Archaic layers from this site produced pollen evidence for cotton horticulture as well as maize.

Two questions may be asked about the Belize Archaic. Were these sedentary villages? It is most likely that they were not; more likely, these sites represent little more than extensive, seasonally occupied camps for the exploitation of local soils and natural resources (including chert). Were these people Maya? Here we can only speculate, but the Texas archaeologists point out that there seems to be no discontinuity between the latest preceramic radiocarbon dates and the first appearance of pottery-using, sedentary villages by 1000 BC. This probably means that we can date the coming of Mayan-speaking, maize-farming people to the lowlands as far back as the third millennium BC.

There is further evidence for the Archaic on the south Pacific coast of Mexico, just beyond the limits of the traditional Maya area, in the region known today as Soconusco (the old Aztec province of Xoconochco). There, Barbara Voorhies and colleagues have traced the lifeways of the people during the Chantuto phase (*c.* 5500–1800 BC), corresponding to the Middle and Late Archaic. During these four millennia, the Chantuto people occupied residential bases on the inner coast, but made frequent forays to the mangrove-lined estuaries of the outer coast in order to collect clams, fish, and probably shrimp that teemed in the shallow lagoons. As a result, huge shell piles accumulated near the lagoons where the Chantuto people camped.

Over time, these foragers gradually made changes that ultimately resulted in the appearance of a new lifestyle. Year-round forays to the coast became limited only to the wet season, a shift that coincides with the first appearance of maize at the shell-mound sites, as evidenced by both phytoliths (microscopic elements of silica produced by the corn and other plants) and tools used to grind the corn kernels into dough. Simultaneously, a shift occurred in fishing practices: an early technique using boats, lines, and shell hooks to catch large, solitary fish was apparently abandoned in favor of catching small, schooling fish by means of nets or traps.

EARLY PRECLASSIC VILLAGES

Effective farming, as expressed by densely inhabited villages, was an innovation of the Preclassic period (*c.* 1800 BC – AD 250). What brought it about? Although some scholars favor the theory that it was a major improvement in the productivity of the maize plant, the adoption of the *nixtamal* process, which enormously increased the nutritional value of corn, may have been of more significance. Whatever the underlying cause, there was clearly some change in the centrality and usefulness of maize, with real consequences for Maya life in the lowlands at *c.* 1000 BC. Villages of thatched-roof houses, not very different from those of the modern Maya peasantry, now dotted the land.

Still, the evidence shows that the advance to Preclassic life did not take place everywhere at the same time. As will be seen, the Maya lowlands were remarkably backward in this respect, remaining for centuries on the preceramic, Archaic level for reasons that are as yet unclear. The crucial area for an understanding of the Early Preclassic in southeastern Mesoamerica is not the Peten or the Yucatan Peninsula, or even the Maya highlands, but the hot, humid Pacific littoral of Chiapas, Guatemala, and westernmost El Salvador, a region of winding rivers, highly fertile soils, and an extensive lagoon-estuary system just set back from the barrier beaches.

Research in this zone has focused on Soconusco, covering part of the coastal plain of Chiapas and adjacent Guatemala, where sedentary villages were foreshadowed by the shell middens of the Archaic, semi-sedentary Chantuto people. The Early Preclassic begins in Soconusco *c.* 1800 BC, and is marked by profound changes in settlement pattern, subsistence, technology, and society. During this period, which lasted until *c.* 1100 BC, settlements were located further inland, and consisted of permanent villages, occupied throughout the year. Significantly, they were placed next to a series of *bajos* which flooded during the rainy season. As they dried up, fish became concentrated in these and could be easily taken; at the height of the dry season, as archaeologists John Clark and Michael Blake have noted, the *bajos* could have served as sunken fields for agriculture, as they retained enough moisture for a third corn crop to be raised in addition to the two that are normal for the fertile Soconusco plain.

What crop or crops were being grown to support these developments? Maize cobs are found in Soconusco sites by *c.* 1700 BC, but these are from small and not very productive ears; further, carbon pathway analysis of human skeletal material has shown that maize was not very important in the diet of these Early Preclassic villagers. Gareth Lowe, of the New World Archaeological Foundation, and Michael Coe once speculated that they might have been relying on manioc or cassava, an ancient root crop of the

13 Reconstructed Barra-phase pottery, Pacific Coast of Chiapas, Mexico.

New World tropics, rather than maize, but the evidence for this remains elusive, and the case is unproven.

From a technological point of view, the most significant innovation was the invention or introduction of pottery, which appears at the beginning of the Barra phase (*c.* 1800 BC) [13]. Although Barra ceramics may well be the oldest in Mesoamerica, they are of remarkable sophistication and beauty. They largely consist of thin-walled, neckless jars (*tecomates*), the remainder comprising deep bowls. Vessel surfaces include monochromes, bichromes, and trichromes, and are decorated by the potter by grooving, incising, and modeling. As Clark and Blake make clear, these were not mere cooking vessels; based on forms and decoration of gourd prototypes, they were more likely containers for liquids and foods used during rituals. Then how did they cook? Discoveries of fire-cracked rock indicate that the technique was stone-boiling: rocks were heated, then dropped into water contained in waterproofed baskets.

Remarkably, chocolate – that great Mesoamerican gift to the rest of the world – had already been discovered by Barra times. This substance is produced by a complex process from the seeds of the cacao (*Theobroma cacao*) tree. It contains the alkaloid theobromine, which has been detected in trace amounts on Barra potsherds by Jeffrey Hurst, a chemist at the Hershey Foods Technical Center. It is thus likely that it was liquid chocolate that was kept in these magnificent vessels.

Barra sites also yield the first fired clay figurines in Mesoamerica, a craft tradition that was to continue throughout the Preclassic. Thousands of these objects, generally female, were made in Preclassic villages of both Mexico and the Maya area, and while nobody is exactly sure of their meaning, it is generally thought that they had something to do with the fertility of crops, in much the same way as did the female figurines of Neolithic and Bronze Age Europe.

Pottery becomes even more complex in the succeeding Locona phase (1600–1500 BC) [14], with the addition of rocker-stamping (carried out by "walking" the edge of a shell in zigzags across the wet clay) and of striping with a pinkish-iridescent slip. True cooking vessels now make their first appearance; more significant, however, is the evidence for the first ranked societies in this part of the New World. Clusters of villages and communities were organized under a single polity, dominated by a large "capital" village, which could have contained over 1,000 people. At one such "capital," excavators found the clay foundations of a very large, long house with apsidal ends and a floor area of 1,313 sq. ft (122 sq. m). This surely was a chiefly residence where public rituals were carried out, perhaps occupied over several generations.

Social differentiation in Locona is also suggested by the burial, found at El Vivero, Chiapas, of a child who had been covered with red pigment and who had a mica mirror on his forehead. Figurines depicting enormously fat men seated on stools and wearing chest mirrors and sometimes animal masks may represent shaman chiefs. Along with this increase in cultural and social complexity, we have the first evidence in Mesoamerica for the worship of a specific god. In 2002, at the site of Cuauhtemoc, Rosenswig excavated a Locona phase *tecomate* fragment with the effigy head of a duck-billed human face. Iconographic research by Karl Taube of the University of California, Riverside, has shown that this chimeric supernatural is the earliest known example of the pan-Mesoamerican Wind God. Locona is also the time in which the first pyramid occurs, as found by John Clark and John Hodgson at Ojo de Agua in Chiapas.

The subsequent Ocós phase (1500–1400 BC), discovered by Michael Coe and his wife in 1958, is in most respects a continuation of Locona, with the addition of a pottery decoration known as cord-marking, made by

14 Early Locona-phase hollow figurine head, from San Carlos, coastal Chiapas. Ht 3.5 in. (9 cm).

impressing the wet surface of the clay with a paddle wrapped in fine cotton twine – a technique unique in Mesoamerica, but common on the most ancient ceramics of east Asia and North America. Ocós figurines are highly sophisticated, many appearing to be almost anatomically perfect human caricatures out of the imagination of da Vinci, but with some armless representations of beautiful young women. After Ocós, the Soconusco region was strongly influenced by the Early Preclassic Olmec civilization of the Mexican Gulf Coast, but that is another story.

Now, Early Preclassic sites with materials and settlement patterns very similar to the Soconusco cultures have been located all along the Pacific littoral of Guatemala as far as El Carmen in El Salvador. In stark contrast, in spite of decades of intensive search and excavation, no pottery-using village culture of this age has yet been uncovered anywhere in the Central and Northern Maya Areas, or, for that matter, contemporaneous with the earliest known Olmec civilization of the Gulf Coast. This is one of the unexplained mysteries of Mesoamerican archaeology.

THE MIDDLE PRECLASSIC EXPANSION

If conditions before 1000 BC were less than optimum for the spread of effective village farming outside of the Pacific littoral, in the following centuries the reverse must have been true. Heavy populations, all with pottery and most of them probably Mayan-speaking, began to establish themselves in both highlands and lowlands during the Middle Preclassic period, which lasted until c. 400 BC. Most Maya at this time were still peasants grouped into as-yet-unclear forms of social organization: there was no writing, only a few buildings that, judged by their scale and necessary labor investment, could be called architecture, and hardly any development of art in its elite form.

Something very different, however, had been taking place in Mexico, on the hot coastal plain of southern Veracruz and adjacent Tabasco. This was the developing Olmec civilization, which emerged in the Early Preclassic, reached its peak toward the end of the Middle Preclassic, and then suddenly collapsed (as would the Maya, much later). So far, the oldest known Olmec site of great size is San Lorenzo, lying near a branch of the Coatzacoalcos River in Veracruz. Excavated by a Yale expedition between 1966 and 1969, and by the Mexican National University ever since, this Early Preclassic site dates back to 1400 BC with a fully developed Olmec culture, represented typically by gigantic basalt sculptures fashioned in a distinctive style [15]. The site is Mesoamerica's first urban capital, covering about 1,235 acres (500 ha), and was built of earth and clay above a natural plateau. By c. 1150 BC, San Lorenzo was destroyed by an unknown

15 (*Opposite*) Monument 52 at San Lorenzo, Veracruz, a representation of the Olmec maize god as an infant. San Lorenzo phase (1400–1150 BC), Early Preclassic period. Ht 35 in. (90 cm).

hand, and its monuments mutilated and smashed; but during the four centuries of its *floruit*, Olmec influence emanating from this area was to be found throughout Mesoamerica, with the curious exception of the Yucatan Peninsula – perhaps because there were few Maya populations at that time sufficiently large to have interested the expanding Olmecs.

However, one area that did interest them was eastern Soconusco on the Pacific coastal plain, where a team led by David Cheetham of the New World Archaeological Foundation has excavated a site called Cantón Corralito. Surely a settlement of Olmec colonists from San Lorenzo, perhaps drawn to the region's rich cacao orchards, these intruders used both imported and locally made ceramics of pure San Lorenzo design.

During the Middle Preclassic, some centuries after the demise of San Lorenzo, the great Olmec center was La Venta, situated on an island in the midst of the swampy wastes of the lower Tonalá River and dominated by a 100 ft (30 m) high mound of clay. Elaborate tombs and spectacular buried offerings of jade and serpentine figurines were concealed by various constructions, as at other Olmec sites. The Olmec art style centered upon the representations of creatures which combined the features of a snarling jaguar with human characteristics, often those of a weeping infant; among these were-jaguars was a maize god, one of the first recognizable deities of the Mesoamerican pantheon, as well as a god of rain. From the unity of the art style, the size and beauty of the sculptured monuments, and the presence and massive scale of public architecture, the conclusion must be drawn that there was a powerful Olmec state on the Gulf Coast which even at this early time was able to command enormous resources both in manpower and in materials.

More relevant to the Maya, there are also good reasons to believe that it was the Olmecs who devised the elaborate Long Count calendar. Whether or not one thinks of the Olmecs as the "mother culture" of Mesoamerica, the fact is that many other civilizations, including the Maya, ultimately drew on Olmec achievements. This is especially true during the Middle Preclassic, when lesser peasant cultures away from the Gulf Coast were acquiring traits which had filtered to them from their more advanced neighbors, just as in ancient Europe peoples in the west and north eventually benefited from the achievements of the contemporaneous Bronze Age civilizations of the Near East. Paradoxically, some of these changes took place during a transitional period after the collapse of San Lorenzo as a power and the rise of La Venta. Did such turbulence induce new, creative experiments in living?

Olmec stone monuments lie scattered all along the piedmont zone of the Pacific Coast, from Chiapas as far southeast as El Salvador, so there can be little doubt that these people had intruded into that fertile zone during the Early and Middle Preclassic. There is even an Olmec rock painting in red and black pigments high on a cliff above Lake Amatitlan, to the south of Guatemala City, showing an encounter between two helmeted dignitaries

16 Olmec rock painting in red and black, Lake Amatitlan, Guatemala. Early Preclassic period.

holding unidentifiable objects [16]. It has recently been dated to *c.* 1250 BC, which, if trusted, places it at the same time as San Lorenzo, and therefore within the Early Preclassic.

PRECLASSIC KAMINALJUYU

One of the greatest of all archaeological sites in the New World is Kaminaljuyu, on the western margins of Guatemala City in a broad, fertile valley lying athwart the Continental Divide. Although it consisted of several hundred great temple mounds in Maudslay's day, all but a handful have been swallowed up by the rapidly expanding slums and real estate developments of the capital. Rescue operations by the Carnegie Institution of Washington, Pennsylvania State University, and the Universidad del Valle have shown that whereas part of the site was constructed during the Early Classic, the great majority of the mounds were definitely Preclassic. The loss to science through the depredations of brickyards and bulldozers has been incalculable.

It has been no easy task, under these circumstances, to work out an archaeological sequence for Kaminaljuyu, but the oldest culture is Las Charcas. The remains of this culture are scattered widely, representing a major occupation of the Valley of Guatemala. Its stratigraphic position underneath deposits of the Late Preclassic, supported by a number of radiocarbon dates, suggests that this culture flourished during the Middle Preclassic, c. 800–350 BC.

The best-preserved Las Charcas remains come from a series of ancient, bottleshaped pits which had been cut through the topsoil into the underlying volcanic ash. No one has a firm idea of the purpose of these excavations. Some may have been cooking pits, and it is entirely possible that, as among the historic Hidatsa Indians of the Great Plains, others were used to store maize and beans. In any case, their final use was surely as refuse containers. Carbonized avocado seeds, maize cobs, and remnants of textiles, basketry and probably mats, and rope fragments have been found within them. The magnificent Las Charcas white ware, manufactured from a kaolin-like clay, is extremely sophisticated, with designs in red showing spider monkeys with upraised arms, grotesque dragon masks, and other more abstract motifs [17].

17 Pottery vessels of the Las Charcas culture, Middle Preclassic period. *a, c*, interiors of red-on-white bowls; *b*, gray-brown bowl with modeled decoration. *a*, diam. 12 in. (30.5 cm); *b, c*, to scale.

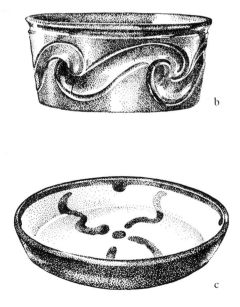

a

b

c

18 Middle Preclassic pottery figurine of a seated woman, from the Las Charcas-culture site of Copolchi. Ht *c.* 4 in. (10 cm).

Las Charcas figurines are predominantly female, with a liveliness of concept seldom found elsewhere [18].

Until recently, it was thought that Las Charcas was merely a culture of simple village farmers, but in 2005 archaeologist Barbara Arroyo of Guatemala's Asociación Tikal began a rescue excavation of Naranjo, located in the hills just to the northwest of Kaminaljuyu. This site, long known for its two rows of plain stone monuments, turned out to be of Las Charcas date. It was clearly a ceremonial center, with a small pyramid and associated platform built of clay, radiocarbon dated to the Middle Preclassic. Many fragments of Las Charcas redzoned pottery were recovered, including one astonishing example incised with the heron-crowned head of the Maya God G1, one of the ancestral deities of Palenque a thousand years later! Arroyo has worked with developers to spare part of the site, but the growth of Guatemala City has been no friend to archaeology.

THE MAYA LOWLANDS

During the tenth century BC, both in the Central and Northern Maya Areas, we now have for the first time substantial evidence for a Maya population. Earlier ceramics may have been found *c.* 1050 BC at Nixtun Ch'ich' near Lake Peten Itza, but these need further study. What is secure, as proven by Takeshi Inomata of the University of Arizona, is that most such dates need compression into shorter periods. In effect, Inomata has replaced a gradual view of change with one that sees bursts of activity across large areas. The spread of Mayan-speakers in the southern lowlands is almost surely to be associated with ceramics of a very early pottery tradition found in the oldest levels at the sites of Ceibal, Cival, Altar de Sacrificios, and Tikal, in the Peten, and at Cahal Pech and Cuello in Belize [19]. These vessels, although somewhat varied in style, include plates with wide, everted, and incised rims, and pierced pottery colanders that were probably used to wash lime-soaked maize kernels in the *nixtamal* process. In the more western sites are found white-slipped ceramics very similar to those at the ancient site of Chiapa de Corzo, to the west of the Maya area proper in the Grijalva

19 Reconstruction drawing of Cunil ceramics, Belize. Beginning of Middle Preclassic. Ht of jar on upper right *c.* 16 in. (40 cm).

drainage of Chiapas. It may well be that the technique of pottery-making had come to the Archaic people of the lowlands from there, perhaps with Mayan-speaking migrants.

Not so long ago, one would have thought that these pioneer Maya groups would have been simple village farmers, with no social differentiation and certainly no temples or pyramids. But evidence from Ceibal, on the Pasión River in the southern Peten, has transformed this picture. During its 1964–68 excavation by a Harvard team, a cache which contained greenstone celts, whose arrangement mirrored a similar deposit at Olmec La Venta, along with a jade Olmec perforating instrument, was encountered almost at bedrock level in a deep stratum of the Real-Xe (Cunil Horizon) phase; this was radio-carbon dated to *c.* 900–800 BC. More recently, in 2009, a team led by Inomata conducted far more extensive excavations in Real-Xe deposits at the site. Not only have they discovered other La Venta style greenstone celt caches, laid out according to cosmic directions, but also that, even at this early date, Ceibal had been organized as a ceremonial center of earth and clay. Early elevated platforms were only later (*c.* 800–700 BC) topped with pyramids, laid out in a particular formation known as an "E-Group" arrangement to archaeologists (discussed in more detail in Chapter 3). This formation was to appear thereafter in many parts of the Maya lowlands. Lifestyle at this time remains a puzzle, however, and Inomata wonders whether larger settlements coexisted with more mobile horticulturalists. Indeed, the earliest architecture may only have been visited intermittently, as parts of sites occupied by relatively few people.

The ceramics of Ceibal lead directly into the so-called Mamom culture (600–400 BC) and its more homogeneous ceramics. Mamom, or something like it, is spread over almost all of the Maya lowlands, and at one time was also interpreted as a simple village culture, since until recently there were no real examples of public Mamom architecture on the scale of La Venta. However, the special conditions of excavation in the Peten must be considered. The lowland Maya almost always built their temples over older ones, so that over the course of centuries the earliest constructions would come to be deeply buried within the towering accretions of Classic-period rubble and plaster. Consequently, to prospect for Mamom temples in one of the larger sites would be extremely costly in time and labor.

The recent discoveries by Richard Hansen at the northern Peten site of Nakbe (to be further considered in the next chapter) indicate that by 600 BC its inhabitants had begun to create substantial buildings with structures and platforms as high as 59 ft (18 m). While these lack the spectacular mask-panels that were to be a hallmark of this and other cities in the Late Preclassic, the Nakbe temples testify that the lowland Maya had begun to develop even at this early date from simple peasant life to a more complex society.

Mamom pottery appears quite simple when compared with Las Charcas, to which it seems related. The commonest wares are red and orange-red monochromes, with polychrome decoration absent. Usually the only embellishment is simple incising on the inside of bowls, or daubing of necked jars with red blobs. The figurine cult, if such it may be called, is also present in Mamom, with a wide range of stylistic treatment carried out by punching and with applied strips of clay. At Tikal, a cache of Mamom ceramics was discovered in a sealed *chultun*. This is a bottle-shaped chamber below the plaza floor, comparable in shape and perhaps in use to those of Las Charcas. *Chultun* are ubiquitous in sites of the Central and Northern Areas, cut down into the limestone marl from the surface. We know that by the Classic they were used as cisterns in the Puuc region, and for burials and perhaps sweat baths in the Central Area. Initially, they could have been utilized as sources of the fine lime employed in construction by Maya architects, but their use as storage pits should not be overlooked, nor the likelihood that most served as cisterns. Whatever the answer to the "*chultun* mystery," they are as old as the Mamom phase.

These early Maya did not "live by bread alone." Many Middle Preclassic pottery vessels have spouts like teapots, and while it was known that they were used for pouring liquids, exactly which liquids remained unknown, until Terry Powis of Kennesaw State University submitted residue from the inside of several vessels excavated at the northern Belize site of Colha for analysis at Hershey Foods. Dating from around 600 BC, Jeffrey Hurst found traces of theobromine, which, as we have seen, is an alkaloid distinctive of chocolate. Because later Mesoamericans highly prized the foam on the chocolate drink, Hurst speculates that the Colha villagers frothed up the liquid by blowing through the spout.

In the southeastern corner of the Central Area, the pioneers who first settled in the rich valley surrounding the ancient city of Copan had very different roots from Mamom. Towards the end of the Early Preclassic, village cultures all along the Pacific littoral as far as El Salvador had become "Olmecized," a tradition that was to continue into the Middle Preclassic, and that was to be manifested in carved ceramics of Olmec type and even in Olmec stone monuments. This Olmec-like wave even penetrated the Copan Valley, during the Middle Preclassic Uir phase (*c.* 800–400 BC), with the sudden appearance of pottery bowls incised and carved with such Olmec motifs as the paw-wing and the "flame eyebrows." In a deep layer of an outlying suburb of the Classic city, William Fash discovered a Uir-phase burial accompanied by Olmecoid ceramics, nine polished stone celts, and over 300 drilled jade objects. Although the rest of the Maya lowlands seem to have been of little or no interest to the Olmec peoples, the Copan area definitely was.

Jade was surely the compelling reason for this intrusion of the Olmec into what in later times was the southeast frontier of the Maya area. It has been known for over 50 years that the Classic Maya obtained their green and often dull-colored jade from alluvial deposits in the drainage of the Río Motagua, to the west of Copan, but this was not the distinctive blue-green jade so prized by the Olmec. The mystery of where the Olmec obtained this material has at long last been solved by the discovery in 2001 of several sources in the Sierra de las Minas, far above the Motagua, by a team including geophysicist Russell Seitz, mineralogist George Harlow, geologist Virginia Sisson, and anthropologist Karl Taube. Since then, subsequent expeditions have found workshop sites near these sources and river-worn cobbles being worked downstream. Control of both the Motagua and Copan valleys would have given the Olmec a virtual monopoly of a material that was as important to this primordial civilization as gold was to be for the Spanish *conquistadores*.

There is still a great deal to understand about the Middle Preclassic, the base on which the flowering of Maya culture took place. It ended in widespread disruptions that have not been explained. Certainly it was during this period when the Maya area became truly "Maya." But full Maya civilization as we know it – the vaulted masonry architecture, the naturalistic painting and relief style, the Long Count calendar and writing – had not even begun to germinate during this epoch.

3

▼▼▼▼▼▼▼▼▼

THE RISE OF
MAYA CIVILIZATION

To archaeologists, it once seemed a very long step from the village or small civic-religious centers that we have thus far been considering to the awe-inspiring achievements of the Classic Maya, but we now realize that this advance took place in what we know of as the Late Preclassic. The more we know about that period, which lasted from about 400 or 300 BC to AD 250, the more complex and developed it seems. From the point of view of social and cultural evolution, the Late Preclassic really is a kind of "proto-Classic," in which all of the traits usually ascribed to the Classic Maya are present, with the exception of vaulted stone architecture and a high elaboration of calendar and script on stone monuments.

Initially, the Maya highlands and lowlands (excluding the Pacific coast) were remarkably backward and provincial compared with the extraordinary and precocious civilization of Mexico's Olmec heartland. It will be remembered from the last chapter that at a time when the San Lorenzo Olmec were carving and moving multi-ton stone monuments, the Yucatan Peninsula was sparsely inhabited by preceramic peoples following an essentially Archaic way of life, centered on hunting and gathering, with some maize and manioc horticulture. Only after 1000 BC did they have villages and pottery, with small temples and their platforms appearing just before 900 BC [20].

As the Olmec civilization went into a steep decline *c*. 400 BC, rapid changes took place in the Maya area. This timing cannot be coincidental but, as explained in the last chapter, its meaning is unclear. What we do know is that, as populations rose, the southern lowlands of the peninsula became the new "hotspot" for complexity in Mesoamerica, resulting in the construction of immense cities, particularly in the Peten's so-called Mirador "Basin" (which is really an upland). Concurrently, we see in this epoch the beginnings of Maya hieroglyphic writing and the calendar, perhaps to record the doings of kings and dynasties – a problematic topic, since we still cannot read the very earliest Maya inscriptions beyond the dates.

As for the origins of Late Preclassic Maya civilization, all indications are that the *fons et origo* was Olmec. That ancient and now-dead culture of the fertile Veracruz–Tabasco plain appears to have been as familiar to, and respected by, the early Maya as Classical Greece and Rome are to ourselves (we shall see direct evidence for this at San Bartolo). In art, in religion, in state complexity, and perhaps even in the calendar and astronomy, Olmec models were transferred to the Maya through direct interaction or by

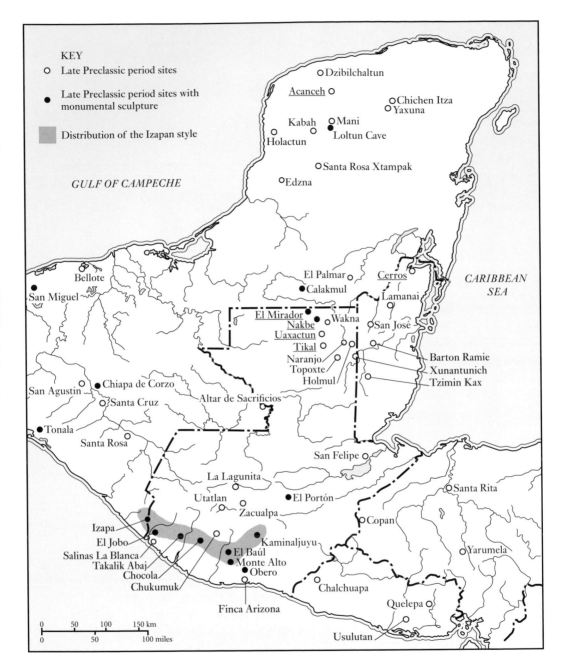

20 Sites of the Late Preclassic period. Underlined sites have giant architectural masks.

means of intermediary groups in Chiapas and Tabasco, Mexico. There is a consistent theme in such interactions, from this period until the time of Spanish contact: if the ancient Mexicans saw the Maya region as a land of great wealth in jades, feathers, and chocolate, the Maya looked to the west, in what is now Mexico, as the enduring locus of civilization. The only exception might be the Late Preclassic, when the immense pyramids of the Maya may have inspired similar examples in central Mexico, including those at the great city of Teotihuacan.

How are we to define the word "civilization"? How do the civilized differ from the barbaric? Archaeologists have usually dodged this question by offering lists of traits which they think to be important. Cities are one criterion. The late V. G. Childe thought that writing should be another, but the obviously advanced Inca of Peru were completely non-literate, or had only string notations, *khipu*, whose function seems largely numerical or mnemonic. Civilization, in fact, is different in degree rather than in kind from what precedes it, but has certainly been achieved by the time that state institutions, large-scale public works, temple buildings, and widespread, unified art styles have appeared. With few exceptions, the complex state apparatus demands some form of record-keeping, and writing has usually been the answer: so has the invention of a more-or-less accurate means of keeping time.

Yet all civilizations are in themselves unique. The Classic Maya of the lowlands had a very elaborate calendar; writing; temple-pyramids and palaces of limestone masonry with vaulted rooms; architectural layouts emphasizing buildings arranged around plazas with rows of stone stelae lined up before some; and a highly sophisticated art style expressed in bas-reliefs and in wall paintings. These traits are now known to have been developed in the Late Preclassic period.

THE BIRTH OF THE CALENDAR

Some system of recording time is essential to all higher cultures – to fix critical events in the lives of the persons ruling the state, to guide the agricultural and ceremonial year, and to record celestial motions. The Calendar Round of 52 years was present among all Mesoamericans, including the Maya, and is presumably of very great age. It consists of two permutating cycles. One is of 260 days, representing the intermeshing of a sequence of the numbers 1 through 13 with 20 named days [21]; these names varied from culture to culture in Mesoamerica but often had the same animal or mythic associations. Among the Maya, the 260-day count was fundamental. It was sometimes called by the *ersatz* term *tzolk'in*, the actual Maya label perhaps being 13 *tuk*. The cycle began with 1 Imix, followed by 2 Ik', 3 Ak'bal, 4 K'an, until 13 Ben had been reached; the day following was Ix, with the coefficient 1 again, leading to 2 Men, and so on. The last day of the 260-day cycle would be 13 Ajaw, and it would

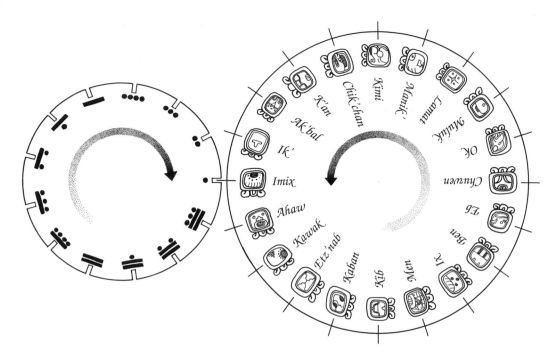

21 Schematic representation of the 260-day count. The day-names are in Yukateko Maya.

repeat once again commencing with 1 Imix. An important point: scholars use Yukateko names for most of the days, a convention that does not necessarily reflect how they were pronounced in other parts of the Maya world. How the 260-day calendar even came into being remains an enigma – it is eerily close to the nine-month span of human gestation – but the use to which it was put is clear. Every single day had its own omens and associations, and the inexorable march of the 20 days acted as a kind of perpetual fortune-telling machine guiding the destinies of the Maya and all the peoples of Mexico. It still survives in unchanged form among some indigenous peoples in southern Mexico and the Maya highlands, under the care of calendar priests.

Meshing with the 260-day count is a "Vague Year" or *Ha'b* of 365 days, so called because the actual length of the solar year is about a quarter-day more, a circumstance that leads us to intercalate one day every four years to keep our calendar in march with the sun. Although the Maya were perfectly aware that the *Ha'b* was shorter than the tropical year, they did not change the calendar accordingly. Within the *Ha'b*, there were 18 named "months" of 20 days each [22], with a much-dreaded interval of 5 unlucky days added at the end. The Maya New Year started with 1 Pop, the next day being 2 Pop, etc. The final day of the month, however, carried not the coefficient 20, but a sign indicating the "seating" of the month to follow, in line with the Maya philosophy that the influence of any particular span of time is felt *before* it actually begins and persists somewhat beyond its apparent termination.

From this it follows that a particular day in the 260-day count, such as 1 K'an, also had a position in the *Ha'b*, for instance 2 Pop. A day designated as 1 K'an 2 Pop could not return until 52 *Ha'b* (18,980 days) had passed. This is the Calendar Round, and it is the only annual time count possessed by the highland peoples of Mexico, one that obviously has its disadvantages where events taking place over a span of more than 52 years are concerned.

22 Signs for the months in the *Ha'b* or 365-day count. The names of the months are in Yukateko Maya.

Pop	Wo	Sip	Sotz'	Sek
Xul	Yaxk'in	Mol	Ch'en	Yax
Sak	Keh	Mak	K'ank'in	Muwan
Pax	K'ayab	Kumk'u		Wayeb

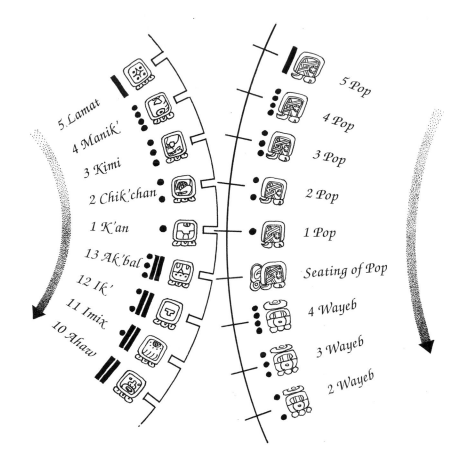

23 Schematic representation of part of the 52-year Calendar Round.

Although it is usually assumed to be "Maya," the Long Count was widely distributed in Classic and earlier times in the lowland country of Mesoamerica; but it was most highly refined by the Maya of the Central Area. This is really another kind of permutation count, except that the cycles used are so large that, unlike the Calendar Round, any event within the span of historical time could be fixed without fear of ambiguity. Instead of taking the Vague Year as the basis for the Long Count, the Maya and other peoples employed the tun, a period of 360 days. The Long Count cycles are:

20 k'ins	1 winal or 20 days
18 winals	1 tun or 360 days
20 tuns	1 k'atun or 7,200 days
20 k'atuns	1 bak'tun or 144,000 days

Long Count dates inscribed by the Maya on their monuments consist of the above cycles listed from top to bottom in descending order of magnitude, each with its numerical coefficient, and all to be added up so as to express the number of days elapsed since the end of the last but one Great Cycle, a period of 13 bak'tuns the ending of which fell on the date 4 Ajaw 8 Kumk'u. The starting point of the last Great Cycle corresponded to 14 August 3114 BC (Gregorian calendar), and its ending point to 24 December AD 2012. Thus, a Long Count date conventionally written as 9.10.19.5.11 10 Chuwen 4 Kumk'u would be:

9 bak'tuns	1,296,000 days
10 k'atuns	72,000 days
19 tuns	6,840 days
5 winals	100 days
11 k'ins	11 days

or 1,374,951 days since the close of the previous Great Cycle, reaching the Calendar Round position 10 Chuwen 4 Kumk'u. Again, to ensure consistency, scholars use labels for these units of time that do not always match those of the Classic period. The bak'tun was actually read *pih* or *pik*, and, in a switch sure to confuse modern readers, the tun was really called *ha'b*!

Epigrapher David Stuart has recently proposed that the 13 bak'tun-long Great Cycle among the Classic Maya was actually embedded in a far larger structure that he has dubbed the "Grand Long Count," enabling Maya calendar specialists to make calculations thousands and even millions of years into the cosmic past and future. Such dizzying super-numbers are rare, but they are carved on monuments in several Maya cities.

Something should also be said about the coefficients themselves. The Maya, along with a few other groups of the lowlands and the Zapotecs and Mixtecs of Oaxaca, had a numbering system of great simplicity, employing only two symbols: a dot with the value of "one" and a horizontal bar for "five." Numerals up to four were expressed by dots only, six was a bar with a dot above, and ten two bars. Nineteen, the highest coefficient in calendrical use, took the form of four dots above three bars. The treatment of higher numbers, for which the "nought" symbol (a sign of unknown origin) was essential, will be discussed in Chapter 9.

It is generally agreed that the Long Count must have been set in motion long after the inception of the Calendar Round, but by just how many centuries or millennia is uncertain. Be that as it may, the oldest recorded Long Count dates fall within Bak'tun 7, and appear on monuments which lie outside the Maya area. At present, the most ancient known is Stela 2 at Chiapa de Corzo, a major ceremonial center which had been in existence since Early Preclassic times in the dry Grijalva Valley of central Chiapas: in a vertical column the numerical coefficients [7.16.]3.2.13 are carved, followed by the day 6 Ben, the "month" of the Vague Year being suppressed as in all these early inscriptions. The initial coefficients are missing but reconstructable. This would correspond to 9 December 36 BC. Five years later, the famous Stela C at the Olmec site of Tres Zapotes in Veracruz was inscribed with the date 7.16.6.16.18 6 Etz'nab.

Now, the sixteenth k'atun of Bak'tun 7 would fall within the Late Preclassic, and we can be sure that unless these dates are to be counted forward from some base other than 13.0.0.0.0 4 Ajaw 8 Kumk'u (as the end of the previous Great Cycle is recorded), which seems improbable, then the "Maya" calendar had reached what was pretty much its final form by the first century BC among peoples who were under powerful Olmec influence, and who may not even have been Maya.

Who might they have been? It will be remembered from Chapter 1 that one likely candidate for the language of the Olmecs was an early form of Mixe-Zoquean; languages belonging to this group are still spoken on the Isthmus of Tehuantepec and in western Chiapas. Some scholars are now willing to ascribe the earliest Long Count monuments outside the Maya area proper to Mixe-Zoquean as well. In 1986, a magnificent stela was found at a place called La Mojarra in southeastern Veracruz; two Bak'tun 8 dates corresponding respectively to AD 143 and 156 are inscribed on it. These are accompanied by a text of about 400 signs, in a script which most epigraphers call "Isthmian," but others term "Epi-Olmec" (the famous "Tuxtla Statuette," also found in southern Veracruz, is inscribed in the same script and dates to AD 162). In 1993, Terrence Kaufman and John Justeson presented their decipherment of the Isthmian script, which they assert is in Mixe-Zoquean, but this decipherment has not been not accepted by the majority of glyph specialists. Unfortunately, we still are in the dark about what language group was responsible for either the Isthmian script or for the early development of the Long Count.

To muddy the picture, the relation between Maya and Isthmian writing remains obscure. The earliest Maya writing, from San Bartolo, Guatemala, comes from c. 300 BC, *prior* to Isthmian writing. The descent of Isthmian to the Maya highlands to the southern lowlands – until recently, the view of most archaeologists – is thus upended. The genealogy of Mesoamerican writing is therefore more complicated than formerly thought, yet the sample of texts is too poor to clarify relations between such writing. Another vital point: the very existence of a beginning date implies a belief not just in cycles, but in *particular events* that took place at this distant time. Later Maya inscriptions, to be discussed in Chapter 9, explain that it was a period when gods erected ritual stones and renovated cosmic hearths. Similar beliefs might have spread across the Isthmus of Tehuantepec and into the Maya region.

IZAPA AND THE PACIFIC COAST

Crucial to answering the question of how higher culture came about among the Maya is the Izapan civilization. Its distinctive, elaborate art style is found on monuments from Tres Zapotes on the Veracruz coast, to the Pacific plain of Chiapas and Guatemala, and up into the Guatemala City area.

Izapa itself is a very large site made up of over eighty temple mounds of earthen construction faced with river cobbles, just east of Tapachula, Chiapas, in the moist, slightly hilly country about 20 miles (32 km) inland from the Pacific shore. Although the language spoken in this area in early Colonial times was Tapachulteko, a Mixe-Zoquean tongue, the religious iconography of Izapa is entirely Maya, and the site was surely created by Maya-speakers – perhaps ancestral Mam.

Izapa was founded as a ceremonial center as far back as Early Preclassic times and was used until the Early Classic, but the bulk of the constructions and probably all of the many carved monuments belong to the Late Preclassic era – Takeshi Inomata of the University of Arizona places these between 100 BC and a century or two later. The Izapan art style consists in the main of large, ambitiously conceived but somewhat cluttered scenes carried out in bas-relief. Some of the activities shown are profane, such as a richly attired person decapitating a vanquished foe, but there are deities as well. One of these is a "Long-lipped God," part human and part fish (most likely shark), who apparently is an ancestral form of Chahk, the ubiquitous Maya patron of lightning and rain. Another supernatural being present at Izapa has one leg ending in a serpent's body and head, and is thus the earliest known representation of the god K'awiil, in Classic times the presiding deity of Maya ruling houses.

But by far the leading figure in the crystallizing Maya pantheon as seen in Izapan monumental art, extending to the giant stucco masks of Late Preclassic temples in the Peten and Belize, is the Principal Bird Deity (PBD), the monstrous form of Wuqub Kaquix or 7 Macaw, an anthropomorphic bird (likely a mythic eagle) [24]. He is prominent in the Popol Vuh as the arrogant "sun" of the creation preceding this one (see box overleaf). On one monument the PBD is seen descending to eat *nantze* fruit while the Hero Twins stand on either side of the tree; on another he perches on his tree, while Hunahpu – blood coursing from the stump of his

24 Stela 2, Izapa. The Hero Twins gesture toward the Principal Bird Deity (Wuqub Kaquix) as he descends to the fruit tree. Late Preclassic, *c.* 100 BC or later.

THE HERO TWINS AND THE CREATION OF THE WORLD

We now know that much of the iconography of the ancient Maya, from the Late Preclassic until the Spanish Conquest, explicitly illustrates a creation story that is fundamentally agricultural, relating to the annual planting and harvest cycle of maize, the Maya staff of life, although there are many other themes adhering to it. Part of the most important episode of the story, that which pertains to a marvelous pair of monster-slaying twins and their Maize God father, is preserved for us in the Popol Vuh, the "Book of Counsel" of the K'iche' Maya. Other parts of what must have been an all-encompassing theogony can be fleshed out with ethnohistoric sources, by analysis of the Maya epigraphic and archaeological record, and by comparison with well-known Mesoamerican cultures such as the Aztec.

• Originally produced from a watery void by a pair of grandfather/grandmother gods (named Xpiyacoc and Xmucane in the Popol Vuh), the universe had passed through various cycles of creation and destruction. Each successive world was peopled by imperfect beings, the last of whom were wooden idols whose doom was brought about because they would or could not give the gods proper praise. At the close of this penultimate creation a great flood covered the world, the sky fell upon the earth, and the sun, moon and stars were extinguished. In the midst of this darkness, a monstrous, arrogant bird-monster (the Popol Vuh's Wuqub Kaquix or "7 Macaw") proclaimed himself the new sun as well as the moon. More of him later on.

• To the old creator couple was born a pair of twins. One of these was the Maize God (Hun Hunahpu or 1 Ajaw); his brother 7 Hunahpu was a mere double or companion. This handsome young god married, and fathered two sons, Hun Batz and Hun Chuwen. Later in the story, the Maize God and his twin were playing ball in a ball court, but the noise angered the lords of the Underworld (Xibalba, "Place of Fright"). They were summoned to the Underworld, where they suffered a series of tests and trials in several dread chambers, one of which was inhabited by Death Bats. Eventually they were sacrificed, and the Maize God's head was hung in a tree (either a calabash or cacao tree).

• One day, a daughter of one of the Underworld lords passed under that tree. The suspended head spoke to her; when she raised her hand, she became magically impregnated. Six months later, she was expelled in disgrace from the nether regions to the earth's surface, and took refuge in the house of the ancient creator divinities, the grandparents of her soon-to-be-born offspring. These children were the Hero Twins, Hunahpu (known as Huun Ajaw in the Classic Period) and Xbalanque: hunters, blowgunners, ball players *par excellence*, and tricksters.

• By means of trickery the Hero Twins turned their jealous half-brothers Hun Batz and Hun Chuwen into monkeys or monkey-men; these latter were also worshipped as gods or demi-gods by the Maya, for whom they were considered the patrons of all the arts including music, dancing, writing and carving.

• As in many other Native American cultures, the main task of the Hero Twins was to rid the world of anomalies and monsters. Hunahpu and Xbalanque began with the formidable Wuqub Kaquix, "7 Macaw." As this gigantic, bejeweled bird descended to a *nantze* tree to gorge on its favorite fruit, Hunahpu shot it with a blowgun pellet that demolished its jade teeth. In the ensuing struggle, the bird-monster ripped off the arm of Hunahpu (which was later recovered), but it was doomed. The grandfather/grandmother replaced its teeth with nothing but soft maize kernels, and it died ignominiously. The Twins went on to destroy two further monsters, one a volcano and the other the producer of earthquakes.

• At last the Twins achieved their final triumph, the defeat of the Lords of Xibalba. Summoned like their slain father and uncle into the Underworld, they were placed in the usual torture chambers. However, by means of tricks and legerdemain they turned the tables on the gods of death, even defeating them in a ball game; but eventually they were killed themselves. The upper world gods did not wish them to die, however, so they were revived, and entered the court of Xibalba disguised as dancers and mountebanks. Through a clever stratagem, the wily youths slew their enemies in a true Harrowing of Hell; following their ultimate victory, they resurrected their father Hun Hunahpu, the Maize God. As he journeyed back to life, the Maize God passed through the Xibalban waters in a canoe, paddled by two aged deities and attended by naked young women who restored to him the jewels and headgear from which he had previously been despoiled. This journey may have been fraught with danger, for two incised Late Classic bones from Tikal show the canoe sinking, its occupants in despair. However, with the assistance of his twin sons, the Maize God emerged through a crack in the earth's surface, pictured as the carapace of a turtle.

It seems clear that this whole mythic cycle was closely related to maize fertility. Towards the end of the dry season, by planting the seed in the hole made with his digging stick, the Maya farmer symbolically sent it to Xibalba, to its temporary death. Thanks to the intervention of the Maize God's twin sons, the maize was reborn and rose again to the surface as a young sprout, to be nourished by the coming of the rains. Small wonder that many Colonial-period Maya identified the risen Christ with the Maize God.

The visible expression of this mythic cycle as well as many others not surviving in the Popol Vuh can be seen in the language of Maya religious iconography during almost every period. The bird-monster 7 Macaw appears on buildings and monuments from the Late Preclassic onwards as the Principal Bird Deity (PBD), sometimes even perched on his tree. The Maize God is recognizable from his silk-like tonsure and youthful appearance. Of his Hero Twin sons, Hunahpu (called Huun Ajaw in Classic texts) has distinctive black spots as his "god-markings," while Xbalanque (the Classic Yax Bahlam or "Young Jaguar") is marked with patches of jaguar skin.

severed arm – gazes at him from below. Certain recurrent elements must represent well-understood iconographic motifs, such as a U-shaped form between diagonal bars above the principal scene, probably an early occurrence of the sky-band so ubiquitous in Classic Maya art.

Izapa, then, is a major center with some of the features which we consider more typical of the lowland Maya already in full flower – the stela-altar complex (seen earlier in Naranjo, near Kaminaljuyu), the Maya rain god Chahk, and a highly painterly, two-dimensional art style which emphasizes historical and mythic scenography with great attention to plumage and other costume details. Writing and the calendar are absent, but as one moves along the Pacific slopes east into Guatemala, one finds sites with inscriptions and Bak'tun 7 dates.

One of these Guatemalan stations is Takalik Abaj, situated in a lush, well-watered Piedmont zone that in the days of the Conquest was a great producer of chocolate, and is now devoted to coffee. It is made up of clay temple-mounds (and a ball court) faced with river cobbles and other rocks, arranged on terraces, and covers an area of at least 2.5 sq. miles (6.5 sq. km). That the Olmecs had once intruded here is apparent from a large boulder located less than a mile from the main group of mounds, carved in relief with a bearded were-jaguar in the purest Olmec style. Stela 1 from the site is purely Izapan but dateless, but Stela 2, now somewhat damaged, bore on its carved face two richly attired Izapan figures with tall, plumed head-dresses, facing each other across a vertical row of glyphs below a cloud-like mass of volutes from which peers the face of a sky god. The topmost sign in the column is beyond doubt a very early form of the "Introductory Glyph" which in later Classic inscriptions stands at the head of a Long Count date. Just beneath is the bak'tun coefficient, which is pretty clearly the number 7. In recent decades, several new texts, some in flamboyant, full-figure style, have come to light in excavations by Miguel Orrego and Christa Schieber de Lavarreda, as well as royal burials equipped with jade necklaces and large figurines.

A more complete Bak'tun 7 inscription appears on Stela 1, the "Herrera Stela," from El Baúl [25], a former coffee plantation

25 Stela 1 from El Baúl, the earliest dated monument from the Maya area proper. On the right a figure in profile stands stiffly posed below a face looking down from a cloud-scroll.

to the southeast of Takalik Abaj in a region noted for its Terminal Classic Cotzumalhuapa centers. On the right, a profile figure is stiffly posed with spear in hand below the visage of an ancestor or deity looking down from a cloud-scroll. In front of him are two vertical columns of glyphs, the right-hand of which consists of little more than empty cartouches that were probably meant to be painted. At the top of the column on the left is the coefficient 12 above a fleshless jaw, a Mexican form of the day sign Eb. Then there are four indecipherable signs, followed by a series of Long Count numbers which can be reconstructed as 7.19.15.7.12, reaching the Calendar Round position 12 Eb. This would be 5 March AD 37, making it the earliest dated monument in the Maya area proper.

We cannot leave the Pacific coastal zone without mentioning a second sculptural tradition that reaches some degree of popularity both there and at Kaminaljuyu. This is expressed in large, crude, pot-bellied statues with closed eyes, collars, as well as puffy faces and lower jaws so inflated that they have been compared with Italy's one-time Fascist leader, Mussolini. At Monte Alto, not far from El Baúl, a group of these monstrous forms is placed in a row along with a colossal head carried out in the same style, and some believe that the entire pot-bellied complex is connected with the Olmec culture and precedes the Izapan. However, since Monte Alto is strewn with Late Preclassic pottery sherds, it is most likely that this was a subsidiary cult that coexisted with the Izapan Rain God, just as Egyptian and Graeco-Roman religious art flourished side-by-side in ancient Alexandria. But a cult to which deity? A fairly good case can be made for this being none other than the Fat God, without known functions but ubiquitous among the peoples of Mexico and the Northern Maya Area in Classic times.

KAMINALJUYU AND THE MAYA HIGHLANDS

A Late Preclassic rival to Izapa in size and number of temple mounds and in the splendor of its carved monuments was Kaminaljuyu during the Verbena and Arenal phases, dating from *c*. 100 BC to AD 150. This, it will be recalled, was once a major ceremonial site on the western outskirts of Guatemala City. Many of the approximately 200 mounds once to be found there were probably constructed at this time; Kaminaljuyu's rulers must have possessed formidable economic and political power over much of the Maya highlands at this time.

Archaeologist Marion Hatch and her Guatemalan colleagues have encountered evidence for the existence of a now-extinct lake [26] around which the earthen platforms of Kaminaljuyu were arranged, as well as a sophisticated system of intensive agriculture. Connected with the lake were various irrigation canals, one of which carried water to an artificial storage basin 52 ft 6 in. (16 m) wide and 36 ft (11 m) deep; leading from the latter were small tributary channels which brought water to the fields, some of which were agricultural terraces on the sides of the ravines. As the lake dried up after the time of Christ, perhaps due to exploitation of the land, or even to tectonic movements (the region is highly earthquake-prone), the city dwindled until its revival during the Early Classic period.

The excavation of two tombs from this period has thrown much light on the luxury to which these rulers were accustomed [27]. Mound E-III-3 at Kaminaljuyu consists of several superimposed temple platforms, each a flat-topped, stepped pyramid fronted by a broad stairway; in its final form it reaches a height of more than 60 ft (18 m). In lieu of easily worked building stone, which was unavailable in the vicinity, these platforms were built from ordinary clay and basketloads of earth and household rubbish.

26 Map of Kaminaljuyu, Guatemala, showing the extent of the lake that disappeared in the Late Preclassic.

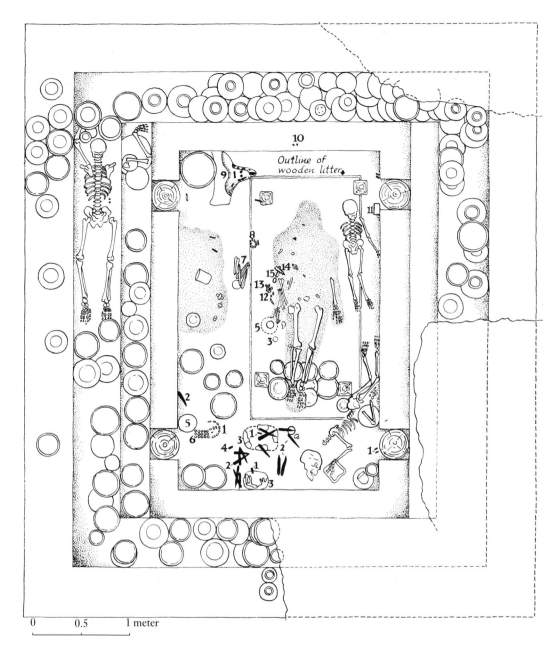

27 Plan of Tomb II, Mound E-III-3, a burial of the Late Preclassic culture at Kaminaljuyu. *1*, jade beads; *2*, obsidian flake-blades; *3*, mica sheets; *4*, jade mosaic element; *5*, stuccoed gourds; *6*, pebbles; *7*, basalt implements; *8*, human teeth; *9*, jade mosaic mask or headdress; *10*, obsidian stones; *11*, pyrite-incrusted sherd; *12*, soapstone implement; *13*, bone objects, fish teeth, and quartz crystals; *14*, stingray spines; *15*, spatulate bone object. All other circular objects are pottery vessels.

Almost certainly the temples themselves were thatched-roof affairs supported by upright timbers. Apparently each successive building operation took place to house the remains of an exalted person, whose tomb was cut down from the top in a series of stepped rectangles of decreasing size into the earlier temple platform, and then covered with a new floor of clay. The function of Maya pyramids as funerary monuments thus harks back to Preclassic times.

The corpse was wrapped in finery and covered from head to toe with cinnabar pigment, then laid on a wooden litter and lowered into the tomb. Sacrifices, both adults and children, accompanied the illustrious dead, together with offerings of an astonishing richness and profusion. In one tomb, over 300 objects of the most beautiful workmanship were placed with the body or above the timber roof, but ancient grave-robbers, probably noticing the slump in the temple floor caused by the collapse of the underlying tomb, had filched, it seems, objects which once covered the chest and head. Among the finery recovered were the remains of a mask or headdress of jade plaques, perhaps once fixed to a wooden background, jade flares which once adorned the ear lobes of the honored dead, bowls carved from chlorite-schist engraved with scroll designs, and little carved bottles of soapstone and fuchsite.

Pottery vessels from E-III-3 and elsewhere belong to a ceramic tradition prevalent throughout southeastern Mesoamerica during the Late Preclassic, from Izapa to El Salvador, and up into the Central and Northern Maya Areas, but differ from this tradition in their refinement and sophistication. Shapes have now become exuberant, with re-curved outlines, elaborate flanges on rims and bodies, and the appearance of vessel feet. Some of the most amusing examples of the potter's art are effigy vessels, a few of which show smiling old men. Painted stucco is often used to achieve effects in colors such as pink and green, unobtainable in fired slips. Most bowls and jars are embellished with engraved and carved scroll designs. A more peculiar kind of decoration which is virtually a marker for the Late Preclassic period in the Maya area is found on Usulutan ware, believed to originate in El Salvador where it attained great popularity. On this widely traded ware, a resistant substance (such as wax or thin clay) was applied to bowls with a multiple-brush applicator; after smudging or darkening in a reducing fire, the material was removed to leave a design of yellowish wavy parallel lines on a darker orange or brown background.

As for stone carving on a large scale, it was once believed that the Verbena-Arenal people made only "mushroom stones." The function of these peculiar objects, one of which was found in an E-III-3 tomb, is unknown. Some scholars see vaguely phallic associations. Others, such as the late Stephan de Borhegyi, connect them with the cult of the hallucinogenic mushrooms still to this day prevalent in the Mexican highlands, and it is claimed that the mortars and pestles with which the stones are so often associated were used in preparatory rites.

But we have much more to go by than that, thanks to the devastation of Kaminaljuyu by the rapid urbanization of Guatemala City. It now appears that there were artists capable of creating sculpture on a large scale, in an Izapan style that prefigured Classic Maya imagery. Moreover, the elite of this valley were fully literate, as shown by a handful of enigmatic texts [28, 29]. Two of these monuments were encountered by accident in a drainage ditch. One is a tall, granite stela embellished with a striding figure wearing a series of grotesque masks of Izapan gods (in a clear example of deity impersonation, the one over his face is the head of the bird-monster Wuqub Kaquix); he carries a chipped flint of eccentric form in one hand. Depicted on either side of him are spiked clay incense burners, examples of which have been found in excavations [30]. The other monument is even more extraordinary [28]. Very likely to have been a throne or altar, its surviving fragments show several Izapan gods, one bearded, surrounding a human figure with downpointing tridents in place of eyes, probably a precursor of a god who later appears at Tikal; he

28 Broken altar from Kaminaljuyu depicting Izapan gods (top) and a human figure in profile, associated with calendrical names in the 260–day count. The text below cannot yet be read.

Monuments from Kaminaljuyu

29 (*Above*) Stone head of an aged divinity with jaguar characteristics. Kaminaljuyu, Late Preclassic. Ht 16.5 in. (42 cm).

30 (*Right*) A ruler impersonating the Principal Bird Deity (Wuqub Kaquix) is carved on this granite stela from Kaminaljuyu. Ht 6 ft (1.8 m).

31 (*Opposite*) Monument 65, Kaminaljuyu. This enormous relief, hacked up anciently, depicts three enthroned rulers, each flanked by a pair of captives with bound hands. All protagonists are identified by their distinctive headdresses. An eroded design with standing figures is on the back. Late Preclassic. Ht 9 ft 6 in. (2.9 m).

too wields an unusual flint. The glyphs associated with these figures may be their calendric names; in ancient Mesoamerica, both gods and men were identified by the days on which they were born. A much longer text in several columns is incised below in a script that contains some recognizable Maya signs – the winal for 20 days or "person" (we all have 20 digits!) is known from an inscription at Chalchuapa, El Salvador – but on the whole, it is utterly opaque in content.

Not only were elaborate stelae and thrones (also found at Izapa and Takalik Abaj) carved by the Verbena-Arenal artisans; they also turned their hand to tenoned figures called "silhouette sculptures," perhaps originally meant to be stuck upright into temple and plaza floors; frog- or toad-effigy figures of all sizes; and many other forms. On Monument 65 (the largest yet found in Kaminaljuyu and probably earlier than the sculptures just discussed) three successive rulers appear seated on thrones, each flanked by kneeling captives [31]; all have different headdresses, apparently emblems of their names, as archaeologist Jonathan Kaplan notes. Once more, the pot-bellied figures are ubiquitous: did they represent a cult of the people, separate from the more aristocratic religion of the rulers? Or do they, as some believe, belong to an earlier horizon? Archaeology has unfortunately arrived on the scene too late to answer this.

Considering the astonishing wealth of the Verbena-Arenal people, their artistic and architectural capabilities, and their obvious relation to the Classic Maya in matters of style, iconography, and script, all leads one to see them as key interlocutors with the lowland Maya. While the pre-eminence of Kaminaljuyu during the Late Preclassic period is plain to see, its star began to sink by the second and third centuries AD, and most of it was left in ruin at the close of the Late Preclassic. It was not until the Mexican invasions of the Early Classic that this great center regained its former splendor.

THE PETEN AND THE MAYA LOWLANDS

While the Maya highlands and Pacific Coast were experiencing an extraordinary cultural efflorescence in the Late Preclassic, the Central and Northern Areas were hardly slumbering. Within the boundless forests, the agricultural economy and society had advanced to such a degree that massive temple centers were already rising in jungle clearings. But it is clear that from the very beginning the people of the lowlands were taking a somewhat different course from that of their kinsmen to the south, and the unique qualities which so distinguish them in the Classic period were soon to be inaugurated.

Although there are minor differences from region to region, a single widespread culture, Chicanel, dominated the Central and Northern Areas at this time. Usulutan ware and vessels with wide, everted lips, elaborate rim flanges, or complex outline are, as in the Southern Area, hallmarks for the period [32]. Most pottery is legless and confined to a simple black or

32 Usulutan ware bowl from Burial 85, Tikal. Chicanel culture. Diam. *c.* 7 in. (20 cm).

red monochrome, with thick glossy slips that feel waxy to the touch. It is strange that figurines are absent from most known Chicanel sites, indicating that there was a change in popular cults. The most unusual feature of Chicanel culture, however, is the high elaboration of architecture. It must be remembered that the Peten-Yucatan shelf is blessed with an inexhaustible supply of easily cut limestone, and abundant flint for tools with which to work it. Moreover, the Maya of the lowlands had discovered as far back as Mamom times that if limestone fragments were burnt, and the resulting powder mixed with water, a white plaster of great durability was created. Finally, they quickly realized the structural value of a concrete-like fill made from limestone rubble and marl.

With these resources at hand, the Maya temple architect was able to create massive constructions. There was an explosion of activity around 100 BC, the lead-up to this frenzy of building spanning the previous two centuries. This vast investment in monumental architecture is one of the great events in human history. At the Peten sites of Uaxactun, Tikal, El Mirador, Nakbe, and Calakmul (the latter just over the border in southern Campeche), deep excavations have shown that major pyramids, platforms, and courts were already taking shape by Chicanel times. Many of these were faced with elaborate stucco friezes and stairways flanked by massive stucco masks, all incorporating the dominant religious iconography of the times – most popularly, the monstrous Principal Bird Deity of the Popol Vuh. There is general agreement, for instance, that the E–VII-sub pyramid at Uaxactun, excavated by the Carnegie Institution of Washington in the 1930s, was built in the Chicanel phase [**33**]; beautifully preserved by the overlay of later structures, this truncated temple platform is faced with brilliantly white plaster and rises in several tiers, each having the apron moldings which are so distinctive a feature of Maya architecture in the lowlands. Inset stairways flanked by great monster masks, apparently

33 The north side of Pyramid E-VII-sub, Uaxactun, a Late Preclassic substructure belonging to the Chicanel culture. On top of this stucco-faced pyramid had once been a pole-and-thatch temple. Ht 26 ft 4 in. (8 m).

representing feathered serpents and depictions of mountains, were centrally placed on all four sides. Postholes sunk into the floor show that the superstructure was a building of pole and thatch.

Facing E-VII-sub across a plaza on the east is a long, low platform oriented north–south, topped by three small structures. It was early on recognized by archaeologists that lines of sight drawn from the pyramid to the corners of these three structures marked sunrise at the solstices and equinoxes, and the arrangement was dubbed the "E-group." As explained in the last chapter, such E-groups have been found at other Middle and Late Preclassic sites in the southern lowlands, but since the alignments at some of these sites are not as precise as at Uaxactun, some have questioned their astronomical function.

Although Group H at Uaxactun was discovered by Carnegie as long ago as 1935, it was only in 1985 that excavations under Juan Antonio Valdés of Guatemala's Institute of Anthropology and History revealed that its major constructions were almost entirely Late Preclassic, with hardly any Classic-period overburden. The South Plaza, the focus of Valdés' research, is essentially a great platform supporting on the east a high, truncated pyramid (H-sub-3) with a central stairway. Flanking it are two buildings with rooms which were once spanned by the corbel vault, or "false arch," while three other buildings faced it on the west, all of them enclosing a small plaza.

Most of the South Plaza structures have huge, perfectly preserved masks and friezes formed of stucco over a stone core, and these were polychromed. On each side of the central stairway of H–sub–3 are two superimposed masks, each 8 ft 9 in. (2.65 m) high. The iconography of the South Plaza is complex – several deities are represented, some of them with quite Olmecoid characteristics.

Even more advanced temples have been uncovered at Tikal, which lies only a half-day's walk south of Uaxactun. Two late Chicanel structures, for instance, had superstructures with masonry walls, and it is possible, though certainly not proved, that the rooms were corbel-vaulted. Some quite extraordinary paintings embellished the outer walls of one of these temples, showing human figures standing in a background of cloud-like scrolls, carried out by a sure hand in black, yellow, red, and pink. Another set of murals, this time in black on a red background, was found inside a late Chicanel burial chamber at Tikal. The subject matter comprises six richly attired figures, probably both human and divine. The two sets, which are thought to date from the last half of the first century BC, are pretty clearly in the Izapan style characteristic of Kaminaljuyu.

Late Preclassic tombs at Tikal prove that the Chicanel elite did not lag behind the nobles of Kaminaljuyu in wealth and honor. Burial 85, for instance, like all the others enclosed by platform substructures and covered by a primitive corbel vault, contained a single skeleton. Surprisingly, this individual lacked head and thigh bones, but from the richness of the goods placed with him it may be guessed that he perished in battle and had been despoiled by his enemies, his mutilated body being later recovered by his subjects. The remains were carefully wrapped up in textiles, and the bundle placed in an upright position. A small, greenstone mask with shell-inlaid eyes and teeth seems to have been sewn onto the bundle to represent the head [34]. A stingray spine, the symbol of self-sacrifice among the Maya, and a spondylus shell were added to the gruesome contents. Packed around the burial chamber were no fewer than 26 late Chicanel vessels, one of which contained pinewood charcoal radiocarbon dated to *c.* AD 1. Later inscriptions trace the origin of the Tikal dynasty to one Yax Ehb Xook ("First Step Shark"), who lived in the first century AD; according to epigraphers Simon Martin and Nikolai Grube, it could well be that this is his tomb. There must have been earlier kings, of course, yet this personage, often mentioned in later texts, may exemplify a change in royal status. A similar shift occurred among Aztec lords in central Mexico. When shown in retrospective documents of the colonial period, they went from modestly dressed chieftains to true kings endowed with fine clothing and jade or turquoise regalia.

The towering achievements of the Classic Maya in building and maintaining their enormous centers have blinded us to the equally remarkable

34 A greenstone mask, with shell-inlaid teeth and eyes, from Burial 85, Tikal. Ht 5 in. (12.7 cm).

florescence of Late Preclassic Maya culture. Two sites in Belize have shed light on this phenomenon. The first is Cerros, a relatively compact site located on a small, narrow peninsula near the mouth of the New River on the southern edge of Chetumal Bay. Excavations and mapping carried out by David Freidel of Washington University have shown that this Late Preclassic center, with four primary pyramidal structures along with a host of other buildings, was surrounded by a moat-like canal which may have been connected with raised agricultural fields. One such pyramid was a two-tiered temple platform; its central stairway was flanked by four elaborate plaster-sculpture masks. Their relationship to the huge platform masks found at Uaxactun and on early buildings at Tikal is obvious. Such sculptures are now being found on a yearly basis, from Cival, where Francisco Estrada-Belli has discovered spectacular masks, to the city of Holtun, excavated by Brigitte Kovacevich and Michael Callaghan of Southern Methodist University. To be sure, challenges of interpretation remain. The masks are sufficiently varied so as to baffle scholars, and it is uncertain who or what they identify. Some may correspond to specific hills, others to presiding gods thought to reside in summit temples.

Far up the New River, a considerable distance to the southwest of Cerros, is the important site of Lamanai (known as "Indian Church" on older maps of Belize), which was excavated by David Pendergast of the Royal Ontario Museum during a series of field seasons beginning in 1974; Elizabeth Graham of University College London has continued that research up to the present. Lamanai lies on a long lake formed by the river, and its 718 mapped structures are stretched in a strip along its shore. Its location and rich remains attest to its entrepreneurial importance in ancient Maya trade. While it was occupied from earliest times right into the post-Conquest period, much of its importance lies in the imposing Late Preclassic temple-pyramids which underlie many of the Early Classic constructions, including one with a plasterwork mask closely resembling those from Cerros.

THE MIRADOR REGION

The full scope of Late Preclassic achievement in the southern Maya lowlands has only come to light at the sites of Nakbe and El Mirador, located in the northernmost Peten, a region with extensive swamps, or *bajos*, that were probably shallow lakes in that era. We have already seen that Nakbe had a precocious development of monumental architecture during the Mamom phase of the Middle Preclassic. El Mirador, some 8 miles (13 km) northwest of Nakbe and connected to it by a causeway which crosses the intervening *bajos*, has turned out to be the earliest Maya capital city, far older than Tikal, which it dwarfs by its size and lessens by its antiquity [III]. It may well have been the seat of an expansive polity of a scale hitherto unknown among the Maya – perhaps, too, its reach coincided with the spread of Ch'olti'an as a prestige language. The investigations and mapping carried out initially by Bruce Dahlin and Ray Matheny, and later by Richard Hansen, have shown that El Mirador is of Late Preclassic (Chicanel) date; it was largely abandoned throughout the Early Classic, though there is evidence of Late Classic reoccupation in the high courtyards of some of its pyramids.

There are two groups of monumental construction, connected by a massive causeway, and in fact a whole network of causeways radiates out from El Mirador across the surrounding swampy landscape. The East Group is dominated by the Danta pyramid and its associated platforms, which cover an area of 44.5 acres (18 ha); the pyramid and the structure upon which it sits reach a height of 230 ft (70 m) and thus with its smaller superstructures must comprise an overall bulk which makes it the largest in Mesoamerica, its only competition the Great Pyramid at Cholula, in Mexico. The Tigre pyramid in the West Group is no less than 180 ft (55 m) high, with an estimated volume of 380,000 cubic meters.

35 Stucco frieze showing impersonators of the Rain God, Chahk. Tecolote Structure, El Mirador. Late Preclassic.

As at Cerros, Lamanai, Uaxactun, Tikal, Cival, and Holtun, gigantic stucco masks of deities flanked stairways at El Mirador; one excavated structure has huge masks representing the Principal Bird Deity (PBD), the great bird-monster so typical of the Late Preclassic, while another has stucco figures of god-impersonators (surely of Chahk) swimming beneath a frieze of water birds catching fish [35]. Typical also of this intriguing period in Maya culture history is the "triadic" pattern of architecture found here and at other similarly early lowland sites: this consists of a principal pyramid, plus two others which face each other, all with stairs leading from a central plaza. The scale and centrality of the triadic pyramids suggest an important function, perhaps even funerary. At Wakna, Guatemala, a triadic building contains a tomb, strengthening this supposition. Another clue comes from El Palmar, also in the Peten. There, James Doyle of the Metropolitan Museum of Art found an Early Classic tomb on the front axis of a triadic building. Did this placement recall or honor a Preclassic burial nearby?

The largest buildings at Nakbe were erected at the beginning of the Late Preclassic (*c.* 300 BC) over Middle Preclassic platforms, although these dates may need review. Hansen has so far uncovered nine monumental architectural masks and panels, including the largest yet known for the Maya;

situated at the base of Structure 1, this is a vast relief of the PBD, over 16 ft (4.9 m) high and 36 ft (11 m) wide, completely polychromed. Another stela, reconstructed from many fragments, shows two important personages facing each other. Their costume links this relief in time and style to the granite stela from Kaminaljuyu.

We now realize that by *c.* AD 150, the Mirador Basin cities had suffered a collapse as disastrous as that which would occur throughout the southern lowlands at the end of the Classic. El Mirador, Nakbe, and other centers were abandoned to the forest, for reasons that remain obscure; but, as in the later case, drastic overpopulation with all its consequences (including the silting up of the *bajos*, compounded by a severe drought). The geographer Nicholas Dunning and colleagues have emphasized that this collapse has many of the hallmarks of the better understood disasters at the end of the Classic period. It was multi-generational, not always occurring at precisely the same time, indicative of chronic heightened vulnerability and reduced resilience. The Maya coast, too, was affected by rising sea levels and groundwater tables. Some cities, such as Tikal, adapted, while El Mirador did not.

SAN BARTOLO

One of the greatest archaeological finds of all time took place in 2001, when William Saturno of Boston University stumbled across San Bartolo, a relatively small Peten site in dense forest some 25 miles (40 km) northeast of Tikal. Taking refuge from the intense sun in the shade of a looter's tunnel that had penetrated a temple-pyramid, Saturno's flashlight illuminated part of an extraordinarily well-preserved fresco that the perpetrators had overlooked in their search for saleable antiquities. This is in fact the earliest Maya painting known, dating to *c.* 100 BC or slightly earlier. In its beauty and sophistication it equals the famous Late Classic murals of Bonampak (Chapter 5). Large sections of the mural's estimated 90 ft (27.4 m) have been revealed or reconstituted from fragments, casting new light on Maya religion and society during the Late Preclassic. In a way, it is the painted, polychrome version of some of the iconography that we see in Izapan sculpture, depicting the creation of humankind and of maize.

The mural is on the upper part of the four inner walls of a modestly sized, flat-roofed structure built onto the back of the "Las Pinturas" pyramid. During one extension of the pyramid, the painted room ("Room 1") was partly demolished and filled with rubble; it is this rubble that has to be cleared by Saturno's project to free the frescoes. Further paintings and large stuccoed reliefs of the PBD adorn the exterior of the structure.

According to the archaeologist Heather Hurst, who has copied the mural, at least two artists' hands are detectable. Painting directly onto the wet plaster in brilliant pigments – red, black, yellow, white, gray, and blue – certain mixes of paint were favored by this or that artist. The north wall

36 Modern rendering of a wall painting of the resurrected Maize God surrounded by female figures. The deity's head is purely Olmec. San Bartolo, Guatemala, first or second century BC. Late Preclassic.

37 Rendering of a detail of the west wall mural, San Bartolo. The Principal Bird Deity perches on a world-direction tree, while one of four Hunahpus perforates his penis before an offering of a slain deer. Late Preclassic.

shows the Maize God removing a bottle gourd of water from the cave; four young women – his harem of corn maidens? – accompany him, one offering maize *tamales* [36]. All stand on a feathered serpent that issues from the maw of a gigantic, anthropomorphic mountain – in effect, a cave. The face of the protagonist, with its slanting eye and downturned mouth, is identical to lifesized jade masks of the Maize God that have survived from the Olmec civilization.

On the west wall are no fewer than four Hunahpus (Hunahpu being one of the Hero Twins), each standing before a world-direction tree, on top of which perches a PBD holding in its mouth a two-headed serpent. One of these has descended to a *nantze* tree to eat its fruit as in the Popol Vuh myth and at Izapa. In each case, the Hero Twin holds his own penis in his hand and perforates it with a long instrument, the blood graphically spurting forth – a royal rite that heretofore we have only known for the Classic and Postclassic Maya (although bloodletters of jade or stingray spines are attested for the Olmecs). Between some Hunahpus and the tree are sacrificial offerings, including a deer [37] and a fish. As Karl Taube has pointed out, the sequence of these offerings is almost precisely the same as scenes in the Dresden Codex from over 1,300 years later, a truly remarkable demonstration of ritual continuity. Then, to the right of these scenes, the Maize God with his Olmec mask beats a turtle shell within a quatrefoil cave, itself placed within a gigantic turtle (possibly representing Earth). Taube interprets this as the birth of music and dance, facilitated by raucous rain gods.

As one approaches the northwest corner of the room, a figure sits on a scaffold during what may be a calendrical ritual, as a lesser personage climbs a ladder to offer him a headdress. Later, in the Classic period at Piedras Negras, Guatemala, such activities correspond to calendrical rites after royal accessions. Does the scene at San Bartolo show an actual king, as many scholars believe, or is it a depiction of an early ritual that was adopted and transformed by later rulers? Whatever the interpretation, the majority of the images in the San Bartolo murals concern mythic beings, not humans. The relatively low, wide room and the didactically positioned paintings – all slanting to within close distance of standing visitors – leads to a speculative possibility. Were they intended for instruction in the mysteries of Maya belief? Young men's houses are known in later Maya civilization, and it may be that the mural building at San Bartolo served a similar purpose in imparting esoteric knowledge to adolescents.

Although there are a few glyphic texts on the walls of San Bartolo, these are sparse and extremely difficult to interpret, since full phonetic writing had not yet been developed by the Maya. Excavations in 2005 by Saturno and his team proved that there were even earlier structures underneath Room 1, and revealed a stone block painted with a vertical column of ten glyphs, one of which may be recognizable as the sign for *ajaw*, "king"; the remaining signs are at present undecipherable, but bear a vague formal resemblance to Isthmian glyphs. Associated radiocarbon dates show that this text is the oldest known writing in the Maya area, and perhaps even the oldest anywhere in Mesoamerica. By at least 300–200 BC, the Maya were a literate people. There is yet more to be found at San Bartolo: Edwin Román of the University of Texas, Austin, has recovered fragments of even finer painting, with an exquisite range of colors, in the so-called Ixim building above the murals room.

FROM PRECLASSIC TO CLASSIC IN THE MAYA LOWLANDS

The splendor of Late Preclassic civilization is found throughout the Peten-Yucatan Peninsula wherever the spade has gone deep enough. Even in the seemingly less-favorable Northern Area, there are enormous constructions which date to this period, such as the great high mound at Yaxuna, a temple substructure having a ground plan of 197 by 427 ft (60 by 130 m). At the site of Edzna in north-central Campeche, research carried out by Ray Matheny has shown that the Late Preclassic occupants had constructed a massive hydraulic system, consisting of 13.75 miles (22 km) of canals radiating out in all directions from the city's center (resembling aquatic versions of Maya ritual roads) and even a moat surrounding a kind of "fortress."

By the terminal Late Preclassic of the second and third centuries AD we are on the threshold of Classic Maya civilization. Temples arranged around plazas, construction with limestone and plaster, apron moldings and frontal stairways on pyramids, tomb building, and frescoes with naturalistic subjects – all had already taken shape by the end of the Late Preclassic. This brief epoch sees the intrusion of new ceramic traits which seem to have been first elaborated across a broad area, the most important of these being the addition of hollow, breast-shaped supports to bowls, hourglass-shaped pot-stands, and polychrome. Maya polychrome is distinguished by a brilliant range of colors applied over a glossy, translucent orange underslip, but wherever it was first invented it certainly was not native to the Peten region. Corbeling of rooms must have evolved from methods employed in the construction of tombs, and by AD 250 began to be in universal use at Peten sites. The principle is simple: above the springline of the walls, successive courses of stones were set in overlapping rows up to the vault summit, which was capped by flat stones. However, there is an inherent structural weakness, and the great thrust from above is taken up in Maya buildings by massive walls and by the strength of the rubble-cement fill. Nevertheless, once adopted it became the badge of Maya architecture in the lowlands, as opposed to the thatched or flat-beam roofs of Mexico.

The list is impressive, but while hieroglyphic writing is sporadically present, Long Count dates are not. Nevertheless, towards the close of the Late Preclassic, some inscribed texts definitely celebrate the doings of great personages. A human figure in relief on the walls of Loltun Cave

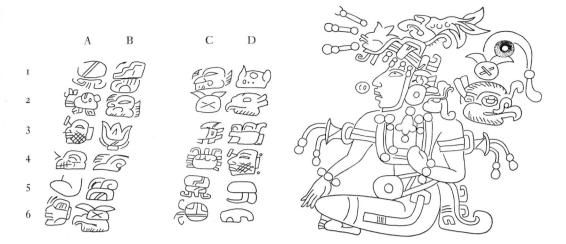

38 Incising on a greenstone pendant. The name of the ruler being "seated" (i.e. enthroned) appears at B6 and again behind his shoulder. Late Preclassic.

in Yucatan (associated with a Maya date that, alas, cannot be placed in time) testifies to this – but literacy and a concern with recording important dates in the lives of rulers did not become really prevalent in the lowlands until the eve of the Classic period. A good example of this would be the greenstone pectoral at Dumbarton Oaks, said to be from Quintana Roo [**38**]. A were-jaguar face on one side indicates that the object was originally Olmec; during the Late Preclassic, the reverse was delicately incised with the seated figure of a richly garbed ruler, facing four vertical columns of hieroglyphs. Next to the personage's shoulder is inscribed his name, almost surely to be read "Sky Owl." The same glyph combination appears twice in the text, once following a sign now known to be a very early form of the verb "to be seated." Epigraphers conclude that the pectoral reverse records the "seating," or accession to power, of the ruler in question.

By the time the Long Count calendar made its debut in the lowlands, at the opening of the Early Classic *c.* AD 250, the life and times of the royal house had come to be the major preoccupation of the Maya state, and full Maya civilization had begun.

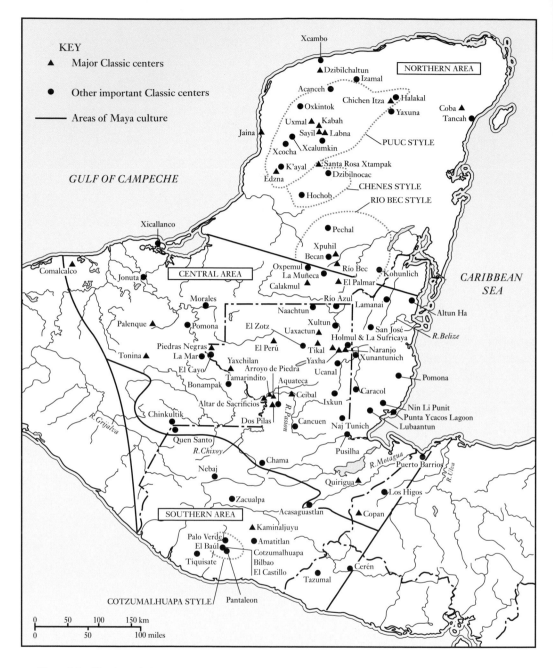

KEY

▲ Major Classic centers

● Other important Classic centers

— Areas of Maya culture

Xcambo

▲ Dzibilchaltun

NORTHERN AREA

Izamal

Acanceh

Chichen Itza Halakal

● Oxkintok

Coba ▲

Uxmal ▲ Kabah Yaxuna Tancah

Jaina ▲ Sayil ▲▲ Labna

Xcocha Xcalumkin PUUC STYLE

K'ayal ▲ Santa Rosa Xtampak

Edzna Dzibilnocac

Hochob CHENES STYLE

RIO BEC STYLE

GULF OF CAMPECHE

Xicallanco Pechal

Xpuhil

Becan

Comalcalco ▲ Oxpemul Rio Bec Kohunlich

Jonuta ● La Muñeca El Palmar *CARIBBEAN*

CENTRAL AREA Calakmul *SEA*

Morales Río Azul

Naachtun Lamanai

Palenque ▲ Pomona El Zotz Xultun Altun Ha

Piedras Negras ▲ Uaxactun San José *R. Belize*

Tonina ▲ La Mar El Perú Holmul & La Sufricaya

El Cayo Yaxchilan Tikal Naranjo

Arroyo de Piedra Yaxha Xunantunich

Tamarindito Ucanal Pomona

Bonampak Aquateca Caracol

Altar de Sacrificios Ceibal Ixkun

Chinkultik Dos Pilas Cancuen Nin Li Punit

Quen Santo Naj Tunich Punta Ycacos Lagoon

R. Chixoy Lubaantun

Nebaj Chama Pusilha

Quirigua ▲ *R. Motagua* Puerto Barrios

Zacualpa Los Higos *R. Ulúa*

Acasaguastlan Copan

SOUTHERN AREA

▲ Kaminaljuyu

Palo Verde ● Amatitlan

El Baúl Cotzumalhuapa

Tiquisate Bilbao Cerén

El Castillo

Tazumal

COTZUMALHUAPA STYLE Pantaleon

R. Grijalva

0   50   100   150 km

0   50   100 miles

39 Sites of the Classic period.

4

▼▼▼▼▼▼▼▼▼▼▼▼

CLASSIC SPLENDOR: THE EARLY PERIOD

During a span of six-and-a-half centuries, from about AD 250 to 900, the Maya left vivid evidence of a new kind of society [39]. Real personalities can be identified in this period, with lives both dramatic and highly textured. The Preclassic period had shadowy kings and palaces or noble residences. By Classic times, full royal courts came into view, as population grew to an unprecedented extent. These courts centered on a ruler and close members of his, or less often her, family. Several courtiers were so mighty as to be magnates, perhaps descended from collateral royal lines. They needed to be co-opted and watched, lest their pretensions got out of hand.

Then, below, came a variety of servants, some priestly, skilled in war, music, and the crafting of images and glyphs. The latter overlapped with what we might call "bureaucrats," the bean counters – quite literally so, of chocolate beans, an item of wealth! They monitored the ebb and flow of goods and services, making sure that the ruler took in tax or tribute to match or exceed his generosity to others. The most bizarre courtiers (at least from our vantage) were dwarves or other malformed people [40]. Surprisingly common in Maya art, they recall the court fools immortalized by Diego de Velázquez in the Spanish court of Philip IV in the sixteenth century AD. And then, invisible in our sources but surely present, were the cooks, sweepers, water-haulers and washers, the real servants at court.

Numbers are hard to guess. Philip IV of Spain surrounded himself with as many as 1,700 people; his later relative, Emperor Charles VI, up to 2,500. Tikal and especially Calakmul probably had smaller courts, perhaps of several hundred courtiers and servants. One reason size is hard to estimate is that many servants probably lived outside the palace, so there is no way to tally them from palace rooms alone; such buildings probably housed only a few people.

Classic-period sources are detailed for some courts. At Piedras Negras, over a hundred people are known. Yet, despite its size, Tikal's record is limited, and the same holds true for Calakmul. Getting at the dynamism of the Maya court involves a mix of evidence, some from Classic texts and images, along with comparisons drawn from other parts of the world, where courts can be studied in more detail. The first thing to understand is that every court had its own history and different emphases. Courts were subject to the whims of rulers, affected by their relative prosperity, and varied by local traditions. Not all rulers were effective. Some governed boldly and

decisively, while others simply reigned in passive ways, presiding over events outside their control. Certain kings wished to contrast with predecessors, while some simply ran out of resources. A living court changed constantly, yet tended also to claim a steady link to the past.

But several shared features are clear. In the first place, courts were often imitative. Through a curious form of standardization, they emulated each other, even those of enemies. Alternatively, they sought conscious contrasts with neighboring kingdoms. The dynasty at Arroyo de Piedra and Tamarindito, Guatemala, took pride in its sculptors, while Dos Pilas, only a few kilometers away, and its cousins at Tikal did not mention a single one. Sons were sent, as from La Corona, Guatemala, to a larger court at Calakmul to polish heirs and, not coincidentally, to serve as hostages securing their fathers' good behavior. No court stood on its own. The replication of its features rippled down to magnates or lesser nobles, who ran their own, albeit far less impressive, provincial establishments. Some of these might have been pleasure retreats for monarchs, but many served those wishing to imitate royal splendor.

Courts heightened inequality in Maya kingdoms. This was true physically, in that access needed to be controlled. A ruler available to anyone, at any time, was unlikely to preserve his or her special status. Royal palaces restricted and channeled movement, via doorways or small patios. By this means, gatekeepers (not always the ruler!) gained leverage over the flow of information and people at court. It was in the ruler's interest to know as much as possible about his kingdom, and some sought power by reserving that knowledge to themselves. During the Classic period, accessibility diminished over time; courts became less and less porous, a goal easier to achieve in larger cities than smaller ones. The quintessential gatekeepers were "favorites," special friends of the ruler. One such individual is known from Piedras Negras, Guatemala, during the final years of the Classic period. Present at court as a young man, he rose to become chief warrior, lord of a subordinate kingdom, and apparent power behind the throne. Usually, favorites were loathed by competitors; when they fell, they fell hard.

Exclusivity was not only physical, but also social and behavioral. Obsessed with protocol, courts sorted people by their relative rank or status. This was done by assigning titles, positions of precedence, or particular tasks, a pattern that becomes clearer as the Classic period progresses. Etiquette and refined speech also marked these boundaries, by identifying those who understood such rules and those who did not. The existence of a "high" language, understood by only a few people, deepened that exclusivity, as did precise knowledge of when to undertake ceremonies and how to conduct them. No Maya pot showed precisely what was done at court; rather, it

40 The finest Maya wood carving known, this seated figure from Tabasco, Mexico, represents a courtier, a moustachioed dwarf with folded arms; traces of hematite remain on the piece. The dwarf probably supported a real mirror, angled for use by a ruler. Ht 14 in. (35.5 cm).

depicted what was supposed to happen, as a lesson in correct decorum. The esoteric knowledge of the Maya did not arise solely for its own sake. It served to separate and elevate people in the know from those denied that privilege.

This attention to refinement extended beyond language and behavior. Maya pots show rulers sniffing bouquets of flowers or bedecked with jewels, and the concern with aesthetics permeated all courtly life. Rulers and noblemen projected an image of beauty in their persons and practices; they discerned and evaluated that which was exquisite. Dances, for example, were likely choreographed rather than improvised, and the principal performer was the ruler himself. Poetry and oration, perhaps not completely comprehensible to the masses, sounded through palace halls and courtyards; dress, ornament, and cuisine contrasted, too, with what might be worn or eaten by lower ranks.

There are suggestions of other kinds of elegance. Mary Miller discovered that musicians in Classic imagery often appear in a set order, beginning with singers and maraca players, followed by drummers, holders of turtle shell rasps, and trumpeters. The ordering might have been purely conventional, but it underscores the complexity of orchestral arrangements. Did Maya courts have their own composers, a Handel at Tikal, or Jean-Baptiste Lully at Palenque? At the same time, such establishments exhibited the opposite of refinement in an unmistakable dehumanization of reviled enemies, a delight in their pain and dishonor [41]. This combination of warrior ethos and aesthetic sensibility would not seem out of place in Japan of the Shogunate. Just as a samurai might craft an exquisite ink painting, a Maya lord at Aguateca, Guatemala, could carve shell or paint like any other great craftsman.

The rivalry within and between courts made them arenas of competition, places of opportunity and danger. Behind every courtier lay, in all probability, a tale of opportunistic success or thwarted ambition. Yet, if comparisons around the world tell us anything it is that courts did not operate by individual action alone. They worked instead through factions pivoting around a high-ranking courtier or member of the royal family. Fierce guardians of secrets and insider information, these groups would favor a certain patron. Where such stratagems typically played out was in royal or noble marriages. A particular match tended to strengthen one cabal and weaken another – after all, external politics always has an internal local dimension too. We can well imagine that when Bird Jaguar IV, ruler of Yaxchilan, Guatemala, married Lady Mut Bahlam of Hixwitz there must have been rejoicing for some and gnashing of teeth for others.

A final observation is that courts functioned as "great households." They were, of course, a little like the homes of humble subjects. In them, people ate, drank, and worked. But, in other respects, they differed greatly. Modest acts in small households had little political consequence. In courts, feasts and gifts helped to bind alliances and keep underlings happy, with effects across the kingdom. Oddly, however, royal rhetoric in the Classic period did not stress this reality. Scenes with food, drink, and tribute focused on the ruler's consumption and acquisition rather than his generosity to courtiers. For the king, it appears, receiving was better than giving. A further contrast between great and small households was in their level of impersonality. In a small setting, most people knew each other, but rulers probably did not recognize all their servants. As in the royal courts of Europe, this gave ample

41 Captive on hieroglyphic stairway from Dzibanche, Quintana Roo, Mexico. He is bound with flowery stalks, hair dishevelled. The text, with a date of 10 August AD 490, refers to his capture under the authority of a Dzibanche king.

room for gross inefficiency and corruption. Presumably, the hemorrhaging of food, drink, and treasure happened among the Maya as well. Yet, for all the emphasis on courtly societies in the Classic, we should remember that there were many areas, often in coastal or more remote regions, that were beyond their control or paid only lip service to dynastic lords.

DEFINING THE EARLY CLASSIC

The Classic is, in fact, defined as the span during which the lowland Maya were using the Long Count calendar on their monuments. In 1864, workmen digging a canal near Puerto Barrios, on the steamy Caribbean coast of Guatemala, came across a jade plaque which subsequently found its way to Leiden, Holland [42]. The Leiden Plaque, which once dangled

42 The Leiden Plaque, a jade plaque found in 1864, shows a Maya king trampling a captive underfoot and, on the reverse side, carries the date 8.14.3.1.12, 1 Eb 0 Yaxk'in, corresponding to 18 September AD 320.

from a ruler's belt, has engraved on one face a richly ornamented Maya lord in dancing position, trampling underfoot a sorry-looking captive, a theme repeated on so many Maya stelae of later times. On the other side is inscribed the Long Count date 8.14.3.1.12, corresponding to 18 September AD 320. As with many such plaques, it may have been a posthumous portrait of an ancestor. The style of the glyphs and the costume and pose of the person depicted call to mind the Late Preclassic monuments of the high-lands and Pacific Coast, but in this case the date is preceded by the typical Maya Introductory Glyph, and the bar-and-dot numbers are followed by the signs for bak'tun and lesser periods. Until 1960 the Leiden Plaque was considered the most ancient object dated in lowland Maya fashion, but now we have Stela 29 from Tikal, erected in 8.12.14.8.15 (9 July AD 292). Thus, the lowland Maya were definitely using the Long Count by the close of the third century AD. From this point until the Classic downfall, we have a very closely dated archaeological sequence derived from carvings on stelae and other monuments, themselves tied, at Uaxactun and other sites, with the construction of floors, building stages, and tombs. The Classic conveni-ently divides into an Early and a Late period at *c.* AD 600; this division is not merely an arbitrary invention of the archaeologist, for not only did a profound upheaval take place in part of the Central Area at that time, but there are considerable cultural differences between the two halves.

TEOTIHUACAN: MILITARY GIANT

Two things set off the Early from the Late Classic: first, the strong Izapan element still discernible in Early Classic Maya culture, and secondly, the appearance in the middle part of the Early Classic of powerful waves of influ-ence, and almost certainly invaders themselves, from the site of Teotihuacan in central Mexico. This city was founded in the first century BC in a small but fertile valley opening onto the northeast side of the Valley of Mexico. On the eve of its destruction at the hands of unknown peoples, at the end of the sixth or beginning of the seventh century AD, it covered an area of over 5 sq. miles (13 sq. km) and may have had, according to George Cowgill, a preemi-nent expert on the site, a population of some 85,000 people living in over 2,300 apartment compounds. To fill it, Teotihuacan's ruthless early rulers virtually depopulated smaller towns and villages in the Valley of Mexico. It was, in short, the greatest city ever seen in the Pre-Columbian New World.

Teotihuacan is noted for the regularity of its two crisscrossing great avenues, for its Pyramids of the Sun and Moon, and for the delicacy and sophistication of the paintings which graced the walls of its luxurious palaces. In these murals and elsewhere, the art of the great city is per-meated with war symbolism, and there can be little doubt that war and conquest were major concerns to its rulers. Teotihuacan fighting men were armed with atlatl-propelled darts and rectangular shields, and bore round, decorated, pyrite mosaic mirrors on their backs; with their eyes sometimes partly hidden by white shell "goggles," and their feather headdresses, they must have been terrifying figures to their opponents.

At the very heart of the city, facing the main north–south avenue, is the massive Ciudadela ("citadel"), in all likelihood the compound housing the royal palace. Within the Ciudadela itself is the stepped, stone-faced temple-pyramid known as the Temple of the Feathered Serpent (TFS), one of the single most important buildings of ancient Mesoamerica, and apparently well known to the distant Maya right through the end of the Classic. When the TFS was dedicated c. AD 200, at least 200 individuals were sacrificed in its honor. Study of their bone chemistry reveals that not a few are certain to have been foreigners. All were attired as Teotihuacan warriors, with obsidian-tipped darts and back mirrors, and some had collars strung with imitation human jawbones.

On the facade and balustrades of the TFS are multiple figures of the Feathered Serpent, an early form of the later Aztec god Quetzalcoatl (patron god of the priesthood) and a figure that may, according to Karl Taube, have originated among the Maya. Alternating with these figures is the head of another supernatural ophidian, with retroussé snout covered with rectangular platelets representing jade, and cut shell goggles placed in front of a stylized headdress in the shape of the Mexican sign for "year." Taube has conclusively demonstrated this to be a War Serpent, a potent symbol wherever Teotihuacan influence was felt in Mesoamerica – and, in fact, long after the fall of Teotihuacan. Such martial symbolism extended even to the Teotihuacan prototype of the rain deity Tlaloc who, fitted with his characteristic "goggles" and year-sign, also functioned as a war god.

This mighty city held dominion over large parts of Mexico in the Early Classic as the center of a military and commercial empire that may have been greater than that of the much later Aztec. Drawing upon historical data on the Aztecs, ethnohistorian Ross Hassig has suggested that Mesoamerican "empires" such as Teotihuacan's were probably not organized along Roman lines, which totally replaced local administrations by the imperial power; rather, they were "hegemonic," in the sense that conquered bureaucracies were largely in place, but controlled and taxed through the constant threat of the overwhelming military force which could have been unleashed against them at any time. Thus, we can expect a good deal of local cultural continuity even in those regions taken over by the great city; but in the case of the lowland Maya, we shall also see outright interference in dynastic matters, with profound implications for the course of Maya history.

That the Teotihuacan empire prefigured that of the Aztecs is vividly attested at the site of Los Horcones, Chiapas, Mexico, studied by Claudia García-Des Lauriers of California State Polytechnic, Pomona [43]. Situated near a spectacular hill, the city lies on the very edge of the great chocolate-producing area known to the Aztecs as the Xoconochco. The southern part of Los Horcones is a dead ringer for the complex composed of the Pyramid of the Moon and the Avenue of the Dead at Teotihuacan, and artifacts and

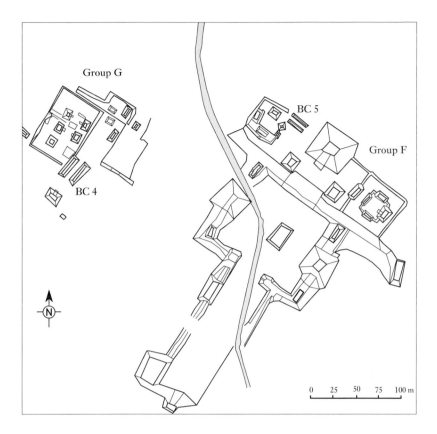

43 Map of Los Horcones, Chiapas.

monuments point to a direct Teotihuacan presence in the region. It is hard to believe that the Aztecs were not the imitators here, and that Teotihuacan was the first to interest itself in the cacao plantations and trade routes of the region. The contact did not stop there, but extended to what may be a Teotihuacan colony at Montana, Guatemala. This settlement, surrounded by others like it within a 3 mile (5 km) radius, is endowed with magnificent incense burners, portrait figurines, and an enigmatic square object known to specialists as *candeleros* or "candle holders," though their function is not known. And Montana was not alone. In 1969 tractors plowing the fields in the Tiquisate region of the Pacific coastal plain of Guatemala, an area located southwest of Lake Atitlan that is covered with ancient (and untested) mounds, unearthed rich tombs and caches containing a total of over 1,000 ceramic objects. These have been examined by Nicholas Hellmuth of the Foundation for Latin American Archaeological Research; the collection consists of elaborate two-piece censers (according to Karl Taube symbolizing the souls of dead warriors), slab-legged tripod cylinders, hollow mold-made figures, and other objects, all in Teotihuacan style [44]. Numerous finds of fired clay molds suggest that these were mass-produced from Teotihuacan

44 Effigy incense burner in Teotihuacan style, Escuintla area, Pacific coastal Guatemala. Early Classic. Ht 18 in. (45.5 cm).

prototypes by military-merchant groups intruding from central Mexico during the last half of the Early Classic.

Contacts must have been intense and conducted at the highest levels. Taube has detected Maya-style ceramics at Teotihuacan, some made locally, perhaps in an ethnic enclave at the city. Legible Maya glyphs from murals in the Tetitla apartment compound at Teotihuacan attest to royal names and rituals of god-impersonation. Very likely, these refer not to mere craftsmen brought from the Maya region, but to dynastic elites. Yet the movement of these people must have been complex. Under the immense Pyramid of the Moon, Saburo Sugiyama and colleagues discovered a burial with three bodies, dating to AD 350–400, accompanied by carved jades and a seated, Maya-like figure of greenstone. The positioning of this figure and the bodies nearby, all buried upright with crossed legs, resembles patterns in tombs at Kaminaljuyu in Highland Guatemala; the date, too, is close to a period of marked contact between Tikal and Teotihuacan-related people. Bone chemistry suggests that at least one of the occupants of the tomb came from the Maya region, but spent much of his life at this important Mexican city.

THE ESPERANZA CULTURE

The disintegration of Maya culture in the highlands began with the close of the Verbena-Arenal period (c. AD 100–150), when building activity slackened at major sites. By the end of the Preclassic, even the great ceremonial center of Kaminaljuyu, focal point of Maya cultural and political affairs in the Southern Area, appears to have been a virtual ruin.

Shortly after AD 400, the highlands fell under Teotihuacan domination. An intrusive group of central Mexicans from that city, or intermediate points like Montana, penetrated Kaminaljuyu and perhaps yet more strongly other sites nearby, like Mejicanos near Lake Amatitlan, a place known for elaborate, aquatic deposits of Early Classic incense burners. An elite class consisting of central Mexican foreigners, and the local nobility with whom they had marriage ties, could have ruled over a captive population of largely Maya descent. Whatever their origin (see below), they were certainly swayed by native cultural tastes and traditions and became "Mayanized" to the extent that they imported pottery and other wares from the Central Area to stock their tombs.

The Esperanza culture which arose at Kaminaljuyu during the Early Classic, then, is a kind of hybrid. There are several complexes of Esperanza architecture at Kaminaljuyu, all built according to a plan which is not in the least bit Maya. Essentially these are stepped temple-platforms with the typical Teotihuacan talud-tablero motif, in which a rectangular panel with inset (*tablero*) is placed over a sloping batter (*talud*). The good building stone which is so abundant in the Mexican highlands is missing at Kaminaljuyu, so that the architect, almost certainly a Teotihuacano himself, had to be content with clay faced with red-painted stucco, sealed with a slurry of

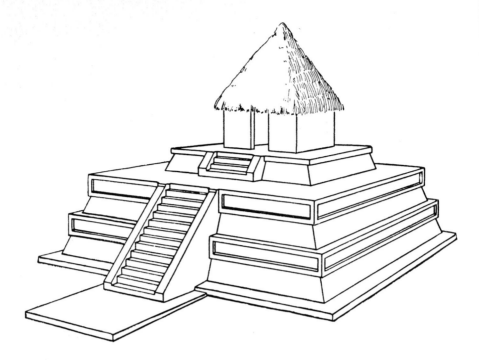

45 Structure A-7 at Kaminaljuyu, a temple-pyramid of the Esperanza culture.

volcanic pumice, a new kind of building technology which may have been introduced by a handful of foreign masons. A single stairway fronted each stage of these platforms, while on top a temple sanctuary was roofed either with thatch or with the more usual flat beam-and-mortar construction of Teotihuacan [45]. Radiocarbon dates from these buildings place them at *c*. AD 500, and they may represent a relatively quick burst of construction.

The lords of Esperanza-phase Kaminaljuyu chose the temple platforms themselves as their final resting places. As with the earlier Verbena-Arenal people, each platform was actually built to enclose the ruler's tomb, a log-roofed chamber usually placed beneath the frontal staircase, successive burials and their platforms being placed in front of older ones. The honored deceased was buried in a seated posture upon a wooden bier, and accompanied not only by rich offerings of pottery and other artifacts, but also by up to three persons sacrificed for the occasion (generally children or adolescents). Surrounding him were rich funerary vessels, undoubtedly containing food and drink for his own use, as well as implements such as *metates* and *manos* needed to prepare them.

Jade ornaments, some in the process of manufacture, were recovered in vast quantity from the Esperanza tombs: beads, complex ear ornaments in the form of flared spools, pendants, and spangles are ubiquitous [46]. One ear jewel names the founder of the Tikal dynasty, indicating close relations with the Peten. The layout of these tomb buildings, oriented to the west

The Esperanza culture

46 (*Above left*) A long jade bead carved with a human figure wearing a crane headdress, from Tomb A-VI, Kaminaljuyu, Esperanza culture. L. 6 in. (15.6 cm).

47 (*Above*) Restored Thin Orange ware vessel in the form of a seated man, from Tomb X, Kaminaljuyu. This ware was manufactured to Teotihuacan taste in northern Puebla, and appears wherever Teotihuacan people had penetrated. Esperanza culture. Ht *c.* 11.75 in. (30 cm).

48 (*Left*) An Esperanza-culture tripod vessel with cover, from Tomb B-II, Kaminaljuyu. The exterior had been stuccoed and painted in buff, red, and light green. The warrior figures on the vessel are Mayoid, while the glyphs on the lid are Teotihuacanoid. Ht 12.5 in. (32 cm).

with shrines above each burial, is first documented in the Peten. The likelihood of direct, historic contact is strong. Underneath one staircase was a 200-lb (90-kg) boulder of jade from which V-shaped slices had been sawn, indicating that the Esperanza elite had access to the Río Motagua valley, the source of this substance so precious to all the peoples of Mesoamerica.

Few of the pottery vessels from the Esperanza tombs are represented in the rubbish strewn around Kaminaljuyu, and so it is clear that they were intended for the use of the elite class alone. Some were actually imported from Teotihuacan itself, probably carried laboriously over the intervening 800 or 900 miles (1,300–1,450 km) on back racks such as those still used by native traders in the Maya highlands. The ceramic hallmarks of the Teotihuacan civilization are: the cylindrical vessel with three slab feet and cover [48]; a little jug with open spout and handle; the florero, named for its resemblance to a small flower-vase; and Thin Orange ware, made to Teotihuacan taste in northern Puebla [47]. All are present in Esperanza, but so are polychrome bowls with peculiar "basal flanges" from the Peten. Certain of the tripod vessels were stuccoed and painted in brilliant colors with feather-bedecked Teotihuacan lords or seated Maya personages, and both Maya and Teotihuacan deities, including the Butterfly Goddess (a symbol of the warrior cult) so popular in Mexico. One Peten Maya polychrome bowl was even overpainted with processional figures in Teotihuacan style, speech scrolls curling from their mouths.

All sorts of other valuables were placed with the dead. That Esperanza pomp, perhaps at the funeral itself, was accompanied by music is shown by shell trumpets and by large turtle carapaces used with antler beaters as percussive instruments. On a large effigy incense burner from one grave, a seated person strikes a two-toned slit drum. Besides jade, the corpse was ornamented with pearls, cut-out pieces of mica, and rich textiles which have long since rotted away. Several tombs contained pairs of jaguar paws, symbols of royal power among the highland Maya. The highest technical achievement is seen in the mirrors made up of pyrite plates cut into polygonal shapes and fitted to each other over a circular disk of slate, which could have been warriors' back mirrors. These are in all likelihood another import from Teotihuacan, but the reverse of one proved to have remarkable carving in an elaborate scrollwork style that is associated with the Classic Veracruz civilization then developing on the Gulf Coast of Mexico. The ability of the Esperanza rulers to amass luxurious objects from the most distant parts must have been considerable.

In an effort to locate the exact origins of the individuals in the Esperanza tombs, Lori Wright of Texas A&M University subjected samples of their bones and teeth to oxygen isotope and strontium analysis. The results were mixed: all but one of the elite occupants appeared to be local, while the sacrifices and decapitated heads came from various places, many in or near the Peten. That pattern fits with the Tikal reference on the earspool mentioned before. Only one body could have derived from Teotihuacan, yet even these results are ambiguous. The Esperanza culture may have its spectacular side, but almost as striking are its omissions. The Long Count calendar had disappeared from the Southern Maya Area for good, which is strange considering its ancient roots here. The figurine cult had utterly disappeared. Nor is there any sure indication of stone sculpture on any scale in Esperanza Kaminaljuyu—rather, Preclassic carvings were reused. At Kaminaljuyu, Early Classic construction is energetic in the monumental center of the city, in strong contrast to the Late Classic, when building technology changed; the deposits are extensive but thin. Who were the people in the Esperanza burials? It seems unlikely that they were invaders from Teotihuacan (or only a few such migrants existed) but they certainly enjoyed ties with that distant city, and with dynasties in the Peten.

CERÉN: A NEW WORLD POMPEII?

For Cerén, a small but prosperous village in western El Salvador near the southeastern limits of the Maya Area, the Early Classic went out with a bang. On an ill-fated day around AD 595, the nearby Loma Caldera volcano erupted, spewing out steam, ash, and eventually volcanic bombs that rained down on the villagers, who fled and abandoned their homes. The entire village of thatched-roofed houses, built of wood and clay, was sealed off by meters of ash; excavations led by Payson Sheets of the University of Colorado have revealed a Pompeii-like situation, uncovering astonishingly complete testimony to the way of life of these early peasants. Through plaster casts, former agricultural fields yielded evidence of cultivation of small-cobbed maize, manioc, and other comestibles, while from kitchens and living areas came evidence for the villagers' cuisines, such as chile peppers and an olla containing chocolate. Two of the houses were certainly devoted to village rituals; Structure 12 in particular had a mask made from a deer skull along with a collection of crystals like those used by modern Maya diviners.

TZAKOL CULTURE IN THE CENTRAL AREA

Early Classic remains in the Central Area are burdened with towering constructions of Late Classic date, and it has only been since the 1960s that the elaboration of Maya civilization during this early period has been fully realized. The Tzakol culture, as the civilization of the Peten and surrounding regions is called, endures until about 9.8.0.0.0 (c. AD 600). From what we can tell, it began with moister conditions. This must have been welcome after the shortfalls in rain that Douglas Kennett and his colleagues detected at the close of the Preclassic period. But a severe dry spell struck just as Teotihuacan engaged with the region in the late third century AD. Droughts have a variety of consequences; while human society is often more flexible and self-adjusting than one thinks, climate deterioration could have played some role in historical changes of the time, if correctly identified.

Many dynasties were founded in the Early Classic period. Several, such as Copan, Honduras, and Caracol, Belize, appear to have hived off from the southern Lowlands. A few families claimed to have far older origins, but such assertions are implausible and the historical figures in question surely mythic in nature (rather like the generations of Adam enumerated in the Book of Genesis). Stelae and altars are carved with dates, and the finest examples, sealed up in the tombs of honored personages, emphasize stylized polychrome designs of cranes, flying parrots, or men [xxi]. These designs often also appear on bowls with a kind of apron or basal flange encircling the lower part. When more elaborate, as on a bowl from the tomb of El Diablo, at El Zotz, Guatemala, the scenes tend to be mythic or watery [xxii]. Most of these pots doubtless held stews or *tamales*. Along with these purely Maya ceramics are vessels which betray the influence of distant Teotihuacan: again, the cylindrical vase supported by three slab legs, the small, spouted jug, and the florero.

There have been two schools of thought regarding the nature of Teotihuacan's presence in the Peten. At first, following the discovery of royal tombs in Tikal's North Acropolis in the 1960s, and of associated stelae, some Mayanists, especially the late Tatiana Proskouriakoff and the art historian Clemency Coggins, argued for a takeover by rulers actually hailing from Teotihuacan. Subsequently, the majority opinion came to be that there was never an actual military intrusion of Teotihuacan people, but emulation by the local Tikal dynasty of the Teotihuacan cult of war, which the dynasts adopted for their own political ends. Generations before this there were Teotihuacan architectural elements and cached obsidians at Tikal and Altun Ha, Belize – the Maya were no strangers to that sprawling, foreign city. But what happened at Tikal from the time when glyphs give us more information? Recent studies by David Stuart strongly suggest that Proskouriakoff and Coggins were right all along.

Dynastic rule among the lowland Maya has some of its deepest roots at Tikal, the great city of the northern Peten whose Classic name was *Mut* (the name "Tikal" only appears in the nineteenth century, perhaps from *ti aka'l*, "at the water reservoir"). Later dynastic annals retrospectively reference a putative founder, who may have lived in the first century AD. According to these inscriptions, the eighth successor to the Tikal throne was an individual known to epigraphers as Chak Tok Ich'aak I ("Great Jaguar Paw"). We know little about him other than his untimely end, which took place on 16 January AD 378. The Maya phrase referring to his demise states that "he entered the water"; that is, the watery Underworld. On that very same day, according to the inscriptions, a figure named Sihyaj K'ahk' ("Fire is Born" or "Born from Fire") showed up on the scene. Significantly, he had previously "arrived" at El Perú, a Peten center on the upper Río San Pedro – this would have been a natural route

49 Ball court marker in Teotihuacan style, from the Mundo Perdido, Tikal, Guatemala. The name glyph of "Spearthrower Owl" appears within the rosette at the top. Early Classic. Ht 3 ft 3 in. (1 m).

for an army marching between the Gulf Coast plain and Tikal. The verb "arrive" is surely a euphemism for something more sinister.

These two events are probably connected. Sihyaj K'ahk', one of the most enigmatic yet momentous figures in Maya history, was in no way a member of the native Tikal dynasty of "Great Jaguar Paw." Rather, he was the liege, perhaps general, of a strange figure whose very non-Maya hieroglyph is a spearthrower conjoined to an owl, a motif well known in the iconography of Teotihuacan [49]. Stuart hypothesizes that "Spearthrower Owl" could even have been a ruler of that fearsome capital. The "arrival" of Sihyaj K'ahk' strongly suggests a Teotihuacan invasion from the west, and the capture and immediate execution of the legitimate Maya ruler.

Whoever "Spearthrower Owl" might have been, within a year his own son, Yax Nuun Ahiin ("First Crocodile") – previously dubbed "Curl Nose" by archaeologists – had been installed, presumably by Sihyaj K'ahk', as the tenth ruler of Tikal. This initiated a new dynasty of patently foreign extraction, at least on the paternal side. Yax Nuun Ahiin was yet a boy when he succeeded to the throne. Strangely, his bone chemistry indicates that he was raised in the southern Maya lowlands, hinting that his father had been meddling in the area for some time. We have not one but two portraits of the young *ajaw* ("king") attired as a Teotihuacan warrior flanking Stela 31, the accession monument of his own son Sihyaj Chan K'awiil, "K'awiil (who is) Born from the Sky," along with a stela from a small site near Tikal that records the death in AD 439 of the latter's grandfather, "Spearthrower Owl." The Maya region had prior contacts with Teotihuacan, but this was something new: cities in the Peten previously independent from, or unconcerned with, Tikal now seemed under its sway or that of Sihyaj K'ahk'. Historians of Rome speak of a "pax [peace] romana," a time of secure imperial control. Perhaps, for a briefer span, the Maya had a similar interval when local squabbles were suppressed by the new rulers of Tikal. What is clear is that, far more than once thought, people moved about in the Early Classic periods: from bone chemistry, Lori Wright estimates that a more than negligible percentage of Tikal's population came from elsewhere, including the introduction of foreign brides for elites. This may have led to its rapid expansion.

The Tzakol culture

50 (*Left*) Polychrome two-part ceramic effigy from Burial 10 (the tomb of Yax Nuun Ahiin) at Tikal. This represents an old god receiving a severed head as an offering. Ht 13.7 in. (35 cm).

51 (*Below*) The tomb chamber of Sihyaj Chan K'awiil II (Burial 48) at Tikal. On its walls is painted the date 9.1.1.10.10 4 Ok (21 March AD 457), together with other glyphs which probably represent flowers and jewels, a fragrant afterworld paradise.

52 (*Right*) Temple cornice, in stucco, with Chahk head and representation of sky in the form of a band. El Zotz, El Diablo Structure F8-1, Sub 1C, north side, *c.* AD 375.

Burials of great richness, filled with luxury offerings of both Teotihuacan and local Maya origin [51], have been uncovered beneath the Tzakol temples of Tikal's North Acropolis – not so much an "acropolis" as the long-revered "necropolis" of the city's earliest kings; these include the tombs of both Yax Nuun Ahiin (who died *c.* AD 404) and his son Sihyaj Chan K'awiil II. Burial 48 is now generally accepted as the final resting place of the latter, following the suggestion by Clemency Coggins. The tomb chamber was cut from the soft underlying bedrock, and contained three interments: Sihyaj Chan K'awiil II himself, and two adolescent victims sacrificed to accompany the dead king. The white, stuccoed walls were covered with glyphs applied in black paint by a sure hand, including the Long Count date 9.1.1.10.10 (21 March AD 457), probably the date of the ruler's death or funeral [51]. Not far away, in a defensive location at the city of El Zotz, is a spectacular tomb some 75 years older. Underneath a shrine, just in front of a building covered with images of Chahk (the rain god) and aspects of the sun in its daytime and nocturnal aspects [52], the tomb probably belonged to the founder of a local dynasty. Depictions of bamboo scaffolds and footprints on its walls suggest it was used in later accession ceremonies – the same features would appear two centuries later at Piedras Negras, Guatemala.

53 Stuccoed and painted "screwtop" jar from Tomb 19, Río Azul. This vessel once held the chocolate drink; the left-hand glyph on the lid spells the Maya word for cacao. Early Classic, fifth century AD. Ht 9 in. (23 cm).

The 1960s and early 1970s saw the apogee (or nadir) of Maya tomb robbery in the southern lowlands. The modestly sized site of Río Azul in the northeasternmost Peten was particularly heavily looted, providing the international market with an extraordinary variety of elite objects of the utmost beauty, mainly (but not entirely) of Early Classic date. Three emptied tombs had Tzakol murals painted in red and black on the bare walls, including glyphic texts of dynastic nature and a scene depicting the undulating surface of the watery Underworld. A project led by Richard Adams of the University of Texas, San Antonio, uncovered several intact tombs with Early Classic offerings, although not of the scale or magnificence of those already stripped of their finery. We now realize that the royal dead, including those of Río Azul, were accompanied by the food and drink to which they had been accustomed in life. One magnificent Río Azul pottery vessel with a screw-on lid was stuccoed and painted with glyphs [53], among which was one read by David Stuart as the word *ka-ka-w(a)*, "cacao," a designation confirmed by the laboratory of the Hershey Foods Corporation who detected traces of both theobromine and caffeine – Q.E.D.!

If, as some scholars believe, Teotihuacanos were present in the Peten cities, might they have tried to impose the worship of their own gods upon the Peten Maya, substituting their own rain god for the native Chahk? To this the upper part of a shattered stela from Tikal [54], showing a large

Tlaloc-like face exactly like that upon the shield of Stela 31 [56] (also from Tikal), might be testimony. However, a more plausible interpretation is that this is a portrait of a foreign overlord attired as the Teotihuacan war god, who we know had Tlaloc characteristics. In fact, Karl Taube argues that the large depictions of this god on slab-like stelae at places like Tikal and Yaxha, Guatemala, reproduce war shields. Blue-faced Tlaloc appears again on finely stuccoed and painted vessels from the Tikal tombs, together with the Mexican god of spring, Xipe Totec, recognizable by his open mouth and pairs of vertical lines passing through the eyes and across the cheeks [55]. Some of these vessels are Thin Orange ware manufactured in the Mexican highlands, another comes from the Tiquisate region on the Pacific Coast of Guatemala, while yet others represent hybrids in shape and decoration, fusing Maya and Teotihuacan traditions. There almost certainly was lively trade between the Peten and the Valley of Mexico, as we can see from Tzakol sherds of basal flange bowls found at Teotihuacan, and green blades struck from obsidian mined at Pachuca in central Mexico placed with the Tikal dead. Sadly, nothing remains of all the perishable products which must have traveled the same routes – textiles, quetzal feathers, jaguar pelts, wooden objects, and so forth.

Maya mural art has its roots in the Late Preclassic wall paintings such as those found at San Bartolo and Tikal, but by Tzakol times it had reached a very high degree of elaboration and naturalism. Destroyed since their discovery in the 1930s, the lovely Early Classic wall paintings of Structure B-XIII at Uaxactun were executed in muted tones of red, brown, tan, and black [VI]. The art is inspired by real life: here two male figures, one a Teotihuacan "visitor" costumed as a warrior, are in conversation, standing before a palace building sheltering three Maya ladies. At one side are two horizontal rows of figures, probably meant to be standing on two levels of a stepped platform, painted with a strong feeling for individual caricature; a few are chattering in excited discourse. Singers shake rattles, while a small boy beats time on a skin-covered drum.

Not only in the northern Peten, but also at many other places in the Central Area, major Maya centers were well established by the fifth century AD and even earlier. At these, Teotihuacan domination is less easy to demonstrate, and one can mistakenly suppose that this was restricted to the Tikal-Uaxactun area alone. Nonetheless, Yaxha, with its shield-like stela, has a city plan which combines the amorphous Maya pattern with formal "streets" laid out in the central Mexican fashion. Some of its proportions date back to the Late Preclassic period, but they were maintained in later periods, too. Yaxha, "green-blue water," is, incidentally, one of the few Classic Maya cities to retain its original name.

Even more convincing evidence for a Teotihuacan military presence in the northern Peten comes from La Sufricaya, a minor site a half mile (0.8 km) to the west of the major Maya site of Holmul. Situated on the northwest corner of a raised platform is a small, flat-roofed building with

Tikal and Teotihuacan

54 (*Left*) Fragmentary stela in the form of a shield from Tikal, showing a ruler attired as Tlaloc, the Teotihuacan war god.

55 (*Below*) Lid of a stuccoed bowl from the tomb of Yax Nuun Ahiin (Burial 10), Tikal. Tzakol culture.

56 (*Right*) Side view of Stela 31 at Tikal, showing the youthful Yax Nuun Ahiin. He is costumed as a Teotihuacan warrior: in one hand he carries an atlatl or spearthrower, and on his left arm a shield with the face of the Teotihuacan war god, Tlaloc.

interior murals. Although in very bad condition, in part due to looters' activity, two of these paintings show rectangular, red grids; within each division stands a Maya individual. Taube makes the plausible case that this grid is a map of Teotihuacan. Another mural appears to be a copy of a hybrid Teotihuacan-Maya book, with footprints on a road to show a journey – this convention is notably central Mexican, not Maya [57]. This may be the closest we get to seeing one of the many books that once existed at Teotihuacan itself. Off to the right side of the larger of these murals are five horizontal, oblong "boxes," in which well-armed Teotihuacan warriors are seated. Standing in another oblong "box" above these is a much-eroded, plumed individual. Another wall in this complex bears a beautifully painted Maya text in red that apparently celebrates the anniversary of the "arrival" (or as we have seen, likely invasion) of the foreigner Sihyaj K'ahk' at Tikal.

Just north of the Peten lies Calakmul, a huge Maya city with ancient roots going back to the Middle Preclassic. According to its excavator, Mexican archaeologist Ramón Carrasco Vargas, by the Early Classic it had already begun to establish a network of alliances that by the Late Classic had made it into a formidable rival of Tikal; indeed, Simon Martin and Erik Velásquez believe the dynasty may even have come from the southern part of the Mexican state of Quintana Roo, where a great number of large and important cities have been investigated in recent years. The immense Structure II on the south side of the main plaza, renovated in the early fifth century AD over an already large Late Preclassic building, attests to its influence and power. Throughout the Classic, Calakmul's history would be recorded on the largest number of stelae known for any Maya site, but most of them, sadly, of low-quality limestone and therefore badly eroded.

Whatever might be the nature of Teotihuacan influence on the political and cultural affairs of the Peten Maya, in the second half of the sixth century AD a serious crisis shook Tikal and Uaxactun. In AD 562, Tikal was attacked and conquered by Calakmul, which prospered as Tikal's fortunes fell. The lone mention of this singular event is at Caracol, Belize, a former ally of Tikal's, with whom it had a messy falling out. No more stelae were erected at Tikal for the next 130 years, and there are signs of widespread, purposeful mutilation of public monuments and, as Simon Martin has recently discovered, profound breaks in the dynasty. It is not clear what all this means, but although no Peten site actually seems to have been abandoned near the close of the Early Classic, there might have been fierce internecine warfare or perhaps even a popular revolt.

57 Modern rendering of a mural from Structure 6N, La Sufricaya, Guatemala. The scene, in hybrid Maya-Teotihuacan style, may copy movements recorded in a now-lost book. Two buildings are shown, one with thatched roof, the other with Teotihuacan-style panels. They are connected by a road marked with small footprints to indicate direction of travel. AD 400.

When the smoke clears in the first decades of the seventh century AD, Classic Maya life is seen to have been reconstituted much as before, possibly with new rulers and new dynasties. But Teotihuacan was now neither a political nor economic force in Peten Maya civilization. Its last embroilment was not with Tikal, but the rather isolated site of Piedras Negras *c.* AD 510. A miraculously preserved wooden box, found in a cave north of the city, may even record a visit to Teotihuacan that lasted 155 days. In some great event (of which we have no written record) the central part of Teotihuacan was destroyed by burning, and the empire of which it was the capital fell. This took place *c.* AD 550–575, and may have been a decisive factor in the Maya disturbances in the closing decades of the Early Classic. However, just as the memory of the achievements of Classical Greece and Rome has remained forever strong in Western civilization, so did the glories of Teotihuacan continue to live in the minds of Maya rulers right through the end of the Late Classic: a Maya king was always proud to take to the field attired as a Teotihuacan-style warrior, fitted with the characteristic War Serpent headdress or helmet. For some dynasties, the founders of their families would be associated for centuries with shrines or buildings tied to Teotihuacan imagery and fire rituals.

COPAN IN THE EARLY CLASSIC

Although relatively isolated, in a remote valley on the southeastern perimeter of the Central Area, not even Copan escaped the heavy cultural grip of Teotihuacan. According to much later inscriptions, the Copan dynasty was founded in the early fifth century AD by K'inich Yax K'uk' Mo' ("Great Sun Quetzal-Macaw"); this royal line was to persist until the death of the sixteenth ruler in AD 820, when kingship probably came to an end at Copan. Yet there must have been earlier chiefs or even kings who failed to be recorded in the annals of the Late Classic.

The key to reconstructing the dynastic history of Copan is the square monument known as Altar Q that celebrates an event in the life of the sixteenth king, Yax Pahsaj Chan Yopaat, which took place in AD 776. Seated around its four sides are this ruler and all the previous fifteen kings in the succession, each upon his own name glyph. Facing Yax Pahsaj Chan Yopaat is the Founder Yax K'uk' Mo' himself, handing him the baton of office. While all of the potentates wear the wrapped turban characteristic of Copan rulership, only the Founder is adorned with the goggles of the Teotihuacan war god. Deciphered by David Stuart, the text on Altar Q's upper surface opens with the "arrival" and accession to office of Yax K'uk' Mo' in AD 426; this brings to mind the "arrival" of Sihyaj K'ahk' in Tikal during the previous century, and it must be more than coincidental that both are given the honorary title of "West Kalomte." Stuart interprets this scene to mean that the Founder was another stranger coming in from the west, perhaps from Teotihuacan.

Early Classic jade

58 (*Left*) Early Classic jade plaque, from Copan, Honduras. This may represent a mythic form of the howler monkey, with reptilian scales. The position is that of a newborn, and the jade may have been intended to lie flat. Ht 4.25 in. (10.7 cm).

59 (*Below*) A jade object shaped like an ear flare from Pomona, Belize, early Tzakol culture. The four glyphs refer to gods. Diam. 7 in. (17.8 cm).

In an extraordinary marriage of epigraphy and dirt archaeology, Copan's modern excavators are beginning to confirm what was previously only known from the inscriptions. Rather than destroying Late Classic buildings to unearth earlier constructions, in recent decades American and Honduran teams have investigated Copan's huge Acropolis by means of tunnels, working in from the great face exposed by past ravages of the nearby Copan River. As shall be seen, the most spectacular discoveries have been made underneath Temple 16, a mighty pyramid now known to have been dedicated to the dynastic Founder, Yax K'uk' Mo' (whose cult there was maintained through the centuries). The excavators, Robert Sharer and David Sedat of the University of Pennsylvania, hit archaeological "pay dirt," the very earliest, most deeply buried structure of all in the Acropolis, nicknamed by them "Hunal." This was a relatively small temple platform in the purest Teotihuacan architectural style, complete with *talud* and *tablero*. Exploring Hunal, they found a vaulted masonry tomb containing a single raised burial slab, on which rested the cinnabar-covered bones of a male individual over fifty years of age, with jade-inlaid incisors; rich offerings of Teotihuacan-style and other ceramics lay nearby. There is every reason to believe that this is Yax K'uk' Mo' himself, the "stranger from the west."

Initially, archaeologists suspected that he was a native of Teotihuacan. Recent isotopic analysis on his teeth, however, indicates that he spent most of his youth neither in the Valley of Mexico nor in Copan, but somewhere in the central lowlands. Indeed, as David Stuart has pointed out, glyphic texts point to his origin at the ancient city of Caracol, Belize, although by adolescence he had moved closer to Copan. When dynasties changed, the new ruler was more likely to be a stranger than someone rising through the ranks. Soon after this burial, Hunal was covered by another temple platform, this time in the familiar apron-molding style of the Peten, and faced with a fine stuccoed and polychromed panel depicting the Maya Sun God. Over this, Copan's second ruler placed an even more splendid platform; known as "Margarita," its western face is adorned with an extraordinary stucco relief of two birds, a quetzal and a macaw – a full figure form of the Founder's name. And within Margarita is probably the richest tomb ever discovered at Copan, belonging to an aged female whom Sharer hypothesizes was the widow of Yax K'uk' Mo'. Among this noble lady's lavish offerings was what the excavators call the "Dazzler Pot," a stuccoed, slab-leg tripod brilliantly polychromed with a Teotihuacan temple design, from the doorway of which peeks a bird face with goggled eyes – could this be the Founder himself?

One of the more exciting discoveries at Copan in recent years was made by Honduran archaeologist Ricardo Agurcia. Dubbed the "Rosalila Structure," this temple dates to the close of the Early Classic, and was buried almost intact by later construction works. It gives Mayanists a good idea of what the splendid exterior of a stuccoed and polychromed

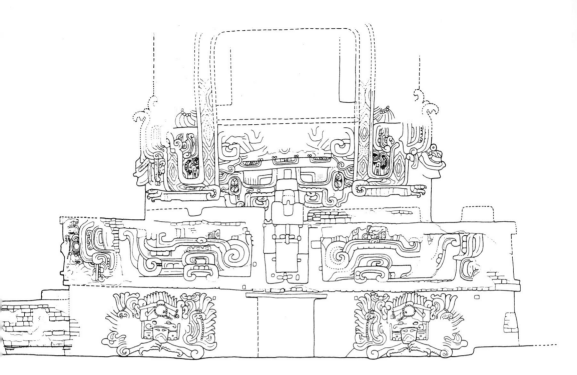

60 Elevation of the west side of the Rosalila Structure, Copan.

temple looked like, before time and the elements do their destructive work. Even part of the roof crest is preserved. On the front, facing west, is the Principal Bird Deity in all his glory [60]. His huge head, with Sun God eyes, is on the second story, and his serpent-bird wings are spread out on the upper facade of the lower one. An archaeological bonus was the find of sacred objects left on the floor of Rosalila, including nine eccentric flints which had been wrapped in blue cloth, some of which still adhered to the flints. As shown by Karl Taube and Barbara Fash of the Peabody Museum at Harvard, the kings of Copan preserved references to the Founder, Yax K'uk' Mo', from the earliest versions of this building to the latest.

Unlike in the northern Peten, there is no "hiatus" at Copan between the Early and Late Classic: the eleventh ruler, Butz' Chan, spans the gap, dying peacefully in AD 628. Although war was eventually to bring a temporary reverse to Copan's fortunes, being on the periphery of great civilizations must have had its rewards.

THE NORTHERN AREA

There is abundant pictorial and glyphic evidence for warfare across the Maya Area during the Early Classic, but proof of warfare is remarkably difficult to derive from "dirt" archaeology. A vivid exception to this rule is provided by Becan in the Chenes region just north of the Peten, which was completely surrounded by massive defensive earthworks sometime between the second and fourth centuries AD. These consist of a ditch and inner rampart, 38 ft (11.6 m) high, and would have been formidable, according to David Webster, if the rampart had been surmounted by a palisade. It would be tempting to see this as a consequence of a putative Teotihuacan invasion of the Chenes, but it is a purely Maya matter as the earthwork was built before the appearance of strong Teotihuacan influence at Becan.

Some 48 miles (80 km) to the east of Becan is the beautifully preserved, Early Classic pyramid-temple of Kohunlich, with its inset stairway flanked by red-painted stucco masks of deities. This and other sites in the Northern Area show burgeoning evidence of a robust Early Classic presence. Izamal, for instance, may have grown to almost 32 sq. miles (53 sq. km) at this time – although its actual population density may have been low – and was linked to the port of Xcambo on the north coast of Yucatan. According to Scott Hutson of the University of Kentucky the densely occupied city of Chunchucmil also thrived at the end of the Early Classic period. Spread across Yucatan and Quintana Roo are further sites with

61 Stuccoed figure of a howler monkey scribal god in Teotihuacan style on the upper facade of an Early Classic building at Acanceh, Mexico.

massive, megalithic buildings, some built in the Preclassic but with construction activity extending well into the Early Classic period. Exterior blocks are a meter long and pillow-shaped, covered by the thick stucco that characterizes major building of the time. One of the earliest centers is Oxkintok at the northern tip of the Puuc hills of western Yucatan. Marked by large buildings and several lintels with laconic texts, it also contains a mysterious labyrinthine building, the "Satunsat," with dark zones for unknown rituals.

Equally impressive is Acanceh, 13 miles (21 km) southeast of Mérida, the present-day capital of Yucatan. On the one hand, there are stepped pyramid platforms with inset stairways and apron moldings of straightforward Peten Maya type. On the other, there is an extraordinary facade stuccoed with relief figures strongly inflected by Teotihuacan style [61]. The scene appears to be a supernatural menagerie of squawking beasts and birds, framed above by conch shells. Among these are a puma, an anthropomorphic bat, birds of prey, a squirrel, a gopher with goggled eyes, and a representation of the Feathered Serpent or Quetzalcoatl, a central figure of Teotihuacan, somehow clutching – quite an accomplishment for a snake! – an obsidian blade, along with a repeated icon that may refer to a "Place of Reeds," that many believe to be Teotihuacan itself. Each creature appears within a stylized hill, perhaps naming that place, or showing that they lurk within: one somewhat fierce rabbit strains to support its hole. Acanceh demonstrates, as does much of the Maya region, that it was never isolated from other parts of Mesoamerica but periodically engaged with neighbors. This foreshadows the great Mexican invasions that were to take place in Yucatan some centuries later.

5

▼▼▼▼▼▼▼▼▼▼▼

CLASSIC SPLENDOR:
THE LATE PERIOD

The great culture of the Maya lowlands during the Late Classic period used to be seen as one of the "lost" civilizations of the world, its hundreds of cities and towns buried under what seemed an unbroken canopy of tropical forest. What was "lost" is now found. That canopy is gone in many places, fallen victim to cattle-ranching and new settlement. The good news is that a great deal is now known about this period, at all levels of ancient society. An unprecedented population, organized into communities large and small, grew to support the courtly societies that can only be glimpsed in preceding times. Glyphic texts, too, reveal much about the dramatis personae of these cities, along with their wars, alliances, rituals, and architectural commissions.

Classic cities have been detected and mapped by two means. The first, survey on foot, is a tried-and-true, yet unimaginably arduous, method. Topographic maps created this way show everything from large masonry buildings to the simple huts of common people; pyramids are obvious, but even modest houses are recognizable as low, rectangular mounds of earth and stone and are therefore easily detected. A newer, highly promising method involves "LiDAR," a word taken from "light" and "radar." Utilized by Arlen and Diane Chase at Caracol, Belize, and increasingly by other researchers, this laser technology pierces the jungle to reveal astonishing surface details, including terraced fields and subtle roads [62]. It is only a matter of time until the forest-covered lowlands are mapped entirely by this technology.

Maya cities are a far cry from the neat gridiron layout of Teotihuacan in central Mexico, which conforms far more to our conventional idea of a city. Instead, as shown by maps of Tikal and Ceibal in the Peten, or Dzibilchaltun in northern Yucatan, they exhibit an almost amorphous pattern of structures. These range from great temple-pyramids and palaces down to individual house mounds arranged around open squares (probably family compounds). Small plazas resembled the large ones at the core of most cities, where ritual dancing processions, displays of captives and tribute, and offerings of incense and human or animal sacrifices on pairs of stelae and altars took place. Ball courts, too, are attested at the larger Maya sites, and a few smaller ones. But the overall appearance is somewhat "colloidal," with occupation becoming progressively less dense at the margins. A few cities, such as Chunchucmil in Yucatan, are amazingly dense, with house lots demarcated by walls; others had extensive space for gardens. Most Maya cities are located on hills or elevated areas, the better

62 LiDAR image of Caracol, Belize, showing the site's center, along with agricultural terraces and causeways.

to see for miles and to be seen by subjects and enemies alike. They look, in fact, rather like artificial mountains. Water was scarce in the Peten, and at huge centers like Tikal there are several artificial reservoirs surrounded by embankments, which provided sufficient water to the city's inhabitants over the winter dry season. Vernon Scarborough of the University of Cincinnati makes the case that, at least to some degree, the Maya configured their urban zones to channel and capture water. At some sites this is understated; but not so at Palenque, which, according to Kirk French of Pennsylvania State University, displayed a remarkable ability to control water pressure through underground conduits that gushed into pools.

Few Maya cities have clear limits. In pre-industrial cities and towns of the Eastern Hemisphere, we are used to seeing city walls, but these are not found at Classic Maya sites. Because of the seemingly unplanned nature of settlements, the boundaries of Maya cities are difficult to determine. Becan, in the Río Bec region, is surrounded by a moat, the Petexbatun site of Punta de Chimino is isolated on its peninsula by a deep ditch, and the neighboring cities of Uaxactun, Tikal, and El Zotz are separated by an earthwork, perhaps never completed; but these cases are exceptions to the rule. When city walls are found, as at Dos Pilas, Ek' Balam, and Uxmal, they seem to date to the final years of the Classic period, when, in places, local conditions became hostile.

The late Sylvanus Morley once classified all known Maya centers, both Classic and Postclassic, according to their supposed degree of relative importance, ranging from Class 1 giants like Tikal and Copan down to Class 4 centers such as Bonampak and Acanceh. In 1946 he listed a total of 116 sites in the Northern and Central Areas, but explorations since then suggest that the figure could probably be doubled. Often, the question is not "how many sites are there," but "what part of the landscape is actually untouched by humans?" Even areas without visible buildings often prove, after excavation, to contain buried structures.

How large were the great cities in terms of size and population? Tikal and Calakmul are the largest of all Classic Maya sites and have been mapped down to the last house mound, although in view of the difficulty of drawing boundaries around any settlement of the lowlands it is hard to say exactly where they end. At Tikal, within a little over 6 sq. miles (15.5 sq. km), there are *c.* 3,000 structures, ranging from lofty temple-pyramids and massive palaces to tiny household units composed of thatch-roofed huts [63]. Estimates of the total Tikal population in Late Classic times vary all the way from 10,000 to 90,000 persons. Few Mayanists accept the latter figure; this would mean a density higher than that of an average city in modern Europe or America. The majority support a more reasonable figure of *c.* 60,000 for Tikal's entire realm. A glance at the site's layout shows that this is, unsurprisingly, a basically dispersed population, with a slight increase in frequency and size of houses as one moves closer to the heart of the city itself, where the dwellings of aristocrats and bureaucrats would have been more splendid than those in the outer regions. These were definitely spacious cities in comparison to the densely urbanized Teotihuacan, or to the Aztec capital, Tenochtitlan. As noted by David Webster, the matter of size has important consequences. If cities were not as large as previously supposed, then doubts about how the Maya would have supported themselves become less pressing. Exact estimates of population will always prove elusive. What is more useful is relative scale, which shows that, in Maya terms, the Late Classic truly was an exceptional period, with populations far in excess of earlier periods.

CLASSIC SITES IN THE CENTRAL AREA

A Classic Maya center typically consists of a series of stepped platforms topped by masonry superstructures, arranged around broad plazas or courtyards. In the really large sites such as Tikal there may be a number of building complexes interconnected by causeways, known to the Classic Maya as *sakbih*, "white roads." Towering above all are the mighty temple-pyramids built from limestone blocks over a rubble core. Although the

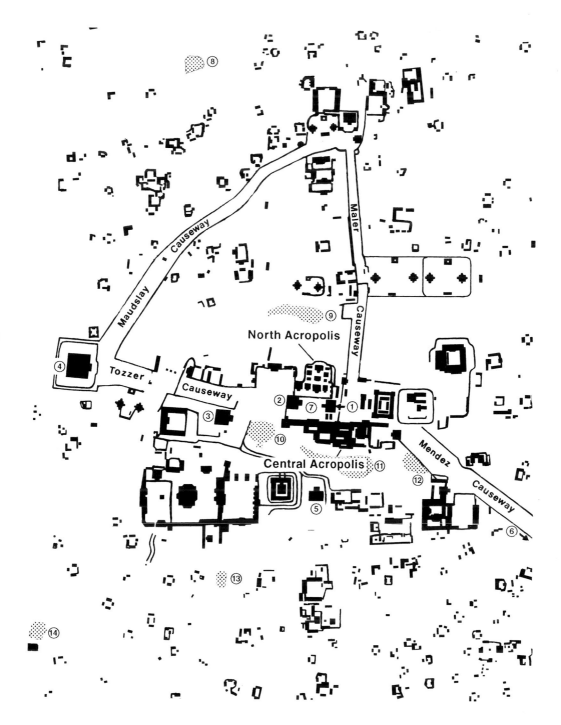

63 Plan of the central part of Tikal (the area covered is slightly over 1 square mile).
1–5 Temples I–V; *6* Temple of Inscriptions; *7* Great Plaza; *8–14* Reservoirs: *8* Bejucal; *9* Causeway; *10* Temple; *11* Palace; *12* Hidden; *13* Madeira; *14* Mundo Perdido.

temple interiors contain one or more corbeled and plaster-covered rooms, these are so narrow that they could only have been used on the occasion of ceremonies meant to be kept from plebeian eyes. Tall they are, but the Maya architects were not content and often added a further extension to the upper temple, a "roof comb," which along with the temple facade was highly embellished with painted stucco reliefs.

The bulk of construction work at Maya sites, however, was concerned with the palaces. These single-storied structures, built on similar principles to the temple-pyramids, were set on much lower platforms and contained more plastered rooms, sometimes several dozen in one building [64]. Occasionally, there may be one or two (or even more) interior courtyards. Palaces were in many cases built up over several centuries as each new ruler in a dynasty added his own palace to what became a single, large complex. Excavations by Peter Harrison at the Central Acropolis of Tikal, along with detailed scenes painted on Late Classic vases, confirm that the palaces were the administrative centers of the city. Seated on benches backed by large cushions covered with jaguar pelts, the *ajaw* ("king") or *kaloomte* (a high title of unknown meaning) dispensed justice, received tribute, entertained ambassadors, feasted, and otherwise acted royally in rooms draped

64 (*Left*) A room in the Five-Story Palace at Tikal, a part of the Central Acropolis group. From a photograph taken by Teobert Maler. These "palaces" are believed to have served both as royal residences and as administrative centers. As seen here, there are usually one or more plastered benches along the back wall of the rooms.

65 (*Right*) Figurines placed in Burial 39, El Perú, Guatemala. The concentric scene corresponds to an idealized or mythic court, including a king, queen, courtiers, dwarves (some boxers), and a deer looming over a kneeling man. The crude figurine at the center was made by a different hand. For full-page enlargements of the figurines, see fig. 66 and plates XXIII and XXIV.

with swagged curtains. In the great courtyards less private activities took place, including dances, ritual bloodletting from the penis and tongue on calendrically important days, and almost certainly sacrifice of high-ranking prisoners by beheading. From the ceramics at a site such as El Perú we get an idea of the palace staff described in Chapter 4: the courtiers and attendants, royal ladies or concubines, and court jesters or dwarves [65, 66, XXIII, XXIV]. The royal cooks and cleaners or other menials do not, however, appear in such imagery – their existence did not merit mention, although they must have been plentiful and their tasks closely monitored. Such staff are certainly known for historically documented cultures elsewhere in Mesoamerica, particularly for the Aztecs and for the Tarascans of Michoacan.

In any Classic center in the Central Area with a claim to importance, standing stelae were placed in the stuccoed floors of the plazas, usually fronting significant temples but sometimes palaces as well. At times the stelae appear on platforms supporting temple-pyramids, but the rule seems to have been that certain stelae were always associated with specific structures, for reasons which until recently were something of a mystery. Generally a stela will have a low, round, flat-topped "altar" standing before it. The subject matter of the relief carvings on one or both stela faces is

66 Figurines placed in Burial 39, El Perú, Guatemala. The scene remains enigmatic, showing a deer with a green necklace, loincloth and raised hoofs, perhaps blessing or even threatening a young male in a subordinate position. Deer are emblems of cuckoldry in Maya imagery, an animal that spirits away luscious young women.

67 Dos Pilas Stela 14, Guatemala, 6 December AD 711. Standing over the captive below, accompanied by a dwarf and water bird, the ruler holds a "manikin scepter" representing the god of rulership, K'awiil.

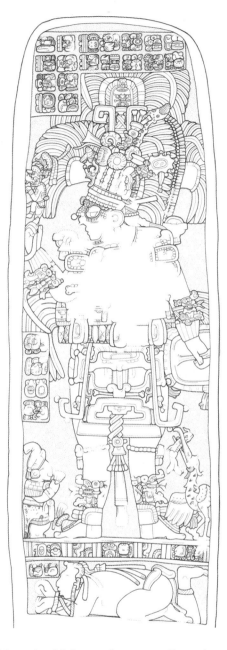

apparently always the same: a richly attired Maya ruler, generally male, carrying peculiar emblems such as the so-called "ceremonial bar," or scepter, in the form of the god K'awiil (in essence, a lightning axe linked to rulership), or else a similarly garbed person equipped with spear and shield and trampling a captive underfoot [**67**]. We shall examine these reliefs and the Long Count dates and glyphs which are inscribed on them in Chapter 9, for the story that they tell is now unfolding.

Ball courts are present at many sites in the Central Area, but they are more frequent and better made in the southeast. These courts are of stucco-faced masonry and have sloping playing surfaces. At Copan, in the southeast, three stone markers were placed on each side and three set into the floor of the court, but the exact method of scoring in the game remains obscure. Toward the western part of the Central Area, in centers along the Usumacinta River, monumental sweat baths are known, the earliest dating to the end of the Early Classic period and the majority appearing, as at Piedras Negras, in the Late Classic.

COPAN AND QUIRIGUA

Certainly one of the loveliest of all Classic Maya ruins is Copan, situated above a tributary of the Río Motagua in a section of western Honduras famed for its tobacco [68]. John Lloyd Stephens, who explored the site in 1839 (and bought it for 50 dollars!) called it "a valley of romance and wonder, where . . . the genii who attended on King Solomon seem to have been the artists." The principal temple-pyramids rest on an artificial acropolis which has been partly carried away by the Copan River, but many of the structures remain intact [69]. Among them is the Temple of the Hieroglyphic Stairway (Temple 25), completed in the eighth century AD, with a magnificent frontal staircase; every one of its 63 steps is embellished with an immense dynastic text, altogether totaling some 2,500 glyphs. This is certainly the longest text known for the Maya, but since most of it was found in extremely jumbled condition, it is difficult to reconstruct. The staircase was constructed in two phases, with very different glyphic style in its two sections, the upper being far more varied in execution than the lower, earlier portion. Most was built by Copan's unlucky thirteenth ruler (of whom more anon), but it was completed in the mid-eighth century by the fifteenth ruler, K'ahk' Yipyaj Kan K'awiil, with a strange "bilingual" inscription, one part Maya and the other a matching text in what some local artist must have imagined to be Teotihuacan hieroglyphs. Even at this late date, a century and a half after the fall of the great Mexican city, memories of Teotihuacan remained strong.

The ball court at Copan is the most perfect known for the Classic Maya, with tenon sculptures in the shape of macaw heads as its markers [70]. But it is the wonderfully baroque qualities of its carving in the round which distinguish this site from all others, for the Copan artists worked in a green-ish volcanic tuff superior to the limestone in use among the Peten centers. Not only were doorways, jambs, and facades of the major temples orna-mented with stone figures of the Rain God, young Maize God, and other deities, but no fewer than 63 stelae were carved and erected in Early and Late Classic times, together with 14 "altars." Many of these were placed in a broad court at the north end of the site, bounded by narrow stepped platforms from which the populace could gaze upon the spectacles involved with the stela cult [71, 72, 73, 74, II].

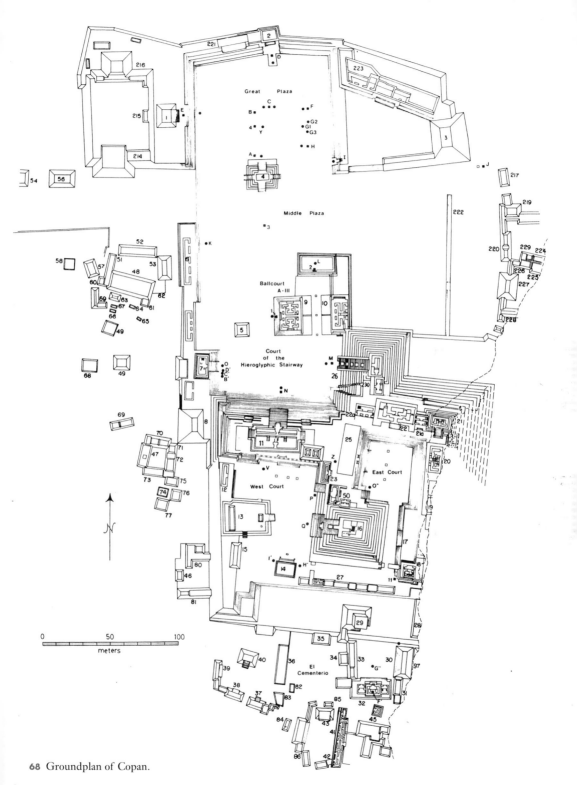

68 Groundplan of Copan.

69 A restoration drawing of the site of Copan, Honduras, by Tatiana Proskouriakoff. To the right is the Acropolis, to the left the Great Plaza. The bulk of the construction shown here is of the Late Classic period.

70 The ball court at Copan from the south. Late Classic period.

71 Monkey-man scribal god, from Copan. He holds a brush pen in one hand, and a conch-shell inkpot in the other. Ht 20.5 in. (52 cm).

72 Stone bust of the young Maize God, Temple 22, Copan. One of the wonderfully baroque sculptures from this site. Ht 28 in. (71 cm).

The glories of Copan

73 Stela D and its "altar," north side of the Great Plaza at Copan, from a lithograph published by Frederick Catherwood in 1844. The "altar" represents the Death God. The stela was erected by the ruler Waxaklahun Ubaah K'awiil to commemorate the tun ending date 9.15.5.0.0 (27 July AD 736). Ht 11 ft 9 in. (3.6 m).

74 Detail of Altar Q, Copan. K'inich Yax K'uk' Mo', the first ruler, faces Yax Pahsaj Chan Yopaat, the sixteenth. Late Classic, AD 776.

The thirteenth ruler of Copan was the man usually known as "18 Rabbit" (his real name was Waxaklahun Ubaah K'awiil, "18 are the semblances of K'awiil"), a great but ultimately unfortunate monarch who took power on 10 July AD 695. During his reign, the Acropolis and ceremonial precinct began to take on their present form, and to him may be attributed the marvelous Temple 22, a structure symbolizing the "Mountain of Sustenance" (well known in the mythology of the later Aztecs), from which all the crops which sustain the human race – above all, maize – are derived. Rising up the corners of the temple's substructure are monstrous faces representing *witz* or mountains, and adorning the temple itself were numerous busts of the young Maize God, some of the finest sculptures ever produced by the Classic Maya.

Like all Classic kings, Waxaklahun Ubaah K'awiil was something of an egoist, and the Great Plaza is crowded with his monuments, including Stela H which depicts him in the jade-bedecked costume of the Maize God. On the fateful day 9.15.6.14.6 6 Kimi 4 Tzek (4 May AD 738), shortly after he had dedicated the final version of the ball court, Waxaklahun Ubaah K'awiil was ignominiously captured and beheaded by K'ahk' Tiliw Chan Yopaat ("Fire-burning Sky Lightning God") of Quirigua, a nearby city which had largely been under Copan's thumb in past centuries.

This sudden downturn in Copan's fortunes, however, was short-lived, and the fourteenth successor, K'ahk' Joplaj Kan K'awiil, took office the following month. Copan's final well-attested ruler was the sixteenth, Yax Pahsaj Kan Yopaat ("First Dawned Sky Lightning God"), seemingly a weak and ineffective lord who allowed the nobility to expand in both number and power [74]. This state of affairs may explain the splendor of the suburban palace complex known austerely as Structure 9N-82, dedicated in AD 781. Devoted to the Monkey-man scribes of the Classic Maya, this palace may well have been inhabited by a high-ranking noble scribe and his family (see Chapter 9). Groups of similar ambition occur in other parts of the valley, including the massive Rastrojón complex that dominates the northeastern entrance to the Copan pocket.

Quirigua lies only 30 miles (48 km) north of Copan, in the lush environs of the Río Motagua, and was a far humbler Classic center that seems, on the basis of its inscriptions, to have periodically been one of the latter's suzerainties. Recent hieroglyphic evidence suggests that in fact it was founded by Copan; certainly the overall layout mirrors Copan's. Quirigua contains a few architectural groups of no great distinction, but its enormous sandstone stelae and carved zoomorphic stones are quite another matter [75, 76]. Stela E, erected late in the eighth century AD, might claim to be the greatest stone monument of the New World, its shaft measuring 35 ft (10.7 m) in height. Its frontal face is carved with the figure of a bearded ruler holding a

75 Altar of Zoomorph O at Quirigua. On the left of this enormous monument, which was dedicated on the k'atun ending 9.18.0.0.0 (12 October AD 790), is the figure of the rain god Chahk dancing in an S-shaped cloud. The zoomorph likely embodies the name of the ruler. L. 12 ft 4 in. (3.8 m).

76 Stela D at Quirigua, Guatemala, from a photograph taken by Alfred Maudslay in 1885. This monument was erected by K'ahk' Tiliw Chan Yopaat on 9.16.15.0.0, or 20 February AD 766. Ht 19 ft 6 in. (5.9 m).

small shield in one hand and a K'awiil scepter in the other, while the sides are covered with texts containing several Long Count dates. The great skill of the Quirigua sculptors can be seen in the grotesque full figures which take the place of cycle glyphs in the inscriptions of several other stelae, in the stone "zoomorphs" representing crouching earth monsters or sky deities with humans seated among their snakelike coils, and in the richly embellished boulders ("altars") associated with them. One set, Zoomorph P and Altar P', embodies the Ruler's name in bold, three dimensional form.

Eventually, however, the worm turned: in AD 725, K'ahk' Tiliw Chan Yopaat ascended the Quirigua throne and pursued a policy of rebellion against the domination of Copan. As we have seen, this culminated sixteen years later with Copan's defeat, and the humiliating capture and execution of its king.

TIKAL

It is more than likely that the ruins of Tikal, in the very heart of the Peten, were first encountered by the brave Father Avendaño and his companions in 1695. Lost and starving among the swampy *bajos* and thorny forests of northern Guatemala, they came across a "variety of old buildings, excepting some in which I recognized apartments, and though they were very high and my strength was little, I climbed up them (though with trouble)." Tikal has now been partly restored by the University of Pennsylvania and the Guatemalan government; a giant among Maya centers, it is one of the largest Classic sites in the Maya area and one of the greatest in the New World. Particularly impressive are its six temple-pyramids, veritable skyscrapers among buildings of their class [77, 78]. From its plaza floor to the top of its roof comb, Temple IV, the mightiest of all, measures 229 ft (70 m) in height. The core of Tikal must be its Great Plaza, flanked on west and east by two of these temple-pyramids, on the north by the Acropolis already mentioned in connection with its Late Preclassic and Early Classic tombs, and on the south by the Central Acropolis, a palace complex [78]. Some of the major architectural groups are connected to the Great Plaza and with each other by broad causeways, over which many splendid processions must have passed in the days of Tikal's glory. The palaces are also impressive, their plastered rooms often still retaining in their vaults the sapodilla-wood spanner beams which had only a decorative function.

Tikal is not particularly noteworthy for its stone sculptures. Among the many limestone stelae lined up in the Great Plaza before the acropolis, most tend to be formulaic, as though copying each other. Nonetheless, there were great artists in the service of Tikal's rulers, for the fortunately preserved sapodilla-wood lintels above the doorways of the temple-pyramids

77 Temple I at Tikal. This is the funerary pyramid of Jasaw Chan K'awiil.

are covered with reliefs of Maya rulers in various poses accompanied by lengthy glyphic texts [**79**]. Artistry of a different sort can be seen in the remarkable offerings accompanying the splendid tomb underneath Temple I, discovered in 1962 by Aubrey Trik of the University of Pennsylvania. In it, a very great ruler named Jasaw Chan K'awiil had been laid to rest with his riches – ornaments of jade and shell and vessels filled with food and drink – and a mighty pyramid built over his remains. But what was really unusual was a large collection of bone tubes and strips which had been delicately incised with scenes of gods and men carried out with the most extreme sophistication [**80, 81**]. According to David Stuart, some of these appear to relate episodes of Early Classic Tikal history around the time of the "arrival" event (see Chapter 4). The fine drawing and calligraphy displayed on these bones give us some idea of what a Classic Maya codex may

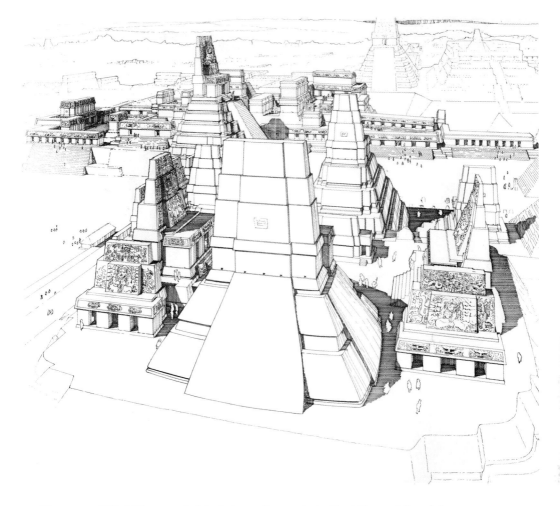

78 The center of Tikal. View over the North Acropolis towards the Great Plaza and Temple I. Beyond lie the royal palace and the massive Temple V and South Acropolis.

have looked like, none of these bark-paper books having survived except in the most fragmentary form in tombs at sites like Altun Ha and Uaxactun.

There are ten reservoirs at Tikal from which the Maya obtained their drinking water, one of which was refurbished by the modern archaeologists in lieu of any other potable source. These are often surrounded by artificial earthen levees, and contain sufficient water throughout the dry season. Some, no doubt, were originally quarries, although the latter are also known in many other places around the site, where outcrops and half-worked blocks of limestone still bear the marks of the crudely chipped tools with which they were hewn by the stone-masons of over one thousand years ago. Finds from areas near Tikal continue to astonish, including, at Holmul, Guatemala, a stucco temple excavated and studied by Francisco Estrada-Belli and Alexandre Tokovinine [82]. Dating to the early seventh century AD,

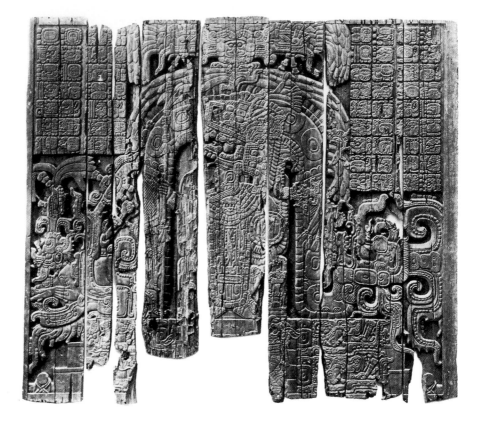

79 (*Above*) Carved wooden lintel from Temple IV, Tikal. Beneath the body of a double-headed serpent the ruler Yik'in Kan K'awiil ("Ruler B") is seated on a war palanquin during a celebration of a great military victory against El Perú on 27 July AD 743. Impersonating a deity, he carries a spear in one hand and a shield on the left wrist. L. in greatest dimension 6 ft 9 in. (2.1 m).

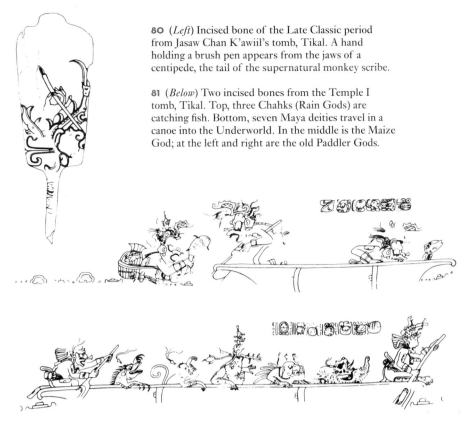

80 (*Left*) Incised bone of the Late Classic period from Jasaw Chan K'awiil's tomb, Tikal. A hand holding a brush pen appears from the jaws of a centipede, the tail of the supernatural monkey scribe.

81 (*Below*) Two incised bones from the Temple I tomb, Tikal. Top, three Chahks (Rain Gods) are catching fish. Bottom, seven Maya deities travel in a canoe into the Underworld. In the middle is the Maize God; at the left and right are the old Paddler Gods.

82 (*Below*) Stucco cornice, Building A, Group II, Holmul, Guatemala. The central figure is the local ruler, who may have been a subordinate of Calakmul. *c.* AD 600.

it shows, front and center, a local ruler on a mythic hill; two snakes slither out of its mouth, perhaps as a kind of breath. The text along the bottom of this scene refers to a contemporary ruler of Naranjo, an immense but little-published and seldom-visited site that was a great rival of Tikal's during the Classic period.

CALAKMUL

Tikal's great rival and, in fact, mortal enemy, was Calakmul, a major city even in the Late Preclassic. As epigraphers Simon Martin and Nikolai Grube tell us, the "golden age" of Calakmul coincided with the fifty-year rule of Yuknoom the Great, which began in AD 636. During this century there were many wars in the Central Area, during which Calakmul not only attacked Tikal, but managed to establish its hegemony over such cities as Piedras Negras, Dos Pilas, El Perú, Cancuen, and Naranjo, to the continued detriment of Tikal, then weakened by a factional split. Glyphic texts from the small city of La Corona (the origin of many looted monuments on the art market) show the extent of Calakmul's influence, documenting the sustained subservience of its local dynasty. La Corona itself may have existed largely to control the southwestern corridor to Calakmul.

Disaster struck Calakmul during the reign of Yuknoom the Great's successor, the ferociously named Yich'aak K'ahk' ("Fiery Claw"). In August AD 695, the forces of "Fiery Claw" attacked the army of Tikal's Jasaw Chan K'awiil, a battle that ended with Calakmul's defeat – an event commemorated at Tikal on a carved wooden lintel atop Temple I. Calakmul and its kingdom, the "Snake" polity, were never to recover their prior eminence. Avoiding intrigue among Maya kingdoms to the south, Calakmul became more oriented towards the Río Bec cities to its north, and there is definite influence of the ornate Río Bec style (see below) in its Late Classic architecture.

As it had been during previous periods, Structure II remained the great state temple of the kingdom, and was chosen to house the tomb of "Fiery Claw," who died c. AD 700. The royal corpse had been virtually swaddled, wrapped in layers of lime, palm, and fine cotton textiles, and fitted with a Teotihuacan War God headdress in jade and shell mosaic. Among the many funerary offerings was a beautiful chocolate vase in "codex style," probably created in the general area of Calakmul. "Fiery Claw" did not make his final journey alone, for he was accompanied by two other individuals – a richly ornamented young woman and an adolescent boy.

In 2004, Mexican archaeologists under the direction of Ramón Carrasco Vargas began excavations into a collapsed mound (Building 1) within a complex known as Chiik Nahb on the north side of Calakmul's ceremonial center. As is typical of Maya pyramids, this proved to have earlier, super-imposed structures within. One of these was a stepped platform with four radial stairways. The outer surfaces of each of the three tiers had been plastered white and then painted in brilliant colors with some of the most extraordinary ancient Maya murals ever discovered. Entirely domestic in subject matter, they show a variety of men, women, and even children involved in the buying and selling of commodities including shelled maize, maize *tamales*, atole (maize gruel), salt, and even vases. Many of the sellers are identified by large glyphs according to what they are offering, such as *aj tz'am*, "salt person," and *aj ix'im*, "maize-grain person." On one panel, a porter with a tumpline around his head carries a bundle of goods [83].

83 Modern rendering of a detail of a mural from the Chiik Nahb complex at Calakmul, showing a traveling vendor with bundle and hat. *c.* AD 600–650.

Most likely dating to the early seventh century AD, these are unique scenes of daily life within a bustling marketplace, which itself must have comprised the entire Chiik Nahb complex, a roughly square enclosure *c.* 490 ft (150 m) on each side. Such markets have been found at a number of other Classic Maya cities (including Tikal and Pueblito in the Peten), either as rooms grouped around courtyards or as modest foundations at the center of their communities. At both Tikal and at the enormous site of Chunchucmil, near the coastal salt flats of northwest Yucatan, excavations have disclosed what most probably are narrow vendors' stalls within the marketplace. Salt was, of course, indispensable to the Maya diet. At Punta Ycacos Lagoon, on the south coast of Belize, Heather McKillop of Louisiana State University has uncovered extensive Late Classic salt works based upon the boiling of seawater, the end product apparently to be loaded onto canoes and traded along the coast, or sent to the great cities via inland waterways. Other sources would have been near the salt domes of Salinas de los Nueve Cerros, where great vats were used to prepare this marketable product.

YAXCHILAN, PIEDRAS NEGRAS, AND BONAMPAK

The many dozens of Classic Maya centers scattered over the Peten and Belize – such as Uaxactun, Nakum, Naranjo, Xunantunich, Caracol, and Altun Ha – are witnesses to the importance of this region before its abandonment. Maya sites are as numerous along the banks of the Usumacinta and its tributaries, in the southwestern part of the Central Area. Yaxchilan is a major center strung out along a terrace of the Usumacinta, with some of its components perched on the hills above. While its temple-pyramids reach no great height, their upper facades and roof combs were beautifully ornamented with figures in stucco and stone. Yaxchilan is famous for its many stone lintels, carved in relief with scenes of conquest and ceremonial life, peppered with dates and glyphic texts providing clues to the real meaning of the Classic Maya inscriptions [84]. Further downstream is Piedras Negras, which has produced similar data [85]. This site is more extensive than Yaxchilan – whose ancient kingdom was, as archaeologists Charles Golden and Andrew Scherer have shown, mostly across the river in what is now Guatemala – and has a large number of particularly fine stelae set in place before its temples, as well as eight sweat baths, complete with stone coffers for heated rocks (they functioned much like Finnish sauna), masonry benches for the bathers, and drains to carry off water used in the baths.

84 Lintel 25, Yaxchilan, Mexico. The scene depicts a bloodletting rite which took place on 24 October AD 681, the accession day of Itzamnaaj Bahlam II ("Shield Jaguar the Great"). Shown here is the kneeling figure of his wife, Lady Xok, holding a bowl in which a stingray spine and bloodied paper have been placed. Before her rises a double-headed snake from whose mouths appear a warrior and a head of Tlaloc, the Teotihuacan god of war. Ht 4 ft 3 in. (1.3 m).

85 Stela 14, from Piedras Negras, Guatemala. The monument marks the accession to the throne in AD 758 of Yo'nal Ahk III, the young lord seated in the niche. At the foot of the platform stands a middle-aged woman, perhaps the new king's mother. Ht 9 ft 3 in. (2.8 m).

86 A Maya king is seated on a dais above three lesser figures on this engraved stone from Bonampak, Mexico. One hands him the "Jester God" headband of rulership. Dedicated AD 692. Ht 38.5 in. (98 cm).

Few discoveries in the Maya area can rank with that of Bonampak, politically important during the Early Classic, but by the Late Classic an otherwise insignificant center clearly under the cultural and political thumb of Yaxchilan [86]. Bonampak, which lies not far from the Río Lacanha, a tributary of the Usumacinta system, was first stumbled across in February 1946 by two American adventurers who were taken there by Lakandon Indians among whom they had been living. Three months later, the photographer Giles Healey was led by a group of Lakandon to the same ruins, and became the first non-Maya to gaze at the stupendous paintings which cover the walls of three rooms in one of the structures.

The Bonampak murals, which can be dated to shortly before AD 800 on the basis of Long Count texts and stylistic considerations, may have been commissioned by the local ruler Yajaw Kan Muwaan, although seemingly highlight his main heir, Kooj, "Puma," along with two other men, perhaps his younger brothers. Indeed, the building itself savors of a young men's house, a place of repose and instruction, known in later Maya sources and throughout Mesoamerica. What is certain is that the murals obviously relate a single narrative: the story of a battle, its aftermath, and the victory celebrations [XV, XVI, XVII]. Against a background of stylized jungle foliage, a skirmish takes place among magnificently arrayed Maya warriors, while musicians blow long war trumpets of wood or bark. The scene shifts to a stepped platform in Bonampak itself; the miserable prisoners have been stripped, and are having the nails torn from their fingers or their hands lacerated. An important captive sprawls on the steps, perhaps tortured to exhaustion, and a severed head lies nearby on a bed of leaves. A naked figure seated on the platform summit pleads for his life to the central figure, Yajaw Kan Muwaan, clad in jaguar-skin battle-jacket and surrounded by his subordinates in gorgeous costume. Among the noble spectators is a lady in a white robe, holding a folding-screen fan in one hand. Yajaw Kan Muwaan's principal wife, she is identified by the glyphic text as coming from Yaxchilan, as did the sculptor of at least one of the lintels of the mural building: the suspicion is strong that the painters, too, came from the city of Bonampak's overlord. One of the ceremonies includes a group of dancers fantastically disguised as gods of wind and water, accompanied by an orchestra of rattles, drums, turtle carapaces (struck with antlers), and long trumpets. Perhaps the culminating scene is the great sacrificial dance performed to the sound of trumpets by noble young men (*ch'ok*) wearing towering headdresses of quetzal plumes; in preparation, white-robed Maya ladies seated on a throne draw blood from their tongues, and a strange, potbellied, dwarf-like figure standing on a palanquin is carried on-stage.

No verbal description could do justice to the beautiful colors and to the skill of the hand (or hands) which executed these paintings. Suffice it to say Bonampak has thrown an entirely new light on the warlike interests of the Maya leaders, upon social organization and stratification in a Maya center, and upon the magnificence of Late Classic Maya culture in general, before time destroyed most of its creations. Bonampak was abandoned before the murals were finished, and the artists dispersed as Maya civilization in the Peten went into eclipse.

THE PETEXBATUN

Another important group of sites occurs atop an escarpment overlooking the shallow Lake Petexbatun, south of the Río Pasión (one of the main branches of the Usumacinta). These are Tamarindito, Arroyo de Piedra, Punta de Chimino, Aguateca, and Dos Pilas; the latter city seems to have dominated the rest, and, in fact, to have begun putting together a large-scale state as early as the seventh century AD, when a noble lineage arrived from Tikal and established a royal dynasty. The family was clearly adroit in its political maneuvers, switching from an allegiance to their cousins at Tikal to one with Calakmul, its arch-enemy. So powerful had Dos Pilas become that, on 4 December AD 735, its ruler had the audacity to attack Ceibal, a far larger and more ancient city located on a bluff above the Pasión; the next day, Ceibal's king fell captive to Dos Pilas.

By the mid-eighth century AD, warfare had in fact become a real problem to all the major Petexbatun sites, and a system of defensive walls (mapped in 1986 by Stephen Houston) topped by wooden palisades was constructed around and within them, often with little regard for the functions that particular structures had once served. Aguateca, in spite of its placement on the edge of an escarpment with a wide view over the countryside to the east, was attacked and burned to the ground, probably at the beginning of the ninth century AD. For Takeshi Inomata, this was a godsend, as he has found a vast quantity of artifacts in situ on the floors of houses abandoned by their occupants, a "Pompeii-like" situation that has enabled him to identify specialized areas, such as a house which was probably that of the chief scribe of the city.

PALENQUE

Sylvanus Morley considered Palenque to be the most beautiful of all the Maya centers, albeit of no great size in comparison with a giant like Tikal. It has now been mapped in full under the direction of Edwin Barnhart of the University of Texas. The setting is incomparable: Palenque lies at the foot of a chain of low hills still covered with tall rainforest, just above the green flood plain of the Usumacinta. Archaeologist Rodrigo Liendo Stuardo has even found evidence of road systems running along the base of those hills, connecting the far reaches of the Palenque kingdom. Parrots and macaws of brilliant plumage fly at treetop level; on rainy days the strange roar of howler monkeys can be heard near the ruins. Although it is relatively compact, it now appears that because of topographical constraints, Palenque was one of the most densely occupied of Classic Maya cities, with over 1,000 structures of various sizes. Here is a good example of the sometimes extensive modification of streams or watercourses by the Maya engineers, by means of channels and aqueducts. One of these, the Río Otulum, is carried underneath the eastern flank of the principal complex, the Palace, by a corbel-vaulted aqueduct.

A veritable labyrinth, the Palace is c. 300 ft long and 240 ft wide (91 by 73 m), and consists of a series of vaulted galleries and rooms arranged about interior courtyards or patios, dominated by a unique four-story square tower with an interior stairway [87]. It has been suggested that the tower was used as an observatory, but it commands a wide view and could also have served as a watchtower. Along the sides of two of the patios are grotesque reliefs, almost caricatures of prisoners showing submission by the usual means (one hand raised to the opposite shoulder) and it could have been in these courts that the captured enemies of Palenque were arraigned, tortured, and sacrificed.

The Palenque artists excelled in stucco work, and the exteriors of the pilasters ranged along the galleries of the Palace are marvelously embellished in that medium, with Maya lords in relief carrying the symbols of their authority, while lesser individuals sit cross-legged at their side. All these stuccoes were once painted, and the noted Palenque authority Merle Greene Robertson has identified a definite color code: for instance, the exposed skin of humans was painted red, while that of gods was covered with blue [88].

87 The Palace and Tower at Palenque, viewed southwest from the Temple of the Inscriptions. In the distance is the floodplain of the Usumacinta River.

88 Stucco-decorated pier on the Palace, Palenque. Pakal the Great, attired as the Maize God, dances on the left; both figures grasp a fantastic serpent.

Of the temple-pyramids of Palenque, three were constructed on more or less the same plan, and must have served somewhat the same function. These are the Temples of the Sun [90], the Cross [89], and the Foliated Cross, arranged around three sides of a plaza on the eastern side of the site. Each temple rests on a stepped platform with frontal stairway, has a mansard roof with comb, and has an outer and an inner vaulted room. Against the back wall of the latter is a "sanctuary," a miniature version of the larger temple; in its rear stands a magnificent low relief tablet carved with long hieroglyphic texts. Each exhibits the same motif: two individual males, one taller than the other, face each other on either side of a ceremonial object. In the case of the Temple of the Sun, the most perfect of all Maya buildings, this central object is the mask of the Jaguar God of the Underworld, the sun in its night aspect, before two crossed spears. The two

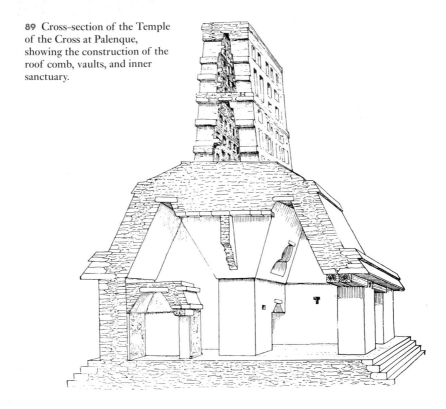

89 Cross-section of the Temple of the Cross at Palenque, showing the construction of the roof comb, vaults, and inner sanctuary.

other temples have in its place a branching, bejeweled World Tree (which bears an astonishing resemblance to the Christian cross) surmounted by a supernatural bird. The exterior pilasters of the sanctuaries also bear stone reliefs of standing figures, the one on the right side of the Cross "sanctuary" unusual in that it shows God L, the patron of warriors and traders, smoking a cigar.

Today's archaeologists may call the inner structures of these three buildings sanctuaries, but epigrapher Stephen Houston has found that the Maya called them something else: *pibnal*, meaning "sweat bath." We know from modern ethnology and ethnohistoric accounts that the Mesoamerican peoples administered such baths to women before and after childbirth, and Houston's interpretation of this strange name is that it was symbolic of the birth of the god to whom each building in the Cross Group was dedicated. We will touch upon this "Palenque Triad," and the inscriptions in the "sanctuaries," in Chapter 9.

Linda Schele and David Freidel have shown us that there is a further, deeper meaning to the three structures of the Cross Group. At the northern apex of the triangle that they form, the inscription of the Temple of the

90 (*Right*) View of the Temple of the Sun, Palenque, from the northeast. Late Classic.

Cross records the events at the beginning of the current era and the history of the Palenque dynasty, surrounding the World Tree in the form of a cross. On the eastern side, the panel of the Temple of the Foliated Cross celebrates the Tree of Maize and the Mountain of Sustenance; while the Temple of the Sun on the western side was consecrated to the birth of war. The Temple of the Cross in particular is notable for the discovery of large supports for incense burners, some evidently consecrated to gods, others to deceased noblemen.

Thanks to some remarkable advances in our understanding of the Palenque inscriptions, we now know why these three temples are so similar: the tablets in their sanctuaries all record the accession in AD 684 of the king known as Kan Bahlam (or "Snake Jaguar"), and the two flanking figures are *both* his portraits, but at different ages – as a six-year-old boy, and at his accession at the age of forty-nine.

From time to time over the sixty years that excavations have been carried out at Palenque, finds have been made of fairly well-stocked tombs that intruded into temple platforms and into the Palace itself. But these are nothing compared with the remarkable discovery made in June 1952 by Mexican archaeologist Alberto Ruz. The Temple of the Inscriptions rests on a 65-ft (19.8-m) high stepped pyramid approached by a noble frontal stairway. On the walls of its portico and central chamber, three panels contain a total of 620 hieroglyphs with many dates, the most recent corresponding to AD 692. The floor of the temple is covered by large stone slabs, but Ruz was particularly curious about one which had a double row of holes provided with removable stone stoppers; on removing this, it was clear that he had hit upon a vaulted stairway leading down into the interior of the pyramid, but intentionally choked with rubble. In four field seasons he completely cleared the stairs, which changed direction halfway down, finally reaching a chamber on about the same level as the base of the pyramid. It too had been filled, but on its floor lay the skeletons of five or six young adults, probably all sacrifices. At its far end, the passage was blocked by a huge triangular slab which filled the entire vault.

Upon removing this slab Ruz first looked into the great Funerary Crypt, a discovery rivaling that of Bonampak in importance [93]. The chamber is 30 ft long and 23 ft high (9 by 7 m), and its floor lies underneath the frontal stairway but below the level of the plaza, some 80 ft (24 m) beneath the floor of the upper temple. Around its walls stride stucco relief figures of men, perhaps distant ancestors of the deceased. A huge rectangular stone slab, 12 ft 6 in. (3.8 m) long and covered with relief carvings, overlaid a monolithic sarcophagus within which an ancient Maya ruler had been put to rest [94]. A treasure trove of jade accompanied the corpse: a life-sized mosaic mask of jade was placed over the face, jade and mother-of-pearl disks served him as earspools, several necklaces of tubular jade beads festooned the chest, and jade rings adorned his fingers [92]. A large jade was held in each hand and another was placed in the mouth, a practice documented for the late Yukateko Maya, the Aztecs, and the Chinese. Two jade figures, and two sensitively modeled heads in stucco, were placed on the floor of the funerary chamber.

Epigraphic detective work eventually revealed that the man in the Funerary Crypt was the mightiest of all of Palenque's rulers: K'inich Janahb Pakal ("Great Sun Flower [?]-Shield"), the father of Kan Bahlam. Now popularly known as Pakal the Great, he ascended the throne when he was twelve years old and died in AD 683 at the venerable age of eighty. It is immediately evident that this great man had the Funerary Crypt built to contain his own remains; further, that he might have had the entire temple-pyramid above it raised in his own lifetime, to be completed by his son in an act of filial piety. Thus it seems that the Temple of the Inscriptions was a funerary monument with exactly the same primary function as the Egyptian pyramids.

During the 1990s, a new and unexpected Palenque king burst upon the scene: K'inich Ahkal Mo' Nahb, who was born in AD 678 and acceded to the throne in AD 721. Following a lengthy dip in Palenque's fortunes, this ruler – a grandson of Pakal the Great – was responsible for the revitalization of the city, and for the construction of major temples on a ridge extending south from the Cross Group; along with the latter three temples, each of these was consecrated to a single god among the triad of divinities from whom the Palenque dynasty claimed descent. Ahkal Mo' Nahb had some extraordinary artistic talent at his disposal, as attested by two of the most expert Maya reliefs ever produced. One of these was a slab-sided bench or

91 Detail of a relief on a bench in Temple XIX, Palenque. K'inich Ahkal Mo' Nahb III leans to receive the "Jester God" headband of rulership from a subordinate.

Lord Janahb Pakal of Palenque

92 (*Left*) Jade funerary mask and jewelry of Pakal the Great, from his tomb in the Temple of the Inscriptions, Palenque. AD 683, Late Classic.

93 (*Right*) Funerary Crypt in the Temple of the Inscriptions, Palenque, dated to AD 683. The sarcophagus of the king Pakal the Great lies below and supports the carved stone slab. Around the walls of the corbeled chamber are nine stuccoed figures.

94 Drawing of the relief carving on the upper surface of the Sarcophagus of the Temple of the Inscriptions, Palenque. The youthful-appearing Pakal the Great (the eighty-year-old king interred within the tomb) falls through gigantic fleshless jaws into the Underworld; above him rises the World Tree, surmounted by the bird–monster Wuqub Kaquix. Surrounding the scene is a band depicting celestial bodies and ancestral figures. AD 683.

throne discovered by archaeologist Alfonso Morales in Temple XIX [91]. It depicts no fewer than 10 seated individuals along with a text of 220 glyphs telling us that this was a re-enactment rite of the king, centering on the accession of one of the three founding gods in 3309 BC.

The other relief, also a facing of a throne or bench, was found by archaeologists Arnoldo González Cruz and Guillermo Bernal Romero in Temple XXI. At the center of the scene is the revenant Pakal the Great, the reincarnation of a legendary ruler who had supposedly reigned in 252 BC; he holds in his hand a large stingray spine for self-sacrifice. Flanking the tableau are two strange deities with rodent heads. To Pakal's immediate right is his grandson Ahkal Mo' Nahb, and to his left his great-grandson Upakal K'inich, the heir apparent. This young man is shown in a magnificent, polychrome stucco relief on a pilaster of Temple XIX, on which he strides along wearing the costume of a gigantic waterbird [v].

The discovery of Pakal's crypt in the Temple of the Inscriptions, Jasaw Chan K'awiil's in Tikal's Temple I, and that of "Fiery Claw" in Calakmul's Temple II leads one to ask whether many Maya temple-pyramids might have functioned as sepulchral monuments, dedicated to the worship of deceased kings. Such a conclusion is backed up by many finds in the Central Area, and not just at the really large sites. Altun Ha, for example, is a relatively small center in northern Belize, with an antiquity reaching back into Preclassic times. It has no stelae and played no great role on the Classic political stage, but some fairly spectacular finds have been made there by David Pendergast of the Royal Ontario Museum. One of these was the famous "Sun God's Tomb," constructed in a modestly sized funerary pyramid. Before the interment of the honored deceased (an adult male), virtually the entire crypt had been draped in cloth. The corpse had then been placed on a wooden platform, accompanied by the skins of jaguars or pumas, matting and cordage, and necklaces and pendants of jade and spondylus shell. The *pièce de résistance* was the largest carved jade ever found in Mesoamerica, a *c.* 6-in. (14.9-cm) high effigy head of the "Jester God," a royal jewel used at accession. Too heavy to be worn, it may at least have been passed into the hands of the new ruler.

COMALCALCO AND TONINA

As with Copan on the southeast Maya frontier, the cities of the far southwestern lowlands often display considerable innovation in art and architecture in comparison to the more staid central Peten sites. Comalcalco, for instance, on the alluvial plains of Tabasco, is unique in the pre-Conquest New World for its use of fired brick in construction, a practice that began in the sixth century AD; clearly an adaptation to a virtually stoneless environment. Many of these bricks were incised while wet, some with naïve drawings of everyday scenes, others more sophisticated [95]. By the Late Classic, Comalcalco's brick acropolis supported a palace, and reached a height of 128 ft (39 m). In buildings of the North Plaza archaeologist Ricardo Armijo found a large

95 Incised brick from Comalcalco, Tabasco, Mexico. An amateur artist has doodled a portrait head, a hunchback, an illegible day sign, and a square shield or textile. Late Classic.

number of royal burials in clay urns, most with rich offerings; one of these included an inscribed sting-ray spine recording a penis-perforation ceremony by an eighth-century ruler named Aj Pakal Tahn, who was then subject to Palenque's rule.

Tonina specialized in three-dimensional sculpture to an extent not seen since the demise of the Olmec civilization. In 1991, Mexican archaeologist Juan Yadeún uncovered an extraordinary stucco relief there, in which the skeletalized Death God brandishes the severed head of an important captive, apparently Hunahpu, one of the Hero Twins of Maya mythology. This great city, in the hill country of central Chiapas, boasts an enormous acropolis and two ball courts, and must have been a feared military power, for in AD 711 its ruler, Baaknal Chahk, managed to capture K'an Joy Chitam, king of the great city of Palenque and second son of the renowned Palenque *ajaw* Janahb Pakal ("the Great"); he must have been magnanimous, for rather than decapitating his captive, he eventually allowed Joy Chitam to return to Palenque.

CLASSIC SITES IN THE NORTHERN AREA: RÍO BEC, CHENES, AND COBA

The forests of southern Campeche and Quintana Roo form the wildest part of the Maya region, but scattered through them are many ruined centers which have as yet been untouched by pick or spade. Our knowledge of these sites, as Tatiana Proskouriakoff pointed out, is owed "to the gumchewing habit of our sedentary city-dwellers," for it is the chicle hunters who have come across them while searching for the sapodilla trees from which gum is extracted. Several share in an aberrant architectural style named after the large site of Río Bec. Here showiness rather than function was apparently favored, for characteristic of this style of the Late Classic is the decoration of perfectly ordinary small "palaces" with high towers imitating the fronts of temple-pyramids; these towers, however, are solid, the steps being impossibly narrow and steep, and the "doorway" at the summit leading to nothing. It is as though the Río Bec architects wished to imitate the great Tikal temples without going to any trouble. In the Río Bec sites, such as Hormiguero and Xpuhil, we begin to see on facades and roof combs an

96 North facade of Structure V at Hormiguero, Mexico, from a photograph taken by Karl Ruppert in 1933. The figure stands before the doorway of the one-room temple, entered through the jaws of a monstrous mask. On the west side are the remains of a false tower. Río Bec culture.

elaborate ornamentation that emphasizes masks, iconographically designating these temples as "Flower Mountains" (see next chapter) [96, 97]. This is a concept that becomes increasingly common among Maya architects as one moves further north into the Yucatan Peninsula.

Between the Río Bec area and the Puuc Hills of Yucatan is the Chenes, a well-populated zone of northern Campeche. Like those of Río Bec, with whom they must have been in close contact, the Chenes architects lavishly ornamented facades with sky-serpent masks and volutes, but the false towers of the former are missing. And, as at the Puuc sites to the north (see Chapter 6), the ornamentation consists of hundreds of small sculptural elements set into the buildings. One enters the front room through fantastic jaws, and is faced with tiers of masks, one over the other, on the corners.

While the two sub-areas that we have been discussing are intermediate in space and style between the Peten and the terminal Late Classic Puuc styles, there are centers in the wild eastern half of the peninsula which were direct extensions of central Peten ideas and perhaps peoples. One of these is Coba, a name implying something like "ruffled waters," a fitting epithet since it was built among a small group of shallow, reedy lakes in

97 Palace at Xpuhil, from a reconstruction drawing by Tatiana Proskouriakoff. The three towers are completely solid and served no other function than decoration. Río Bec culture.

northern Quintana Roo. Until the middle of this century the zone was frequented only by Maya hunters who occasionally burned incense before the stelae scattered among its ruins. Coba is not a single site but a whole group linked to a central complex by long, perfectly straight masonry causeways usually called by the Maya term *sakbih* or, in local Yukateko Maya, *sakbe* ("white road"). There are more than sixteen of these, but what motivated their construction we cannot even guess, for quite often a *sakbe* several miles in length will reach a ruin of very paltry dimensions. *Sakbe* No. 1 is the strangest of all, for it continues west from Coba in a generally straight direction for no less than 62 miles (100 km), finally reaching the site of Yaxuna, some 12 miles (19 km) southwest of Chichen Itza. Some have claimed that the Maya *sakbe* were arteries of commerce, but a purely ceremonial function is far more plausible.

The buildings of Coba are in a sorry state of preservation, but there appear to have been temple-pyramids and palaces resembling those of the Peten. It continued to be inhabited into Postclassic times; there are a few structures similar to those of Tulum (a very late town on the east coast of the peninsula), and in late Maya legends, Coba is associated with the Sun God.

ART OF THE LATE CLASSIC

Late Classic Maya art evolves directly out of that of the early half of the period, but excepting the demonstrably Terminal Classic sculpture of the Puuc, there is very little outside influence to be seen. Maya artists now were free to go their own way, developing a remarkably sophisticated style as introspective as that of Asia and almost as "naturalistic" as that of Europe and the Mediterranean. But the Maya were not always interested in three-dimensionality, although they used it when they wished to give depth to a scene by foreshortening, and to figures by backlighting. Their art is essentially a painterly one, narrative and baroque, tremendously involved with ornament and grotesques but preserving what Proskouriakoff has called "order in complexity." Finally, the Late Classic Maya were, with their predecessors the Olmecs and their contemporaries the Moche of Peru, the only American Indians interested in rendering the uniqueness of individual characters through portraiture [XVIII, XIX].

The Maya artists excelled in low-relief carving, and that is what most Maya sculpture is, whether on stelae, lintels, or panels. By the eighth century AD, they had achieved a complete mastery of this medium, posing their figures in such a manner that in place of the rigid formality prevalent in earlier monuments, a kind of dynamic imbalance among the different parts of the composition was sought which leads the eye restlessly along.

A lintel from Kuna-Lacanha, a site only a few miles from Bonampak, provides a magnificent example of such artistic contraposition, showing a goateed Maya resting on one leg and leaning forward clasping a ceremonial bar [98]; but surely the pinnacle of relief carving was attained on the Late Classic tablets from Palenque, particularly the Tablet of the Slaves which shows K'inich Ahkal Mo' Nahb seated upon the backs of two barbaric-looking captives [99]. Naturally, over such a wide area there were specializations: real schools of carvers at various sites. Copan, as has been mentioned, had a notable development of three-dimensional sculpture (as did Tonina in the Chiapas hills), while Palenque, at the other end of the Central Area, concentrated on reliefs carried out with extremely sophisticated use of carved and engraved lines.

Pottery objects of Late Classic manufacture run the gamut from crude, mold-made figurines and the ordinary pots and pans of everyday life to real works of art [100]. Among the latter are the fantastic supports for incense burners, found at Palenque and in the caves of Chiapas and Tabasco. These tall, hollow tubes were modeled with the figures or heads of gods, particularly the Jaguar God of the Underworld, sometimes placed one on top of the other like Alaskan totem poles [101]. Vertical flanges were placed on either side, and the whole painted in reds, ochers, blues, and white, after firing.

Jaina, a small limestone island just off the coast of Campeche and separated from the mainland by a tidal inlet, is one of the most enigmatic archaeological sites in the Maya area. For reasons known only to themselves,

98 Stone lintel from the Late Classic site of Kuna-Lacanha, Mexico. The protagonist is a *sajal*, an official subordinate to the king of Bonampak; he holds a "ceremonial bar," a stylized, double-headed sky-serpent. In the text is carved the tun ending 9.15.15.0.0 (5 June AD 746). Ht 27.25 in. (68.8 cm).

99 Detail from the Tablet of the Slaves, dated to AD 730. Shown here is the head of Ahkal Mo' Nahb III.

100 (*Above*) Small pottery tobacco flask. On one side, the god K'awiil (left) faces God L, the deity of tobacco, and patron of traveling merchants. Containers of this sort were filled with pounded tobacco (*may*) and slaked lime. Late Classic. Ht 3.3 in. (8.5 cm).

101 (*Right*) Tall pottery censer, probably from Tabasco, Mexico. The face of the Jaguar God of the Underworld is surmounted by the heads of other deities, including a Bat God. Dozens of incense burners of this type have been found in Palenque's temples. Late Classic. Ht 45.25 in. (115 cm).

the ancients used it as a necropolis, serving as the resting place for the rulers and nobles of the Puuc sites inland (Chapter 6). Certainly the puniness of the temples constructed on the island is not in keeping with the great number of graves, or with the magnificence of the offerings found in them; the delicate, sophisticated figurines in particular have made Jaina famous among archaeologists and looters alike [104]. All are hollow and fitted with whistles at their backs. The faces were usually made in molds, but these and other details were embellished by the fingers of the artist. At one level, the emphasis is upon portraiture of real persons, perhaps the occupants of the graves: haughty nobles and armed warriors, some with tattooed or scarified faces, beautiful young women and fat old matrons. But at another level, these might also represent deities, as with two common (and rather Freudian) motifs. One depicts a woman, perhaps some kind of mother goddess, sheltering a grown man as though he were her child [102]; while the other, an ugly old man making advances to a handsome female must be an aged Underworld divinity and his consort, the young Moon Goddess. Another common supernatural in Jaina collections is the enigmatic Fat God, who seems to have been popular among the Maya of Campeche [103].

At some point in the Late Classic the lowland Maya invented a brilliant blue pigment which survives on Jaina figurines, on effigy incense burners, and in the murals of Bonampak. This is the famous Maya Blue, now proven through physical and chemical analysis to have been produced by mixing indigo (a vegetable dye) with a special clay, and heating the combination. The resulting pigment is extraordinarily stable, and – unlike modern blue pigments – highly resistant to the effects of light, acids, and time. Because this particular clay is found only at a place in Yucatan called Sakalum, it was probably there that Maya artists made their extraordinary discovery. Maya Blue continued to be manufactured right through the Spanish Conquest, and has even been found in Colonial murals in central Mexico.

Maya potters achieved chromatic effects of great brilliance in their vessels by firing them at low temperatures, sacrificing durability for aesthetic effect. Late Classic polychromes, generally deep bowls, cylindrical vessels, or footed dishes, are sometimes painted with the same narrative skill as the wall paintings. Most of the greatest paintings, and those signed by calligraphers, come from a small part of the central Peten, near Lake Peten Itza and the center of the Ik', or "wind," kingdom. One vessel is a 10-inch (25-cm) high vase from an otherwise run-of-the-mill grave at Altar de Sacrificios on the border between Guatemala and Mexico, although the pot is clearly from the Ik' kingdom [105]. Justifiably seen as a ceramic masterpiece, six strange figures, all of them dead or wearing the symbols of death and darkness, are painted on its exterior along with glyphs including a Calendar Round date corresponding to AD 754. The figure of an aged supernatural with closed eyes apparently dancing with a sinister, grossly fat snake is so well executed that it suggests the employment of artists of genius in decorating pottery (this figure is now known to be a *wahy*, a subject which will be considered in more detail in

The potters' art

102 (*Left*) Pottery figurine of a woman sheltering a man, Jaina, Mexico. Ht 8 in. (20.3 cm).

103 (*Below left*) Pottery figurine, probably from Jaina. The subject is the Fat God, wearing feathered war costume and carrying a shield. Ht 11.5 in. (29.2 cm).

104 (*Below right*) Pottery figurine from Jaina. A seated man holds an unidentified object, possibly a celt or grinding palette. Like all the finest pieces from Jaina, this figurine was made partly with a pottery mold and partly with the fingers, and was painted after firing. Ht 4.5 in. (11.4 cm).

Ceramic masterpieces

105 (*Right*) Polychrome pottery vase from Altar de Sacrificios, Guatemala, but likely made in the area of Lake Peten Itza. This side shows an old *wahy* supernatural, apparently dead, dancing with a boa constrictor. Five other supernaturals appear on the vase. In the text is a Calendar Round date probably corresponding to AD 754. Ht 10 in. (25.4 cm).

106 (*Below left*) Black pottery jar from the Chochola area of northwestern Yucatan, Mexico. Emulating a wooden original, the vessel has been deeply carved with the figure of the enigmatic deity "GI," perhaps a watery version of Chahk, against a swirling background; red pigment rubbed into the cut-away areas. Ht 5.5 in. (14 cm).

107 (*Below right*) Incised pottery bowl (Slate ware) from the Northern Area. The design, a modified step-and-fret pattern, is carried out in a negative smudging technique. Ht 4.5 in. (11.4 cm).

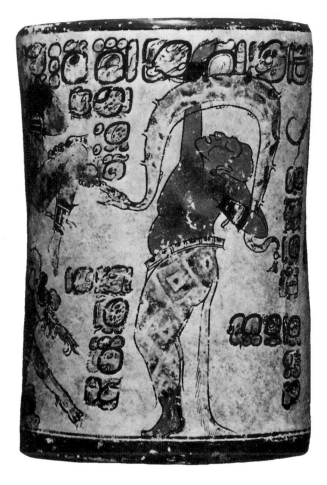

Chapter 9). Vessels could also be carved when leather-hard, just before firing. Some excellent vases in this style from Yucatan depict God G1 – one of the Maya pantheon's more enigmatic gods – seated among swirling volutes [106].

It is natural that the Maya lavished upon jade, the most precious substance known to them, their full artistry [xiv]. That jades were traded over considerable distances is evident from Late Classic Usumacinta-style pieces which were tossed into the Sacred Cenote (see Chapter 7) at Chichen Itza during the Postclassic period, and some from the lowland Maya even found their way to Oaxaca and the Valley of Mexico. Brigitte Kovacevich of Southern Methodist University found non-elite workshops of this material at Cancuen, Guatemala, just at the boundary between the Alta Verapaz and the Peten; at sites like Piedras Negras, desperate for this scarce material, they crafted "jade" jewelry out of fired clay daubed with Maya Blue. The picture is considerably illuminated by recent work near the actual sources of the material, along the Motagua River valley. There, archaeologist Erick Rochette detected jade working, especially of beads, at all levels of society, without convincing evidence of elite control or restricted specialization. Most of the finer, pictorial jades in the Maya region are very thin plaques with low-relief carving on one face, probably executed by tubular drills of cane used with jade sand, garnet or quartz grit. A plaque from Nebaj in the Southern Area must be the product of a Central Area artist, showing a recurrent theme: a richly dressed noble seated upon a throne leaning forward to chat with a dwarf, perhaps a court buffoon [108].

Not only jade, but also calcite was worked by the lowland Maya lapidaries; but it must have been a rare substance, for objects made from it are found infrequently. A fluted vase of translucent calcite, incised in Late Classic style, is a fine example of the genre [109]. It is somewhat doubtful whether the well-known marble vessels from the Ulua region of western Honduras, dating between AD 650 and 850, are to be considered Maya at all, but fragments from them have been found in deposits assigned to the Terminal Classic in Belize and Peten sites. That the Maya could impose their artistic conventions on any medium is apparent in the "eccentric" flint blades chipped to include divine faces in profile, and small blades of obsidian incised with the gods of the Maya pantheon; these were favorite objects for placing in caches under stelae, or beneath temple floors in Central Area sites [111]. Along the coast of Campeche, above all at Jaina, art in carved shell was highly skilled, the Maya typically painting the lily by inlaying these objects with small pieces of apple-green jade [110].

It should always be borne in mind, however, that almost all Maya art that has survived the vicissitudes of time is in imperishable materials. Classic murals and pictorial ceramics testify that the vast majority consisted not of stone, jade, and pottery, but of carved wood, and woven and painted textiles. Every temple, every palace room was surely festooned with curtains and wall hangings. Virtually all of this has disappeared without a trace in the tropical environment. There must have been many thousands of Classic Maya books

108 This carved jade plaque from Nebaj, Guatemala, is emerald green with white clouding, and represents a Maya lord in conversation with a palace dwarf. Mythic trees with the decapitated head of the Maize God appear to either side of him. W. 5.75 in. (14.6 cm).

109 Calcite bowl from the state of Campeche, Mexico. A row of incised glyphs encircles the rim. Below, on the fluted sides, are incised a lord (shown here), his wife, and their son, going by the title *aj k'uhu'n*. Each figure holds a symbolic object.

110 (*Right*) Carved shell pendant, probably from Jaina. A young man with the flattened head so highly esteemed by the Maya appears above a fantastic fish, the body of which is covered with name glyphs. The cut-away areas were once inlaid with jade. Ht *c.* 3 in. (8 cm).

111 (*Below*) Incised obsidians from an offering placed beneath a stela at Tikal, Late Classic. The flat side of a crude flake has in each instance been engraved with the figure of a deity or with a simplified mat design. The god K'awiil appears at upper left and right; the Sun God K'inich Ajaw at lower right.

written on bark-paper, but not a single one has come down to us, represented only by unsalvageable traces occasionally found in elite graves. All of this, and more, perished in the great cataclysm described in the next chapter.

6

▼▼▼▼▼▼▼▼▼▼▼

THE TERMINAL CLASSIC

Maya civilization in the Central Area reached its full glory in the early eighth century AD, but it must have contained the seeds of its own destruction, for in the century and a half that followed all its magnificent cities had fallen into decline and were ultimately abandoned. This was surely one of the most profound social and demographic catastrophes in human history. Yet ironically, during the terrible era that saw the Classic collapse in the southern lowlands, the Maya exerted an altogether unprecedented influence over the Gulf Coast and even the central highlands of Mexico. And it is clear that no similar decline affected the Northern Area. To the contrary, in the Puuc region and at Chichen Itza, cities achieved a remarkable florescence, erecting some of the finest architecture ever seen in the pre-Conquest New World, and were only snuffed out by what may have been foreign invasion.

The Terminal Classic, *c.* AD 800–925, was therefore a time of tragedy and triumph: old thrones toppled in the south as a new political order took shape in the north; southern cities fell into the dust as northern ones flourished. It was an era marked by widespread movements of peoples and goods, during which the destinies of central Mexico and the Maya area became as closely intertwined as they had been in the days of Teotihuacan's hegemony, setting the stage for the rise of a new power in Mexico: the Toltecs.

THE GREAT COLLAPSE

The collapse of Maya civilization in the southern lowlands at the end of the Late Classic is indisputable, being abundantly documented in the archaeological record. What is in dispute is the "why?" Generations of scholars have tried to account for the Great Collapse, explanations ranging from epidemic diseases to invasion by foreigners from Mexico, social revolution to the lowering of the water table, droughts, and even earthquakes and hurricanes. Unfortunately, the last Classic inscriptions throw little light on the problem, since their parsimonious carved texts never deal with such mundane matters as censuses or agricultural production figures.

From AD 751 to *c.* 790, long-standing alliances began to break down, interstate trade declined, and conflicts between neighboring city-states increased (as illustrated vividly by the Bonampak murals, commemorating the battle of 792). From 790 to 830, the death rate of cities increased, while after 830 construction largely stopped throughout the Central Area, with the exception of peripherally located sites like Lamanai. The k'atun ending date 10.3.0.0.0 (AD 889) was celebrated by inscriptions at only five sites; the k'atun ending 10.4.0.0.0 (AD 909) appears only on a monument at Tonina, and incised on a jade from a site in southern Quintana Roo. The very last Maya date found in the Peten was carved on a stela at Itzimte, and corresponds to 16 January AD 910. One by one the lights of Classic urban civilization had winked out.

We know from the downfall of past civilizations, such as the Roman and Khmer empires, that it is fruitless to look for single causes. But most Maya archaeologists now agree that three factors were paramount in the downfall: endemic internecine warfare, overpopulation (and accompanying environmental collapse), and drought. All three probably played their part, but not necessarily simultaneously. Warfare seems to have become a real problem earlier than the other two. Rulers and their entourages had conducted military campaigns against their rivals as far back as the Preclassic, but by the late eighth century in the Petexbatun region, these activities intensified and began to destroy the prevailing social contract, going far beyond the mere taking of a few royal captives for sacrifice. The systems of palisaded fortifications encountered at sites like Dos Pilas and Aguateca date to between AD 760 and 830, by which time many of the palaces and temple superstructures had been reduced to rubble, and the inhabitants (probably augmented by refugee villagers from the rural hinterlands) lived a fearful existence in mere thatched huts huddled within the city walls. At Aguateca, Takeshi Inomata and Daniela Triadan have even found an unfinished pyramid, with a large cavity, perhaps a royal tomb. There was a real devolution of settlements, as cities involved in regional alliances became warring centers, reduced to minor sites and inevitably to tiny villages, all within half a century.

Dramatic confirmation of the role of war in the Great Collapse may have been uncovered at Yaxchilan on the Usumacinta River by archaeologist Akira Taneko. The ruined West Acropolis stands on a natural hill 165 ft (50 m) high. Within the rubble covering its stairways and inside its lowest building (a weak point in its defenses), Taneko found 217 projectile points; almost all were of flint, and had been used on darts propelled by atlatls – mute testimony to a final battle sealing the city's death. Other cities in the Central Area eventually fell victim to the same cycle of violence, characterized by the systematic mutilation and smashing of stone monuments – the eyes and mouths of rulers are often pecked out, as if to cancel their power.

What had happened to Classic Maya society? Archaeologist Arthur Demarest lays it to an intensification of inter-elite competition, manifesting itself in different ways: not only in "wasteful architectural extravagance," in Balkanization of political authority, and in senseless regional wars, but also in ecological over-exploitation. This last factor may have found confirmation in research undertaken by Kevin Johnston at the site of Itzan, on a small tributary of the Río Pasión. Thanks to a long road bulldozed through a residential part of the site, Johnston has determined that about half of all domestic house floors were not located on top of house mounds, and thus would have been invisible to the usual archaeological surface survey. What this might mean is that we may have to double our previous population estimates for the Central Area, which already run into the many millions. As we have seen, other archaeologists, particularly David Webster, argue forcefully for very light populations during the Late Classic, a debate that points up the uncertainties when no actual census records are available for an ancient people.

Nonetheless, one can conclude that by the end of the eighth century, the Classic Maya population of the southern lowlands had probably increased beyond the carrying capacity of the land, no matter what system of agriculture was in use. There is mounting evidence for massive deforestation and erosion throughout the Central Area and Copan, only alleviated in a few favorable zones by dry slope terracing. In short, overpopulation and environmental degradation had advanced to a degree only matched by what is happening in many of the poorest tropical countries today. The Maya apocalypse, for such it was, surely had ecological roots.

Very recently, a research team led by botanist David Lentz of the University of Cincinnati sampled wooden beams and lintels in the major temples and palaces of Tikal. What they found was that in the temples that had been built before AD 741, the raw material of preference was sapodilla (*Manilkara achras*), a tall, straight tree that can grow to 100 ft (30 m). The sapodilla produces *chicle* sap for chewing gum, an edible fruit, and an extremely strong and durable wood that is easy to carve when freshly cut. In the decades following that date, beams were made from the far smaller logwood tree (*Haematoxylum campechianum*), which offers an inferior, gnarly wood that is almost impossible to carve. The botanists conclude, with one caveat, that the Tikal Maya had largely demolished the tall monsoon forest by the 740s. The caveat is this: in AD 810, sapodilla was again the species of choice, but beam widths were far smaller than they had once been. Apparently Tikal's rulers had set aside protected groves of their favorite tree or managed to import it from some distance (a pattern also suggested, with some recent debate, for Chaco Canyon in the prehistoric southwest of the United States).

The final factor in the Great Collapse may have been drought; in Chapter 1 we described the recent, highly convincing, geochemical evidence that there had been a major episode of droughts in the Maya lowlands. These came in bursts. After less severe droughts in the eighth century AD, mostly of short duration, a longer spell afflicted the Maya region from AD 820 to 860. A relatively moist period followed, but then the climate became much worse. A brief yet intense drought took hold around AD 930, and then, from AD 1000 to 1100, there arrived a truly terrible spell; the worst ever experienced by this agricultural people. Compounding the social, political, and ecological stresses already in effect in the Central Area, these droughts might have been the final blow that finished off Classic culture in the Peten once and for all. Year after year the increasingly desperate peasantry may have planted their dwindling supply of seed corn, only to see it wither as soon as it sprouted from the parched earth. With the Maya ruling elites no longer able to call down the rains from Chahk, they would soon have lost "the mandate of heaven"; social revolutions, hypothesized by Eric Thompson, could have been the final act in the tragedy. The entire institution of kingship had lost its relevance to the everyday lives of the Maya people.

It was not just the "stela cult" – the inscribed glorification of royal line-ages and their achievements – that disappeared with the Collapse, but an entire world of esoteric knowledge, mythology, and ritual. Much of the elite cultural behavior to be described in Chapter 9, such as the complex mythol-ogy and iconography found on Classic Maya pictorial ceramics, failed to re-emerge with the advent of the Postclassic era, and one can only conclude that the royalty and nobility, including the scribes who were the repository of so much sacred and scientific knowledge, had "gone with the wind." They may well have been massacred by an enraged populace, their screen-fold books consumed in a holocaust similar to that carried out centuries later by Bishop Landa, and their monuments smashed.

New investigations have shown that at least some of the Central Area population survived the debacle, for instance in a modest village at El Zotz, Guatemala, and in the valleys of the Belize and New Rivers. Nonetheless these dwindling groups would have known little about the glories of the Classic past, and some would have been wanderers among the now-empty centers, camping out like savages (or archaeologists) in the rooms of forgot-ten palaces – peoples like the Lakandon, burning copal incense before the strange depictions of mortal men and women who had now become gods.

But what happened to the bulk of the population who once occupied the Central Area, apparently in the millions? This is one of the great mysteries of Maya archaeology, since we have little or no evidence allowing us to come up with a solution. The early Colonial chronicles in Yukateko speak of a "Great Descent" and "Lesser Descent," implying two mighty streams of refugees heading north from the abandoned cities into Yucatan, and Linda Schele and Peter Mathews, like Sylvanus Morley before them, believe that this account reflects historical fact. Some may have migrated in a southerly direction, particularly into the Chiapas highlands. So far, however, this puta-tive diaspora seems to have left no real traces in the archaeological record.

CEIBAL AND THE PUTUN MAYA

The great city of Ceibal on the Río Pasión apparently recovered from its defeat at the hands of the far smaller Dos Pilas. Indeed, it appears to have absorbed a good deal of the local population, in a manner rather like the Spanish system of "reduction" (Chapter 10). By this practice, populations were forced or somehow induced to move into easily controlled settlements. The city is thus like no other community before or since in this part of the

Peten. Ceibal presents another mystery too. During the Terminal Classic it seems to have come under the sway of foreigners, as seen in the strong influence of non-Maya forms of art and writing. The evidence is to be found in the part of the site known as Group A; in its South Plaza sits an unusual four-sided structure with four stairways. In front of each stairway is a stela, and a fifth stands inside the temple. All five record the k'atun ending 10.1.0.0.0 (1 December AD 849), and have as their protagonist an individual with the name "Wat'ul." Two of them show him in very non-Maya fashion, with clipped moustache and pageboy haircut, but wearing Classic Maya regalia. There are more "foreign"-looking stelae at Ceibal which belong to this period, with non-Maya calendrical glyphs and iconography; on one, a figure wears the bird-mask of the central Mexican wind god, Ehecatl, with a Mexican speech scroll curling from the beak.

Who were these people? We have much to learn about the ninth century in the southern Maya lowlands, but could Eric Thompson have been right in thinking that the Putun or Chontal Maya of the Tabasco and southern Campeche plains had begun taking over some of the more important sites in the southern Peten, such as Ceibal, perhaps moving into a power vacuum? These somewhat Mexicanized merchant-warriors controlled the great Gulf Coast entrepot of Xicallanco where Mexican and Maya traders met, and were known to the later Aztecs as "Olmeca-Xicallanca." There is now evidence that the Putun had not only penetrated into the lowland Maya "heartland," but had also reached the central highlands of Mexico. Excavations at the hilltop site of Cacaxtla, ascribed by the mestizo chronicler Diego Muñoz Camargo to the Olmeca-Xicallanca, have uncovered a ninth-century palace with brilliant polychrome murals in Maya style [xx]. Among other things, these show dignitaries in Maya costume bearing Maya "ceremonial bars," which are in the style of the Putun-influenced stelae of Ceibal, and a great war between two contending factions, which immediately recalls the battle scene of Bonampak.

Linda Schele and Peter Mathews gave a different interpretation of Wat'ul. According to them, the texts on his monuments imply that he was not a foreigner from the west, but had been placed in Ceibal by the ruler of Ucanal, a city of the eastern Peten. This, however, does not answer the question of the patently Mexican hieroglyphs on other Ceibal monuments. And regardless of what these texts may tell us about who supposedly sent him from the east, the Fine Orange ceramics typical of this period at Ceibal and other Terminal Classic sites in the Peten definitely originated in the west – on the Gulf Coast plain, in Putun country. One stela records that a ceremony involving Wat'ul was "witnessed" by a visitor from Puh, or "Place of the Reeds." While Schele and Mathews identify this as Chichen Itza, it was more likely Tollan/Tula, the Toltec capital in far-off central Mexico.

The question remains: if these were Olmeca-Xicallanca or Putun Maya, what were they doing here, almost 500 miles (800 km) from their homeland? For that matter, why are there bas-reliefs showing seated figures in Maya style on the ninth-century Temple of the Feathered Serpent at Xochicalco in Morelos, just south of the Valley of Mexico? It is now evident that the ninth century was a time of turmoil over much of Mesoamerica, with the power of Teotihuacan having long since withdrawn, and the old order in the Maya lowlands breaking down. In this power vacuum, the Putun, seasoned businessmen with strong contacts ranging from central Mexico to the Caribbean coast of Honduras, must have played a very aggressive role in a time of troubles, and their presence in the Mexican highlands may have played a formative role in what was to become the Toltec state.

PUUC SITES IN THE NORTHERN AREA

"If Yucatan were to gain a name and reputation," wrote Bishop Landa in 1566, "from the multitude, the grandeur and the beauty of its buildings, as other regions of the Indies have obtained these by gold, silver and riches, its glory would spread like that of Peru and New Spain." Landa was not exaggerating, for ruins there are by the hundreds. Sylvanus Morley saw this as evidence for what he called a "New Empire" founded by refugees from the derelict civilization of the Central Area, which he dubbed the "Old Empire," and he claimed to find references in the late Maya chronicles to a double-pronged migration from the south. However, ceramics recovered from excavations, along with a better reading of the ethnohistoric sources, led Eric Thompson and George Brainerd to the view that many of the Yucatecan sites were coeval with the Peten centers which were claimed to pre-date them. Modern scholarship has found that both schools were partly right and partly wrong: the great era of Yucatecan culture was the Terminal Classic, when many Peten cities had fallen into ruin, but there never was a real "empire" among the Maya, as Morley had believed.

It will be remembered that a group of very low hills, the Puuc, is to be found in southwestern Yucatan, a region that has deep and fertile soils, in fact the best in the northern part of the peninsula (though according to Nicholas Dunning, this did not prevent the Maya from soon exhausting them). By perhaps the Late Preclassic, the Maya of this region had learned how to construct *chultun*, or bottle-shaped cisterns, to secure otherwise scarce drinking water over the dry season, and over the Classic period populations began to expand. During the Late Classic itself, the Puuc was fragmented into many relatively small major centers controlling domains that included pockets of particularly productive soil.

It was in the Puuc that the dominant Terminal Classic style of the peninsula developed. The problem of dating is acute, for some of these centers are mentioned in the chronicles by late upstart lineages who claimed to have founded them, but there are truncated Long Count dates painted on capstones in the late ninth and early tenth bak'tun; the very latest reads 10.3.17.12.1, or 5 October AD 906, but Thompson believed that the Puuc style may have lasted until 10.8.0.0.0 (AD 987), when Toltec invaders usher in the Postclassic.

Characteristic of Puuc buildings are facings composed of very thin squares of limestone veneer over a cement-and-rubble core; boot-shaped vault stones; decorated cornices; round columns in doorways; engaged or half columns repeated in long rows; and the exuberant use of stone mosaics on upper facades, emphasizing the usual masks with long, hook-shaped snouts, as well as frets and lattice-like designs of criss-crossed elements. In the perfection of architectural facades, the Puuc is far ahead of the more sloppy Peten style.

Thanks to the research of Karl Taube, it is now clear what these abundant architectural masks represent. Long thought to be faces of the Maya rain god Chahk, they are actually iconographic mountains (*witz*), the descendants of the corner masks placed on Classic-period monuments like Copan's Temple 11. On some Puuc buildings, and at Chichen Itza, they often have bands containing stylized flowers above the eyes. In effect, they transform each Puuc and Chichen Itza building where they are found into the "Flower Mountain" – in Taube's words, "a solar celestial paradise, a shining place of flowers and beauty." This is a concept widely disseminated throughout Mesoamerica from at least Teotihuacan times, and even into the Pueblo cultures of the American Southwest.

Uxmal is by far the largest Puuc site, and one of the triumphs of Maya civilization [112]. Traditionally, this was the seat of the Xiu family, but this was a late lineage of Mexican origin that could not possibly have built the site. The archaeological and epigraphic evidence implies that Uxmal had emerged as the capital of a large, Terminal Classic state centered in the eastern Puuc between AD 850 and 925. Uxmal is dominated by two mighty temple-pyramids, the Great Pyramid and the House of the Magician, the upper temple of the latter entered through a monster-mask doorway like those of the Chenes. Next to the House of the Magician is the imaginatively named Nunnery, actually a palace group made up of four separate rectangular buildings arranged around an interior court; although the complex could be entered from the corners, the principal gateway with its corbel arch lies on the south side [113]. The mosaic elements which make up the masonry facades of the Nunnery Quadrangle are particularly interesting; they include miniature representations of the thatched-roof huts of the ordinary folk of the time.

The House of the Governor sits below the Great Pyramid, on its own artificial terrace, and is the finest structure at Uxmal, embodying the culmination of the Puuc style. The upper facade of the three long, interconnected structures of this building is covered by a fantastically elaborate mosaic of thousands of separate masonry elements set into the rubble core, a symphony of step-and-fret, lattice-work, and Flower Mountain mask motifs combined into a single harmonious whole.

In contrast to this masterful architecture, there are only a handful of carved stelae at Uxmal, which are sloppily executed, and in a sorry state of preservation. Nevertheless, Kowalski has been able to work out a

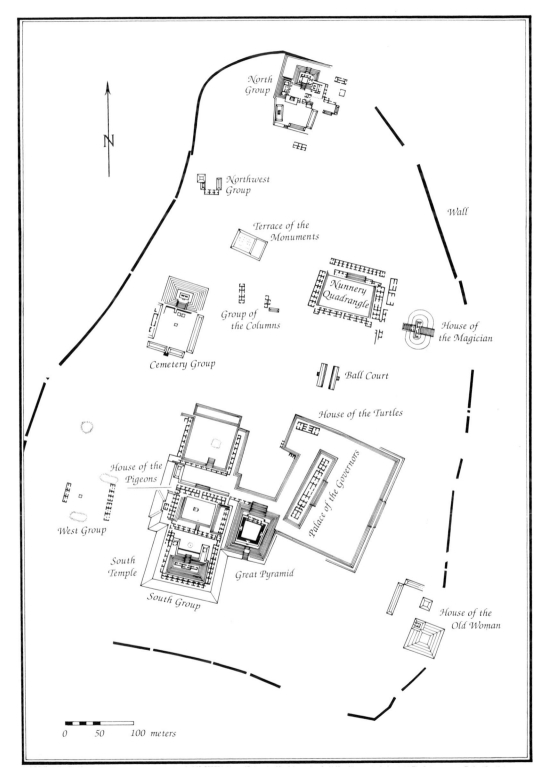

112 Plan of central Uxmal, by far the largest Puuc site.

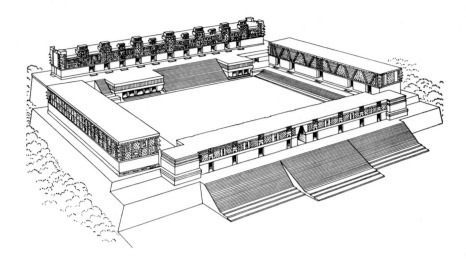

113 (*Above*) The Nunnery Quadrangle at Uxmal, looking northeast.

114 (*Opposite, above*) Arch at Labna, a Puuc-culture site in Mexico, from a view published by Catherwood, 1844.

115 (*Opposite, below*) The five-storied structure at Edzna, Campeche. Terminal Classic period.

partial dynastic history dominated by the figure of Lord Chahk, during whose reign the House of the Governor was built, probably to serve as his administrative headquarters.

A causeway, or *sakbih*, 11.25 miles (18 km) long runs southeast from Uxmal through the small site of Nohpat to Kabah, so presumably the three centers were connected at least ceremonially if not politically. Kabah is noted for its Kotz' Po'op palace, with an extraordinary facade made up of hundreds of Flower Mountain masks, and for its freestanding arch. Sayil, a city to the south of Kabah, is dominated by a magnificent three-story palace. It has the additional distinction of being one of the few Puuc sites to be completely and intensively mapped; Jeremy Sabloff of the Santa Fe Institute, who headed the project, estimates that *c.* 10,000 people lived in an urban core of 1.7 sq. miles (4.5 sq. km), with an additional 7,000 in the zone surrounding this core. To the east of Sayil is Labna, another sizable Puuc city, with an elaborate freestanding arch (far more impressive than Kabah's) [114], a palace group, and a lofty temple-pyramid. Other cities with a far richer inventory of texts are Oxkintok and Xcalumkin, the former with its own distinct lordly epithet, the latter with an unusual emphasis on a title, *sajal*, used solely by secondary lords in cities along the Usumacinta and in Chiapas.

Edzna is the southernmost of the Puuc sites, and is best known for its unusual five-storied structure which combines features of pyramids and palaces [115]. Presumably its Late Preclassic canal-and-moat system,

described in Chapter 2, remained in use throughout the Terminal Classic. Whatever its function, the Puuc sites represent one of the great architectural legacies of the ancient New World, with many buildings of highest finish and masonry of almost unparalleled quality, all in unusual state of preservation. Yet they differ from cities to the south, frustratingly so, by their more limited texts, leaving us in the dark about much of their elite history.

THE TERMINAL CLASSIC AT CHICHEN ITZA

The great site of Chichen Itza in east-central Yucatan proves that the Puuc style reached east as well as north. A number of buildings at this otherwise Toltec-Maya center closely resemble those found in the west, although Puuc veneer masonry is seldom present. These are largely located in "Old Chichen" (the southern zone of the city), and include the three-storied Nunnery [116], the Ak'ab Tz'ib ("dark writing," named for the reliefs containing glyphic texts on one of the doorways), the Casa Colorada, the Temple of the Three Lintels, and the Temple of the Four Lintels. Lintels in the Nunnery and other buildings contain quite extensive hieroglyphic texts. These were inscribed within a very brief period, spanning only the second half of the ninth century, and celebrate not the dynastic history of individual kings (as in the southern lowlands) but rather temple dedication rituals such as bloodletting and drilling of new fire, a rite of renewal. A well-attested personage in these texts is K'ahk'upakal K'awiil, "Fiery Shield K'awiil"; later Colonial sources mention a K'ahk'upakal, described as a valiant Itza captain, which raises the question of whether this may be one and the same person. If so, then he might have been an Itza Maya; but we will defer the treatment of these enigmatic people until the next chapter. Could the rulers of Terminal Classic Chichen have been Putun? There are certainly distinct iconographic links between the late monuments of Ceibal and those of Chichen, even in the Toltec-Maya period. Regardless of ethnic

Opposite
XII Lintel 24 from Yaxchilan, Mexico. In a bloodletting ritual that took place on 29 October AD 709, the ruler Itzamnaaj Bahlam II "Shield Jaguar" holds a torch, while his wife Lady Xok draws a thorn-studded rope through a hole in her tongue. Screenfold books rest in the basket at her knees. Late Classic period.

Overleaf
XIII Jaina figurine of a beautiful, barebreasted woman who may be the young Moon Goddess or a courtesan. The pigment on her skirt and body is the famous Maya Blue – a unique combination of indigo and a special clay. Late Classic period. Ht *c.* 9 in. (22.5 cm).

XIV Jade mosaic vase with portrait head of the Maize God, from Burial 196, a royal interment of the Late Classic period at Tikal, Guatemala. The pieces once adhered to a wooden interior, which has long since disintegrated. Ht 9.5 in. (24.2 cm).

Modern renderings of the Bonampak murals

XV (*Above*) Part of the wall painting in Room 2 at Bonampak, *c.* AD 790.
On a terraced platform stands Yajaw Kan Muwaan, king of Bonampak, his
subordinates, and his wife and mother (or daughter?). Below, captives taken
in a jungle battle are being tortured by having their fingers crushed and
lacerated.

XVI (*Opposite, above*) A detail from the painting in Room 1, Bonampak.
Servants adjust the jade bracelets on a royal prince, preparatory to his
participation in a ritual dance. Hundreds of resplendent quetzal feathers
fan out from his back.

XVII (*Right*) In this detail from the wall painting in Room 1, Bonampak,
a procession of musicians sings and beats time as they advance toward
three dancing princes. The hieroglyphic text above records the date in
AD 790 when "Shield Jaguar" IV of Yaxchilan oversaw the accession of a
Bonampak lord.

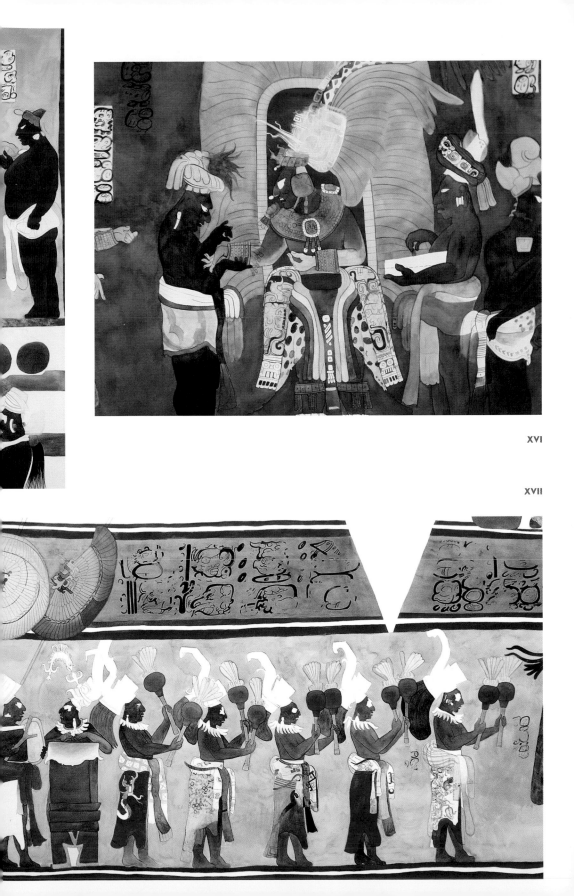

XVI

XVII

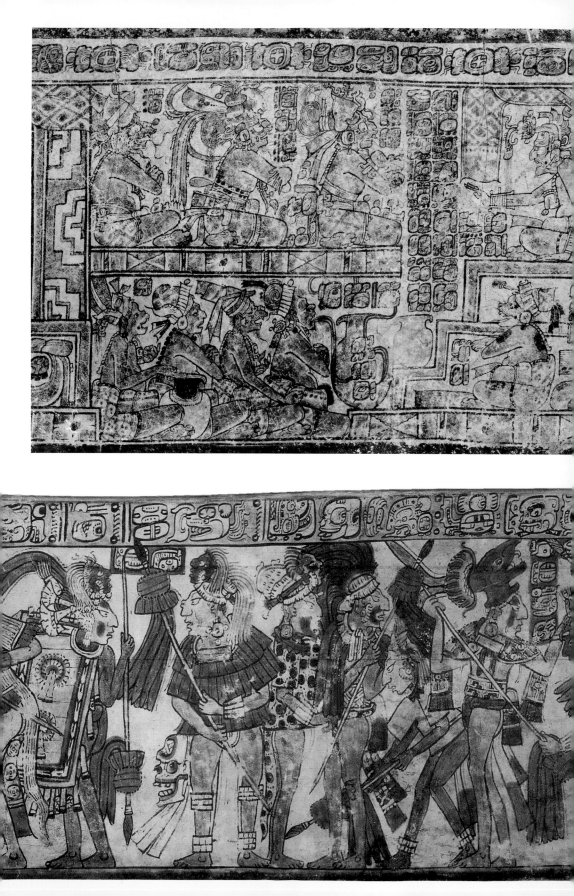

XVIII (*Left*) Rollout of a Late Classic cylindrical vase. This palace scene shows three gods seated before an enthroned high god. The subordinate deities grasp their upper arms in gestures of respect. To lower left are four monkey scribes. One of them speaks, as signaled by a volute from his mouth; the glyphs record that oration. To the right sit three other scribes in animal form. The opossum, *uch*, cradles a book on his lap, while the vulture, *us*, holds up a paper sheet with numbers.

XIX (*Below*) A stylized battle is taking place in this rollout scene from a Late Classic chocolate vase said to come from Nebaj, Guatemala. Several captives are being taken by noble warriors armed with spears; the names of some of the figures are revealed in accompanying texts. Below the rim is a text naming the patron or owner of the vase.

XX Putun Maya influence is powerfully present on this representation of a young Eagle Warrior from Cacaxtla, a hilltop acropolis in Tlaxcala, Mexico. His eagle feet rest on the back of a Feathered Serpent, and he carries in his arms a Maya "ceremonial bar" with open centipede jaws that contain stylized flints; the bar is emblematic of rulership. AD 800–850, Terminal Classic period.

116 East wing of the Nunnery at Chichen Itza, Mexico, from a lithograph by Catherwood.
Puuc culture.

affiliation, there is a possibility that from *c.* AD 870 to 890, K'ahk'upakal
K'awiil was paramount in Chichen, since in the texts he is given the title of
k'uhul ajaw, "holy king."

One of the strangest and most intriguing structures ever raised by the
Maya is the Caracol (Spanish for "snail"), located in the Puuc section
of Chichen [VIII]. Once stigmatized by Eric Thompson as a "two-decker
wedding cake on the square carton in which it came," it is nevertheless one
of the outstanding monuments of the Terminal Classic. The Caracol has
long been described in the popular literature as an observatory, and this has
been proved beyond a shadow of a doubt by measurements taken by the
archaeoastronomers Anthony Aveni, Sharon Gibbs, and Horst Hartung.
The ancient Maya used lines of sight taken from its platforms and door
and window jambs to plot the rising and setting positions of the sun, the
moon, and, above all, the planet Venus. As will be seen in Chapter 9, Maya
astronomers had a remarkably accurate knowledge of the apparent motion
of Venus, and it may be that at least some of that learning derived from
observations carried out in the Caracol.

EK' BALAM

Located some 32 miles (53 km) northeast of Chichen Itza, the site of Ek' Balam is a compact but impressive center dominated by a large acropolis. The triple defensive wall that surrounds the site indicates that conditions in this remote part of the Maya lowlands were dangerously unsettled in the Terminal Classic. Excavations at Ek' Balam began in the 1980s under William Ringle and George Bey, and have continued under the direction of Mexican archaeologists Leticia Vargas de la Peña and Victor Castillo Borges. Many spectacular finds here have thrown altogether unexpected light on Terminal Classic culture in the Northern Maya lowlands; especially the discovery of the abundant hieroglyphic texts painted on the walls and capstones of Ek' Balam's buildings.

According to these, and to a slightly garbled tradition recorded in early Colonial times, the history of Ek' Balam (like certain other Maya cities) began with the "arrival" of a founder from some other place. In this case, it was an individual called Ek' Balam ("Star Jaguar" or "Black Jaguar") who "arrived" on 8 April AD 770, and after whom the place was anciently named. It is possible that he came to the north from the Central Area. According to Spanish epigrapher Alfonso Lacadena, the first real king in these records was Ukit Kan Le'k Tok', who took the throne in the following month. Ukit Kan Le'k Tok' is specifically named as the *k'uhul ajaw* of the kingdom, which bears the name Talol. This man, probably even more powerful in his day than the rulers of Chichen Itza, had a very long reign – perhaps more than four decades – and seems to have been responsible for most of what can be seen at the site today.

The principal monument raised by Ukit Kan Le'k Tok' and his successors is the Acropolis, 525 ft (160 m) long and 102 ft (31 m) high, a very complex structure with many superimposed building stages, with corbel-vaulted rooms on various levels connected by an intricate system of stairways and passages. An extraordinary and perfectly preserved frieze in white stucco forms the facing of the upper levels. During the tenure of Ukit Kan Le'k Tok', entrance was through the stuccoed, befanged maw of a gigantic Flower Mountain mask in pure Chenes style [117]. Magnificent life-sized stucco humans are arranged about the mask, one fetchingly seated within the mask's left eye.

A number of Acropolis rooms have capstones painted with figures of the seated K'awiil, god of royal descent, or a bird-like Itzamnaaj deity (see Chapter 9), along with a text giving the date on which the capstone was placed, and the "owner" of the room or building – usually Ukit Kan Le'k Tok', king of Talol. About AD 814, the corpse of the great king himself was laid out on a jaguar pelt in the most important of these rooms, which was then sealed as a tomb. With him was the richest array of offerings ever found in the Northern Area, including animal and human sacrificial victims, a gold frog (possibly an import from Panama, and one of the

117 Part of the elaborate white stucco facade of the Acropolis, Ek' Balam. In its entirety it represents a gigantic mask of the Flower Mountain monster, its maw surrounded by gigantic teeth.

earliest-attested metal objects yet discovered for the Maya), and, next to his head, a stuccoed ceramic vessel with an incised text, part of which reads ". . . the chocolate vase of Ukit Kan Le'k . . . Holy Lord of Talol." Significantly, on the room's capstone the ruler is portrayed not as K'awiil, but as the youthful Maize God, perhaps a conscious evocation of Pakal the Great's sarcophagus lid in distant Palenque – a representation celebrating resurrection and apotheosis.

Ek' Balam's heyday lasted at least until September AD 896 (the date of its final inscription) but its fate was finally sealed by the arrival of the Toltec army on the Maya scene, and the dominance of the Yucatan Peninsula by a new Maya-Toltec warrior caste based at Chichen Itza.

THE COTZUMALHUAPA PROBLEM

The Pipil have always been an enigmatic people. Their language is Nahuat, a close relative of Nahuatl, the official tongue of the Aztecs, differing mainly by a substitution of *t* in place of *tl*. Having intruded into the Maya area during the Postclassic period from an unknown region in Mexico, by the Spanish Conquest the Pipil had established a major settlement in a small zone within the well-watered Piedmont zone just above the Pacific plain of Guatemala. From traditions recorded in Colonial times, however, it is known that their domain had once extended to the west into lands later claimed by the Kaqchikel Maya.

This once-Pipil territory is the locus of a vanished civilization which was at one time mistakenly ascribed to them, centering upon the town of Santa Lucía Cotzumalhuapa, in a region which once was famed for its production of cacao, the chocolate beans used not only for drink but also as currency. According to Yale University archaeologist Oswaldo Chinchilla Mazariegos, there are only three Cotzumalhuapan sites known (El Baúl, El Castillo, and Bilbao), or perhaps just one large one, for all lie within a tiny area of only 20 sq. miles (52 sq. km). Each is a compact ceremonial center consisting of temple substructures arranged on a single platform measuring only a few hundred yards on its long axis. These structures have earthen cores faced with river cobbles, but stairways and some courts were occasionally covered with dressed stone. They are connected by a network of causeways and stone bridges. Chinchilla believes that the large acropolis at El Baúl could have been the royal residence of the Cotzumalhuapan rulers.

The stone sculpture of this culture is more widely disseminated, being found even in the Antigua Basin, in the highlands to the west of Guatemala City. While it may have its roots in the Late Classic, based on the evidence of art style and pottery the Cotzumalhuapan culture must have flourished in the Terminal Classic, prior to the arrival of the Pipil. To some eyes, a harder and more cruel sculptural style can hardly be imagined, or one less Maya in its general aspect [118]. As Eric Thompson noted, the Cotzumalhuapan sculptors evidently had "a haunting preoccupation with death." Reliefs of skulls and manikin figures of skeletons are not uncommon. Their second obsession was the rubber ball game. Secure evidence for the game comes from certain stone objects that are frequent in the Cotzumalhuapan zone and in fact over much of the Pacific Coast down to El Salvador. Of these, most typical are the U-shaped stone "yokes" which represented the heavy protective belts of wood and leather worn by the contestants; and thin heads or *hachas* with human faces, grotesque carnivores, macaws, and turkeys, generally thought to be markers for the zones of the court, but worn on the yoke during postgame ceremonies [119]. Both are sure signs of a close affiliation to the Classic cultures of the Mexican Gulf Coast, where such ball game paraphernalia undoubtedly originated.

118 (*Above*) A stone relief of a figure emerging from the carapace of a crab, from El Baúl. On either side are the Mexican dates 2 Monkey and 6 Monkey. Cotzumalhuapa culture. Ht 3 ft 3 in. (1 m).

119 (*Right*) A thin stone head (*hacha*) from El Baúl. Objects of this sort were probably ball court markers. Cotzumalhuapa culture. Ht *c.* 1 ft (30.5 cm).

120 A ball player salutes the Moon Goddess. Monument 4 from Santa Lucía Cotzumalhuapa. Cotzumalhuapa culture, Terminal Classic period.

The reliefs and sculptures of the Cotzumalhuapan sites include representations of some purely Mexican gods, along with curious composite entities such as one jaguar-iguana. On some magnificent stelae, ball players wearing "yokes" and protective gloves reach up to celestial deities, usually the Sun or Moon [120]. From the bodies of gods and men may sprout the fronds and pods of cacao, the apparent source of Cotzumalhuapan wealth. In addition to their religion, even their very calendar was more Mexican than Maya. The majority of the glyphs on the monuments are recognizable as the kind of day-names prevalent among the peoples of southern Mexico, while the numbers and coefficients are expressed in the Mexican fashion by dots or circles only; only rarely does the bar-and-dot numeration so characteristic of the Maya occur. As in the highlands of Mexico, individuals (and perhaps gods, too) were identified by the day of their birth. There are suggestive connections with the Gulf Coast plain, where communities similarly concentrated upon the ball game, death, human sacrifice, and the cultivation of cacao. But exactly how and where this distinctive culture originated, and what language was spoken here, remain a puzzle.

THE END OF AN ERA

Beyond the continuing mystery which surrounds the demise of civilization in the Peten and neighboring regions, there is still much to be learned about the Terminal Classic. In many respects, what transpired in the Puuc area was a replay of the Great Collapse which had taken place a century earlier in the southern lowlands: for reasons which are yet unclear (but which may also include overpopulation and a growing inability of the Puuc rulers to feed their people), all of its cities and lesser centers were virtually abandoned by the end of the tenth century, and when first encountered by the Spaniards, they were in ruins. There was one great exception to this second collapse. To the east of the Puuc, Chichen Itza was to gather new strength, and to become the largest and perhaps even the most powerful Mesoamerican city of its day, as the transition was made from Classic to Postclassic.

7

THE POSTCLASSIC

By the close of the tenth century AD the destiny of the once proud and independent Maya had, at least in northern Yucatan, fallen into the hands of grim warriors from the highlands of central Mexico, where a new order of men had replaced the supposedly more intellectual rulers of Classic times. We know a good deal about the events that led to the conquest of Yucatan by these foreigners, and the subsequent replacement of their state by a resurgent but already decadent Maya culture, for we have entered into a kind of history, albeit far more shaky than that which was recorded on the monuments of the Classic Period. The traditional annals of the peoples of Yucatan, and also of the Guatemalan highlanders, transcribed into Spanish letters early in Colonial times, apparently reach back as far as the beginning of the Postclassic era and are very important sources.

But such annals should be used with much caution, whether they come to us from Bishop Landa himself, from statements made by the native nobility, or from native lawsuits and land claims. These are often confused and often self-contradictory, not least because native lineages seem to have deliberately falsified their own histories for political reasons. Our richest (and most treacherous) sources are the K'atun Prophecies of Yucatan, contained in the "Books of Chilam Balam," which derive their name from a Maya savant said to have predicted the arrival of the Spaniards from the east. The "history" which they contain is based upon the Short Count, a cycle of 13 k'atuns (13 x 7,200 days or 256.25 years), each k'atun of which was named according to the last day (always Ajaw) on which it ended. Unfortunately, the Postclassic Maya thought largely in cyclic terms, so that if certain events had happened in a K'atun 13 Ajaw, they would recur in the next of the same name. The result is that prophecy and history are almost inextricably entwined in these documents that sometimes read like divine revelation; one such history, for example, begins:

This is the record of how the one and only god, the 13 gods, the 8,000 gods descended, according to the words of the priests, prophets, Chilam Balam, Ah Xupan, Napuc Tun, the priest Nahau Pech, and Ah Kauil Chel. Then was interpreted the command to them, the measured words which were given to them.

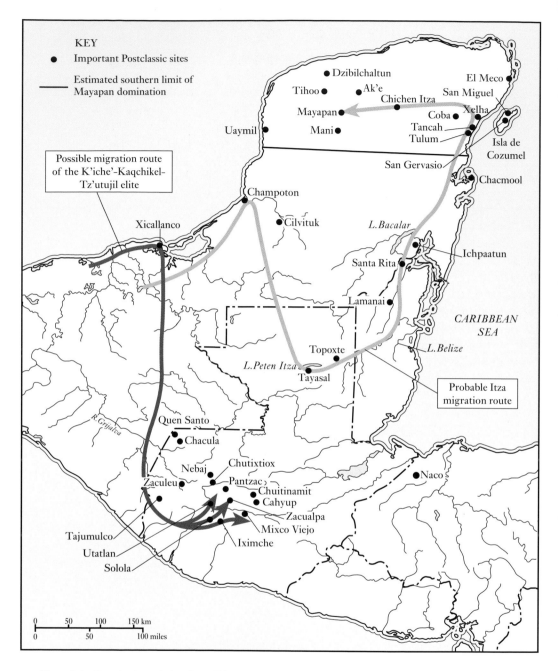

KEY

● Important Postclassic sites

— Estimated southern limit of Mayapan domination

Possible migration route of the K'iche'-Kaqchikel-Tz'utujil elite

Probable Itza migration route

Dzibilchaltun
Tihoo
Ak'e
Chichen Itza
Mayapan
Mani
Uaymil
El Meco
San Miguel
Xelha
Coba
Tancah
Tulum
Isla de Cozumel
San Gervasio
Chacmool
Champoton
Cilvituk
Xicallanco
L. Bacalar
Ichpaatun
Santa Rita
Lamanai
CARIBBEAN SEA
Topoxte
L. Belize
L. Peten Itza
Tayasal
Quen Santo
R. Grijalva
Chacula
Nebaj
Chutixtiox
Zaculeu
Pantzac
Chuitinamit
Cahyup
Zacualpa
Mixco Viejo
Iximche
Tajumulco
Utatlan
Solola
Naco

0 50 100 150 km
0 50 100 miles

121 Sites of the Postclassic period and possible late migration routes.

THE TOLTEC INVASION AND CHICHEN ITZA

Into the vacuum created by the collapse of the older civilizations of central Mexico moved a new people, the Nahua-speaking Toltecs, whose northern origins are proclaimed by their kinship with the non-agricultural barbarians called the Chichimec. Shortly after AD 900 they had settled themselves at the key site of Tula ("Tollan" in Nahuatl, or "Place of the Reeds"). The city, which was the administrative center of an empire spanning central Mexico from the Atlantic to the Pacific, has been securely identified as an archaeological site in the state of Hidalgo, some 50 miles (80 km) northwest of Mexico City, so that a good deal is known about Toltec art and architecture in its place of origin. Everywhere the Toltec went, they carried with them their distinctive style, in which there is an obsession with the image of the Toltec warrior, complete with pillbox-like headdress with a down-flying bird in front and a stylized bird or butterfly on the chest, carrying a feather-decorated atlatl in one hand and a bunch of darts in the other. Left arms were protected by quilted padding, and the back by a small shield shaped like a round mirror. Prowling jaguars and coyotes, and eagles eating hearts, dominate the reliefs which covered their principal temple-pyramid, a testimony to the importance of the knightly orders among these militarists. We have already seen these orders in Early Classic Teotihuacan – the Eagles, the Jaguars, and the Coyotes. They paid homage to the war god Tezcatlipoca ("Smoking Mirror") rather than to the more peaceable Quetzalcoatl; these orders would play a significant role in later Mexican history.

According to somewhat obscure, retrospective histories, the city was founded under the leadership of a king named Topiltzin, who also claimed the title of Quetzalcoatl or "Feathered Serpent," the culture hero of Mexican theology. According to a number of quasi-historical accounts of great poetic merit, a struggle arose between Topiltzin Quetzalcoatl and his adherents on the one hand, and the warrior faction on the other. Defeated by the evil magic of his adversary Tezcatlipoca, the king was forced to leave Tula with his followers, in AD 987 or thereabouts. In one version well known to all the ancient Mexicans, he made his way to the Gulf Coast and from there set across on a raft of serpents for Tlapallan ("Red Land"), some day to return for the redemption of his people. Wracked by further internal dissensions and deserted by most of its inhabitants, the Toltec capital was finally violently destroyed in AD 1156 or 1168, but its memory was forever glorious in the minds of the Mexicans, and there was hardly a ruling dynasty in Mesoamerica in later days which did not claim descent from the Toltecs of Tula.

Now, it so happens that the Maya historical sources speak of the arrival from the west of a man calling himself K'uk'ulkan (k'uk'ul, "feathered," and kan "serpent") in a K'atun 4 Ajaw ending in AD 987, who wrested Yucatan from its rightful owners and established his capital at Chichen Itza; this must surely be our Topiltzin. According to the late Maya scholar Ralph Roys, the accounts of this great event are seriously confused with the history of a later people called the Itza, who moved into the peninsula during the next K'atun 4 Ajaw, in the thirteenth century, and gave their name to the formerly Toltec site of Chichen. In any case, the Maya credited K'uk'ulkan and his retinue with the introduction of idolatry, but the impressions left by him were generally good. Bishop Landa states:

> They say he was favorably disposed, and had no wife or children, and that after his return he was regarded in Mexico as one of their gods and called Quetzalcoatl; and they also considered him a god in Yucatan on account of his being a just statesman.

The goodwill contained in these words is almost certainly due to most of the ruling houses of later times being of Mexican rather than Maya descent, for surely the graphically rendered battle scenes of Chichen Itza tell us that the conquest of Yucatan by the supposedly peaceful Topiltzin Quetzalcoatl and his Toltec armies was violent and brutal in the extreme. The murals found in the Temple of the Warriors at Chichen Itza and the reliefs on some golden disks fished up from the Sacred Cenote at the same site tell the same story [122, 123, 126]. The drama opens with the arrival of the Toltec forces by sea, most likely along the Campeche shore, where they reconnoiter a coastal Maya town with whitewashed houses. In a marine engagement, the Maya come out in rafts to meet the Toltec war canoes, to suffer the first of their defeats.

122 Rendering of a wall painting from the Temple of the Warriors, Chichen Itza. Canoe-borne Toltec warriors reconnoiter the Maya coast.

123 Drawing of a repoussé gold disk from the Sacred Cenote, Chichen Itza. Two Toltec men-at-arms attack a pair of fleeing Maya. Diam. 8.75 in. (22.2 cm).

Then the scene moves onto land, where in a great pitched battle (commemorated in the now-ruined murals of the Temple of the Jaguars) fought within a major Maya settlement, the natives are again beaten. The final act ends with the heart sacrifice of the Maya leaders, while the Feathered Serpent himself hovers above to receive the bloody offering.

The Yucatan taken over by the Toltec exiles was then in its Puuc phase, but following the invasion Uxmal and most other important Puuc centers, along with Ek' Balam, must have been abandoned, perhaps under duress. The wall encircling the center of Uxmal may have been built as result of these instabilities. Chichen Itza, which in those days may have been called Uukil-abnal ("Seven Bushes"), became, under the rule of Topiltzin Quetzalcoatl, the supreme metropolis of a united kingdom, a kind of splendid recreation of the Tula which he had lost [124, 125]. New architectural techniques and motifs were imported from Toltec Mexico and synthesized with Puuc Maya forms. For instance, columns were now used in place of walls to divide rooms, giving an air of spaciousness to halls; a sloping batter was placed at the base of outside walls and platforms; colonnades of pure Tula type were built, which included low masonry banquettes covered with processions of tough Toltec warriors and undulating feathered serpents;

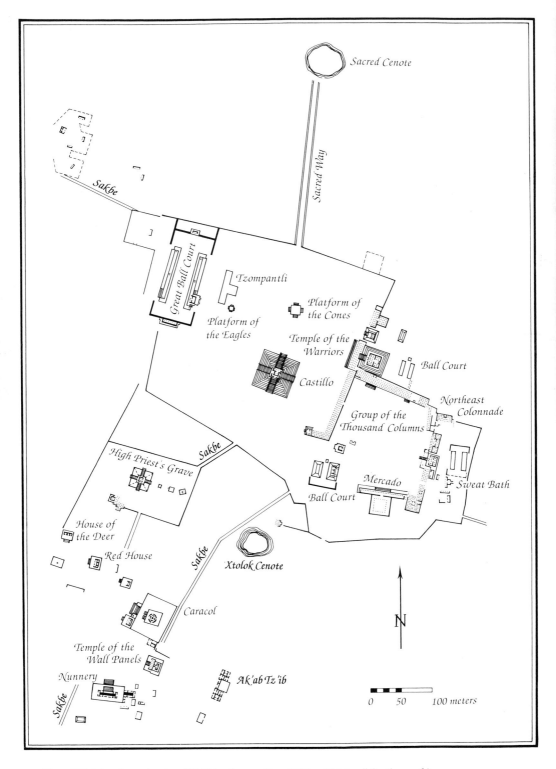

124 Plan of Chichen Itza, showing "Old" (to the north) and "New Chichen" (to the south).

125 View of the main monuments at Chichen Itza, looking northeast from the Nunnery. In the foreground is the Caracol; beyond it to the left, the Castillo or Temple of K'uk'ulkan; and to the right, the Temple of the Warriors.

126 Toltec warrior emerging from the jaws of a cloud-serpent. Detail from a gold disk from the Sacred Cenote, Chichen Itza.

and walls were decorated with murals in bands. And everywhere, the old Maya Flower Mountain masks were incorporated in these new buildings.

For not only was there a synthesis of styles at Chichen Itza, but also a hybridization of Toltec and Maya religion and society. Jaguar and Eagle knights rub elbows with men in traditional Maya costume, and Mexican astral deities coexist with Maya gods. The old Maya order had been overthrown, but it seems obvious that many of the native princes were incorporated into the new power structure. This model is not accepted, however, by all scholars, some preferring to see the contact in more neutral terms, as the result of trade or even a religious cult focused on the feathered serpents that adorn buildings and balustrades at Chichen. Yet there may be some bias here: Maya archaeologists have traditionally been averse to the idea that any historical forces outside of their area – such as the Olmec, the Teotihuacan state, or the Tula Toltec – could have influenced the Maya, or even taken over their territory. Yet there are extremely close iconographic links between "New Chichen" and Tula, as well as a shared, totally non-Maya writing system. And to deny that the Toltec had existed at all, as some Mayanists do, would relegate most of the ethnohistoric accounts that we have of the Toltec, from peoples as diverse as the Aztec and the highland Maya, to little more than fiction. At the same time, there is little doubt that most people at Chichen were Maya, the building technologies and pottery descending from what came before.

What has made resolving the Toltec/Maya problem so difficult has been, until very recently, the dearth of stratigraphic excavations at Chichen Itza, a site very poorly known in spite of its size and renown. To add to the confusion, there are relatively few radiocarbon dates available. However, a pioneering essay by Beniamino Volta and Geoffrey Braswell of the University of California, San Diego, has offered a definitive solution. Based on a statistical analysis of all available stratigraphic, epigraphic, ceramic, and radiocarbon data, they conclude that there is no chronological overlap whatsoever between the older, Puuc-style part of the city ("Old Chichen") and the northern sector of the city ("New Chichen"). The latter was entirely constructed in the Early Postclassic; the Castillo, or "Castle," was erected in the second half of the tenth century, and the Great Ball Court *c*. AD 1000.

The Castillo stands at the hub of Toltec Chichen [x]. It is a great four-sided temple-pyramid which Landa tells us was dedicated to the cult of K'uk'ulkan. The corbel-vaulted temple at the summit of the four breath-taking stairways is a curious mixture of indigenous and foreign; Flower Mountain masks embellish the exterior, while reliefs of tall war cap-tains from Tula are carved upon the door-jambs. An earlier Toltec-Maya pyramid has been discovered inside the Castillo, with beautifully preserved details. Its superstructure's chambers contain a stone throne in the form of a snarling jaguar, painted red, with eyes and spots of jade and fangs of shell; atop the throne rested a Toltec circular back-shield in turquoise mosaic. Before it is a "chacmool," a reclining figure with hands grasping a plate-like receptacle held over the belly, perhaps for receiving the hearts of sacrificed victims. Chacmools are ubiquitous at Tula and Chichen, and are a purely Toltec invention [127].

From the Castillo may be seen the Temple of the Warriors, a splendid building resting upon a stepped platform and surrounded by colonnaded halls, its magnificence restored by the Carnegie Institution in the early twentieth century [128]. It was closely modeled on Pyramid "B" at Tula, but its far greater size and the excellence of the workmanship lavished upon it suggest that the Toltec intruders were better off in Yucatan, where they could call upon the skills of Maya architects and craftsmen. The building is approached on the northwest through impressive files of square columns, which are decorated on all four faces with reliefs of Toltec officers. At the top of the stairs a chacmool gazes stonily out upon the main plaza, while the entrance to the temple itself is flanked by a pair of feathered serpents, heads at the ground and tails in the air. Beyond them lies the principal sanctuary with its table or altar supported by little Atlantean Toltec warriors. Frescoes emblazon the interior walls with lively scenes related to the Toltec conquest of Yucatan.

127 A "chacmool" figure at the head of the stairs of the Temple of the Warriors. Reclining figures of this sort were introduced by the Toltec, and are thought to be connected with the cult of heart sacrifice. Ht 3 ft 6 in. (1.1 m).

In 1926, just as restoration of the Temple of the Warriors was near completion, another such structure came to light underneath it. From this, the Temple of the Chacmool, were recovered relief-carved columns still bearing the bright pigments with which they were painted. Two benches in the temple interior had been painted, one with a row of Toltec leaders seated upon jaguar thrones identical to that in the interior of the Castillo, but the other with Maya nobles seated upon stools covered with jaguar skin and bearing manikin scepters in Maya fashion. Could these have been quisling princes?

The splendid ball court of Toltec Chichen is the largest and finest in all Mesoamerica [129]. Its two parallel walls measure 272 ft long and 27 ft high (82.6 by 8.2 m), and are 99 ft (30 m) apart. At either end of the I-shaped playing field is a small temple, the one at the north containing extensive bas-reliefs of Toltec-Maya life. That the game was played "Mexican-style" is confirmed by the two stone rings set high on the sides of the walls, for a

128 (*Left*) The Toltec Temple of the Warriors, Chichen Itza, from a doorway of the Castillo. The building is a grandiose replica of Pyramid B at Tula in Mexico, and a symbol of Toltec ascendancy over Yucatan.

129 The Toltec-Maya ball court at Chichen Itza. With walls 27 ft (8.2 m) high, and an overall length of about 490 ft (149 m), this is the largest court in Mesoamerica. The rings set high on either wall were used in scoring the game.

130 Doorway of the Temple of the Jaguars, overlooking the ball court, Chichen Itza. Shown here are one of two Feathered Serpent columns which support the lintel, and a door jamb with a relief figure of a Toltec warrior.

Spanish chronicler tells us that among the Aztecs whichever team managed to get the ball through one of these not only won the game and the wager but also the clothing of the onlookers. Above the east wall of the court is the important Temple of the Jaguars, whose inner walls were once beautifully painted with Toltec battle scenes, so detailed and convincing that the artist must have been a witness to the Toltec invasion [130]. Decades of neglect have resulted in their almost total ruin.

Landa describes "two small stages of hewn stone" at Chichen, "with four staircases, paved on the top, where they say that farces were represented, and comedies for the pleasure of the public," surely to be identified with the two Dance Platforms whose facings are covered with themes directly imported from Tula, such as eagles and jaguars eating hearts [131]. Human sacrifice on a large scale must have been another gift of the Toltecs, for near the ball court is a long platform carved on all sides with human skulls skewered on stakes [132]. The Aztec name given to it, Tzompantli ("skull rack"), is certainly apt, for in Postclassic Mexico such platforms supported the great racks upon which the heads of victims were displayed. Each of the six ball court reliefs depicts the decapitation of a ball player, and it is entirely possible that the game was played "for keeps," the losers ending up on the Tzompantli.

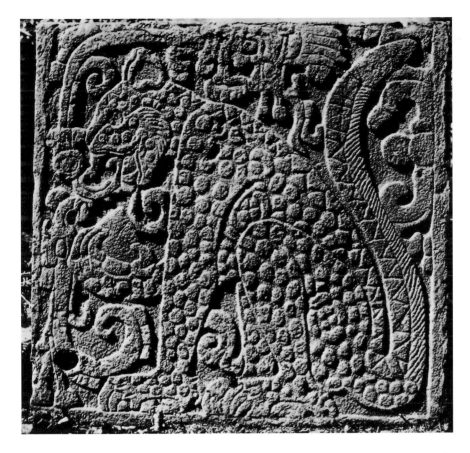

131 (*Above*) Toltec relief panel of a jaguar eating a heart, from the Dance Platform of the Eagles, Chichen Itza. Such a theme is also known at Tula in the Toltec homeland, and is symbolic of the military order of the Jaguars.

132 (*Right*) Bas-relief of skulls skewered on a rack, from the Tzompantli, Chichen Itza.

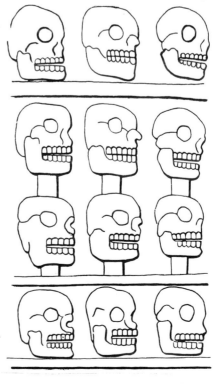

Chichen Itza is, however, most renowned not for its architecture, but for its Sacred Cenote, or "Well of Sacrifice," reached by a 900-ft (274-m) long causeway leading north from the Great Plaza. From Landa's pen comes the following:

> Into this well they have had, and then had, the custom of throwing men alive as a sacrifice to the gods, in times of drought, and they believed that they did not die though they never saw them again. They also threw into it a great many other things, like precious stones and things which they prized.

Shortly before the Spanish Conquest, one of our Colonial sources tells us that the victims were "Indian women belonging to each of the lords," but in the popular imagination the notion has taken hold that only lovely young virgins were tossed down to the Rain God lurking below the Sacred Cenote's greenish-black waters. The late Earnest Hooton, who examined a collection of some fifty skeletons fished up from within, commented that "all of the individuals involved (or rather immersed) may have been virgins, but the osteological evidence does not permit a determination of this nice point." A goodly number of the skulls turned out to be from adult males, and many from children, while pathology showed that "three of the ladies who fell or were pushed into the Cenote had received, at some previous time, good bangs on various parts of the head . . . and one female had suffered a fracture of the nose!"

As the great Mayanists Ralph Roys and Alfred Tozzer stressed, the peak of the sacrificial cult at the Sacred Cenote was reached after the decline of Toltec Chichen, and continued into Colonial times and even later. Nonetheless, many of the objects dredged from the muck at the bottom of the Cenote are of Toltec manufacture, including some marvelously fine jades and the gold disks already mentioned [123, 126]. For metals had now appeared in the Maya area, although were probably cast and worked elsewhere and imported. The many copper bells and other objects from the well were of Mexican workmanship. The local lords brought treasures of gold from places as far afield as Panama to offer to the Cenote.

The Rain God's cult is also strikingly evident in the underground cavern of Balankanche, located 2.5 miles (4 km) east of Chichen Itza [133]. In a deep, hot, and humid chamber which they later sealed, the Toltec priests had placed almost a hundred incense burners of pottery and stone, most of them at the base of an enormous stalagmitic formation – resembling some great World Tree, as Nikolai Grube notes – in the center of the chamber. Twenty-six of these censers are hourglass in shape, and had been modeled with the goggle-eyed visage of the Mexican Rain God, Tlaloc, and polychromed. Off to one side they had made an offering of miniature *metates* with their *manos*, and it is tempting to speculate that there might once have been 260 of these, the number of days in the sacred calendar.

133 Chamber in the cave of Balankanche, Yucatan. In the center, stalactite and stalagmite have united in an immense pillar resembling a World Tree; around it were placed Toltec incense burners of pottery and stone.

The heyday of Chichen has been detected at other places in the Yucatan Peninsula. At about this time there appears a glazed trade ceramic called Plumbate ware, produced in kilns along the Guatemala–Chiapas border area near the Pacific shore. Plumbate vessels must have been made in part to Toltec taste, for they often take the form of Toltec warriors, but many are animal effigies or simple, pear-shaped vases supported on hollow legs, very much like the carved and painted vessels also associated with the Toltec period in Yucatan [134, 135, 136]. Nonetheless, Plumbate probably reflects a time of widespread trade in the Postclassic, especially along coasts, by a multitude of groups, some with entrepots occupied by members of the same family or speakers of the same language. (Often, these communities were surprisingly polyglot, an advantage for trade.) Powerful dynasties were no longer in place to monopolize the movement of goods, which now passed into the hands of trading entrepreneurs or local petty lords. It is unlikely that Chichen controlled all such exchange at this time.

In 1984 and 1985, a team led by Anthony Andrews and Fernando Robles C. mapped and excavated Isla Cerritos, a tiny island in the mouth of the Río Lagartos estuary on the north coast of Yucatan. This has proved to be the

Toltec-style pottery

134 (*Left*) A Toltec effigy jar (Plumbate ware) in the form of the god Itzamnaaj, from Jutiapa, Guatemala. Ht 6 in. (15.2 cm).

135 (*Below left*) Hands are depicted in black paint on this X-Fine Orange ware jar from coastal Campeche. Together with Plumbate ware, pottery of this kind is often a marker for the Toltec presence in the Maya area. Ht *c.* 7 in. (17.8 cm).

136 (*Below*) A Toltec tripod jar (Plumbate ware) from coastal Campeche, Mexico. Produced on the Pacific slopes of Chiapas and Guatemala in Toltec style, this glazed ware was widely traded over much of southern Mesoamerica. Ht 7.5 in. (19 cm).

port of Chichen Itza, with a sea wall pierced by entryways on the exposed side, and with ceramics virtually identical to those of the great Toltec-Maya capital. It will be remembered that Yucatan's greatest resource was its coastal salt beds, and Isla Cerritos was certainly strategically located to exploit production and trade of this necessity. But other items also moved along these trade networks; the excavators encountered obsidian from the mines in central Mexico, turquoise which had probably originated in the American Southwest (a luxury item prized by the Toltecs and their cultural heirs the Aztecs), and gold from lower Central America.

What finally happened to the Toltecs? The challenge for us in the Postclassic period is the strikingly small number of inscriptions. Gone are the texts that memorialized the personalities and events of the Classic period. There is no certain understanding of how Chichen was ruled or organized: an earlier view that it was governed by councils rested principally on a now-discredited reading of a few, earlier hieroglyphs. The later sources indicate that Chichen was spent as a political force by a K'atun 6 Ajaw which ended in AD 1224. Its Sacred Cenote continued to be visited as a place for pilgrimage for centuries to come, but Volta and Braswell believe all monumental construction had ceased by c. AD 1100.

Strangely, according to Douglas Kennett and colleagues, this century of rule coincides with a period of terrible drought in the Maya region, the worst yet experienced. Chichen flourished as a Toltec capital precisely when the Maya were under the *most* environmental stress. Was this the opening the Toltec elites needed to impose control? Or, in the long term, did it simply make their rule untenable? Equally odd is that, when the drought ended, the Maya area passed into a time we know least – the middle of the Postclassic. Rather than rebounding, the Maya experienced political disarray and weakened population.

THE ITZA AND THE CITY OF MAYAPAN

The Toltecs may finally have been accepted by the natives of Yucatan, but the Itza were always despised. Epithets such as "foreigners," "tricksters and rascals," "the lewd ones," and "people without fathers or mothers" are applied to them by the Maya chronicles; and the title carried by the Itza war leader K'ahk'upakal, "he who speaks our language brokenly," shows that they could not have been Yucatec in origin. Some scholars have suggested that the Itza were originally a group of Mexicanized Chontal Maya (that is, Putun) living in Tabasco, where commercial connections with central Mexico were deep-rooted. Much hinges on the origin of the word "Itza." Associated later with the central Peten, in Guatemala, a term much like it occurs as a local title in Classic-era texts around Lake Peten Itza. Whether this is the same label or a title taking on new meanings remains entirely unclear. It is certainly no ethnic description in Classic sources. At any rate, the later historical sources have their own story to tell. While the Toltecs lorded it over Yucatan, the Itza were settled in a place called Chakan Putun ("Savannah of the Putun"), probably Champoton on the coast of Campeche. They were driven from this town *c.* AD 1200 and wandered east across the land, "beneath the trees, beneath the bushes, beneath the vines, to their misfortune," migrating through the empty jungles back to the region of Lake Peten Itza, and to the eastern shores of Belize. Finally, this wretched band of warriors found their way up the coast and across to Chichen Itza, where they settled as squatters in the desolate city in K'atun 4 Ajaw (AD 1224–44).

Leading the Itza diaspora to northern Yucatan was a man who claimed the title of K'uk'ulkan, after his great Toltec predecessor of the tenth century; he consciously imitated Toltec ideas, such as the cult of the Sacred Cenote. And yet another cult was initiated, that of the Goddess of Medicine (and childbirth), one of the several aspects of the old goddess Chak Chel, a deity of healing and destruction. Pilgrims from all over the Northern Area voyaged to her shrine on the island of Cozumel.

In K'atun 13 Ajaw (AD 1263–83) the Itza founded Mayapan, though some of the tribe remained behind at Chichen Itza, which had now lost its old name of Uukil-abnal and taken on its present one (meaning "mouth of the well of the Itza"). The wily K'uk'ulkan II populated his city with provincial rulers and their families, thus ensuring dominion over much of the peninsula. However, after his death (or departure), troubles increased, and it was not until *c.* 1283 that Mayapan actually became the capital of Yucatan, after a revolt in which an Itza lineage named Kokom seized power, aided by Mexican mercenaries from Tabasco, the Kanul ("guardians").

Mayapan, situated in the west central portion of the peninsula, is a residential metropolis covering about 2.5 sq. miles (6.5 sq. km) and completely surrounded by a defensive wall, testifying to the unrest of those days. Over 2,000 dwellings lay within, and Marilyn Masson of the University at Albany estimates that between 15,000 and 17,000 persons lived in the city. At the center of Mayapan is the Temple of K'uk'ulkan, a much smaller imitation of the Castillo at Chichen Itza. The colonnaded masonry dwellings of important persons were nearby, just as Landa tells us, and households become poorer as one moves away from the center. Each group of thatched-roof houses probably sheltered a family, and is surrounded by a low property wall. The city "pattern" is haphazard: there are no streets. No arrangement can be discerned at all; it seems as if the basically dispersed Maya had been forced by the Itza to live jam-packed together within the walls. No city like it had ever been seen before in the Maya area; it even lacks a ball court, so prominent at Chichen, although, in several buildings, excavations by the Mexican authorities did reveal bold murals and sculpted figures with niches in place of heads, perhaps so as to position actual skulls.

On what did the population live? One answer is tribute, for Father Cogolludo tells us that luxury and subsistence goods streamed into the city from the vassals of the native princes whom the Kokom were holding hostage in their capital. Others, such as Masson and Carlos Peraza Lope, discern active markets from their excavations at Mayapan. Of supreme importance to the residents of Mayapan, living in such a stony and relatively dry environment, was the location of *cenotes* within the walls, which archaeologist Clifford Brown has discovered were constructed so as to enclose the maximum number of these natural wells. But some *cenotes* may have served for more than drinking water. Brown has found a tunnel leading off from one right underneath the Temple of K'uk'ulkan, bringing to mind the tunnel and secret chamber below the Pyramid of the Sun in Teotihuacan. And deliberately excluded from the walled city is a large *cenote* still held in awe by local people as a holy place inhabited by a monster (one old man has seen a feathered serpent going in and out!).

By this time, the Maya worshiped at shrines and family oratories, in which were placed brightly painted pottery incense burners in a distinct style found across the Yucatan Peninsula, even down into Belize. These represent Mexican gods such as Quetzalcoatl, Xipe Totec (the God of Spring), and the Old Fire God, side-by-side with Maya deities such as Chahk (the Rain God), the Maize God, the Maya version of the Old Fire God of central Mexico, and the Monkey-man scribal god [137, 138].

137 Pottery incense burner from a shrine at Mayapan. This effigy of God B, the Rain God Chahk, carries a small bowl in one hand and a ball of flaming incense in the other. The censer was painted after firing with blue, green, black, red, white, and yellow pigments. Ht 21.5 in. (54.6 cm).

138 Upper part of a pottery incense burner from Mayapan, Mexico. God M, who was the patron of merchants, is shown here, identifiable from his partly broken, Pinocchio-like nose. Red, blue, and yellow paint had been applied to the censer. Ht 9.5 in. (24.1 cm).

In an ill-omened era, K'atun 8 Ajaw (AD 1441–61), fate began to close in upon the Itza. The later, problematic sources claim that Hunac Ceel was then ruler of Mayapan, an unusual figure who achieved prominence by offering himself as a sacrifice to be flung into the Sacred Cenote at Chichen, and living to deliver the Rain God's prophecy given to him there. The ruler of Chichen Itza was a man named Chak Xib Chak. According to one story, by means of sorcery Hunac Ceel drove Chak Xib Chak to abduct the bride of the ruler of Izamal, whereupon the expected retribution took place and the Itza were forced to leave Chichen. Next it was the turn of the Kokom, and revolt broke out within the walls of Mayapan, stirred up by an upstart Mexican lineage named Xiu which had settled near the ruins of Uxmal. The Maya nobles of Mayapan joined the Xiu, and the Kokom game was up; they were put to death and the once great city was destroyed and abandoned for all time. Whether any of this is accurate cannot be readily determined. We do know from excavations at Mayapan that it flourished in the 1200s and 1300s, but experienced occasional burnings or attacks even before its abandonment. It fell just as the Aztecs began to claw their way to great power, hinting at turbulence across Mesoamerica.

Those Itza who were driven from Chichen Itza were to be in evidence for several centuries more, however. Once again they found themselves as outcasts in the deserted forests, this time wandering back, so the sources say, to the Lake Peten Itza which they had seen in a previous K'atun 8 Ajaw. On an island in the midst of its waters they established a new capital, Tayasal (a Spanish corruption of Tah Itza), now covered by the city of Flores, chief town of northern Guatemala. (The only substantial settlement that remains visible from the 1300s is not Flores but the still-impressive city Topoxte, which looks across to Classic-period Yaxha.) Safe in the fastness of an almost impenetrable wilderness, their island stronghold was bypassed by history. Tayasal was first encountered by Hernán Cortés in 1524, while that intrepid conqueror was journeying across the Peten with his army to punish a rebellious insubordinate in Honduras, and he was kindly received by king Kanek', a name borne by a long line of Itza rulers. It was not until the seventeenth century that the Spaniards decided something must be done about this last, untamed Maya kingdom, and several missionaries were sent to convert Kanek' and his people – to no avail.

But two years later, Spanish arms succeeded where peaceful missions had repeatedly failed. It seems almost beyond belief that Tayasal fell to the Spaniards only in 1697; while students at Harvard College were scratching their heads over Cotton Mather's theology, Maya priests 2,000 miles away were still chanting rituals from hieroglyphic books.

THE INDEPENDENT STATES OF YUCATAN

With Mayapan gone, the whole peninsula reverted to the kind of political organization that had been the rule in Classic times, six centuries earlier. In place of a single, united kingdom, sixteen rival states now stood, each jealous of the power and lands of the others, and only too eager to go to war to assert its claims [139]. Visual culture shows the impact of other parts of Mesoamerica. Somewhat inappropriately, the art historian Donald Robertson called the dominant art form an "international style," by analogy with the stripped-down architecture of Modernist buildings in the twentieth century. In fact, this imagery was anything but plain and devoid of local meaning: its underlying concepts were deeply local, and many (but not all) of the gods depicted were Maya. At Santa Rita Corozal, Belize, a set of murals, destroyed soon after their excavation but dating roughly to this period, displays deities presiding over calendrical periods [140]. A few gods are even bound, as though captives, and one horrific scene shows a deity slinging the heads of two gods while another plays a war drum. Mythic place names, each purely and legibly Maya, accompany the figures. Santa Rita also yielded an extraordinary set of ear ornaments in gold and turquoise, perhaps brought from central Mexico [141].

There are few archaeological sites which can be assigned to this final phase, although the life of the times is well described by Landa and other

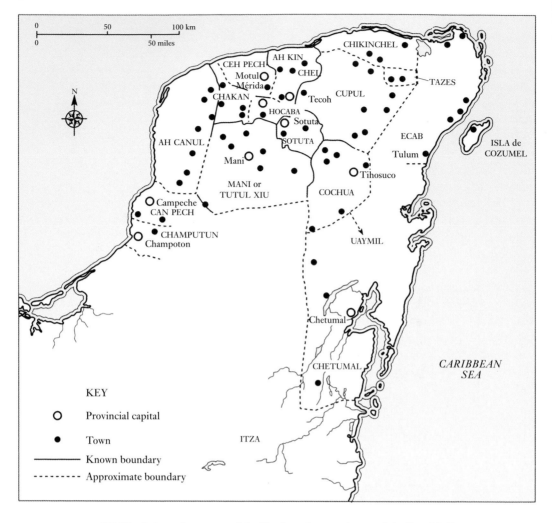

139 The independent states of the Northern Area on the eve of the Spanish Conquest.

early post-Conquest writers able to question natives who had actually participated in that culture. We are sure that there were one or more major towns within each province, but these were chosen by the Spaniards for their settlements and therefore most are buried under centuries of Colonial, and more recent, constructions.

One site which was untouched, however, is Tulum, a small town in the province of Ecab founded in the Mayapan period. Spectacularly placed on a cliff above the blue-green waters of the Caribbean, Tulum is surrounded by a defensive wall on three sides and by the sea on the fourth [142]. Probably no more than 500 or 600 persons lived there, in houses concentrated on artificial platforms arranged along a sort of "street." The principal temple, a miserable structure called the Castillo, and other important buildings are

140 Modern rendering of a mural fragment, now destroyed, from Santa Rita Corozal, Belize. Late Postclassic period.

141 Gold, turquoise, and obsidian ear ornaments, from Santa Rita Corozal, Belize. L. 2.5 in. (6.4 cm).

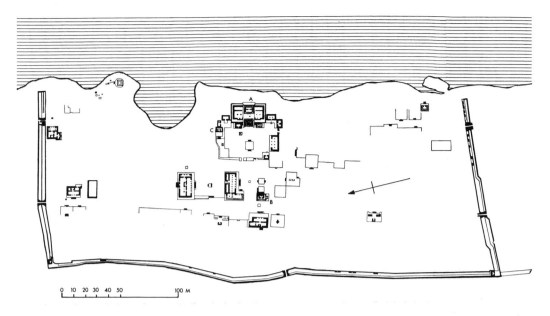

142 Plan of the walled town of Tulum, on the Caribbean coast of the Yucatan Peninsula. *A*, Castillo; *B*, Temple of the Frescoes; *C*, Temple of the Diving God.

143 Temple of the Frescoes, Tulum, from the west, a photograph taken prior to 1923, before the walled site had been cleared. The temple is noted for its wall paintings carried out in a hybrid style. Inset panels over the doorways contain stucco "diving god" figures, while stuccoed faces at the corners of the lower story suggest its dedication to the god Itzamnaaj.

144 Detail of a wall painting in the Temple of the Frescoes at Tulum. An aged goddess, probably Chak Chel, carries two images of the god Chahk.

clustered together near the sea. On the upper facades of many of these dwarfish structures, which are of strikingly slipshod workmanship, are plaster figures of winged gods descending from above. Wall paintings have been found on both the interior and exterior surfaces of some temples, but the best-preserved are in the two-storied Temple of the Frescoes [143, 144]. The style of these is undoubtedly influenced by the pictorial manuscripts of that gifted people from Mexico. Yet the content of the Tulum frescoes is native Maya, with scenes of gods such as Chahk and various female divinities performing rites among bean-like vegetation.

THE CENTRAL AREA IN THE POSTCLASSIC

As noted in the last chapter, not all of the lowland Maya centers and populated regions suffered total decline and abandonment with the Classic collapse (although most certainly did). In fact, Coba in the northeast had a virtual renaissance in the Postclassic, as Tulum-style superstructures were built on top of Classic pyramids. In the Central Area certain towns, including Tayasal, were founded and flourished after AD 1200 on islands in the chain of lakes that extends across the eastern Peten almost to the Belize border. Lamanai, the ancient port town on the New River, saw much construction during the Postclassic, and was occupied well into the Colonial era, as a church built in the sixteenth century (and abandoned in the next) testifies. The ready availability of potable water in all of these places, and the opportunity for waterborne trade, surely had something to do with their survival.

MAYA-MEXICAN DYNASTIES IN THE SOUTHERN AREA

In the mountain valleys of highland Guatemala, there were numerous independent nations on the eve of the Conquest, but the K'iche' and Kaqchikel were the greatest of these. All indications are that they and their lesser neighbors, the Tz'utujil and Poqomam, had been there since very early times. And yet they claimed in their own histories that they had come from the west, from Mexico. As the Annals of the Kaqchikels relate:

> From the setting sun we came, from Tula, from beyond the sea; and it was at Tula that arriving we were brought forth, coming we were produced, by our mothers and fathers, as they say.

This claim may have been pure wishful thinking, similar to that of many Americans who would have liked their forebears to have stepped off the *Mayflower* in 1620. The noted authority on K'iche' Maya culture and history, Robert Carmack, traces the actual origin of the K'iche' elite not to the Toltec diaspora of the late tenth and eleventh centuries, but to a much later incursion of Toltecized Chontal-Nahua speakers (in other words, Putun Maya) from the Gulf Coast border region of Veracruz and Tabasco. These "forefathers" would have arrived as small but very formidable military bands, similar to the Japanese samurai, and terrorized the native K'iche' and Kaqchikel highlanders. Gradually they established an epi-Toltec state, complete with a ruling line claiming descent from Quetzalcoatl. Many of the elite's personal names, as well as names of early places, objects, and institutions, seem to be Chontal rather than K'iche'; and they introduced into the Guatemalan highlands many Nahua words for military and ritual matters.

The *conquistadores* have described the splendor of their towns, such as Utatlan or Q'umarkaj, the K'iche' capital which was burned to the ground by the terrible Pedro de Alvarado, or the Kaqchikel center Iximche [145, 146]. These sites were placed in defensive positions atop hills surrounded by deep ravines, and heavily Mexican down to most architectural details. Typically, the principal building is a large double temple with two frontal stairways, much like the Great Temple of the Aztecs in Tenochtitlan, and there usually is a well-made ball court nearby, confirming the assertion in the Popol Vuh that the highlanders were fond of that game. Lastly, all buildings are covered in Mexican fashion with flat beam-and-mortar roofs, the corbel principle being unknown here.

Best preserved of these late highland centers is Mixco Viejo, the capital of the brave Poqomam nation; this almost impregnable site, surrounded by steep gorges, fell to Alvarado and two companies of Spanish infantry only through treachery.

Utatlan (Q'umarkaj) is the best known of these highland capitals, both archaeologically and ethnohistorically. In it, there was a fundamental social

145 View west of Iximche, the fortified capital of the Kaqchikel state, near Tecpan, Guatemala. This Late Postclassic site is surrounded by ravines, and consists of plazas surrounded by lineage temples, palaces, and residential compounds.

cleavage between the lords and their vassals: these were castes, in the strictest sense of the term. The former were the patrilineal descendants of the original warlords; they were sacred, and surrounded by royal emblems. The vassals served as foot-soldiers to the lords, and while they could and did receive military titles through their battlefield prowess, they were still subject to sumptuary laws. Merchants had a privileged status, but they had to pay tribute. In addition, the free population included artisans and serfs (a growing class of rural laborers). Slaves comprised both sentenced criminals and vassal war captives; in general, only captive lords were considered fit for sacrifice, or for consumption in cannibalistic rites.

There were 24 "principal" lineages in Utatlan, closely identified with the buildings or "Big Houses" in which the lords carried out their affairs. The functions carried out in them were ceremonial lecturing; the giving of

146 Group C, Chuitinamit, Guatemala, looking west; restoration drawing by Tatiana Proskouriakoff. The K'iche' built an impressive stronghold here after driving out the Poqomam Maya. The double pyramid is a typically Mexican feature of the late highland centers.

bride-price; and eating and drinking associated with marriages between the lineages. The K'iche' state was headed by a king, a king-elect, and two "captains," but there was also a kind of quadripartite rule (known also in Yucatan) embodied in four chiefs, one from each of the four major Utatlan lineages.

Documentary evidence unique for the ancient Maya enables us to associate specific ruined temples at Utatlan with gods revered by the K'iche'. The major cult structures faced each other across a plaza, and were dominated by the Temple of Tojil, a Jaguar deity connected with the sun and with rain. In the same plaza was a circular temple dedicated to the Feathered Serpent, while the Ball Court of Utatlan represented the Underworld. There was a palace elaborating the idea of the Big Houses in honor of Utatlan's ruling lineage, the Kawek ("Rain") dynasty; other Big Houses can be identified as the range structures so typical of highland towns. Perhaps we have a clue here to the functions played by the "palaces" in Classic sites of the southern lowlands.

THE SPANISH CONQUEST

"The raised wooden standard shall come!" cried the Maya prophet Chilam Balam, "Our lord comes, Itza! Our elder brother comes, oh men of Tantun! Receive your guests, the bearded men, the men of the east, the bearers of the sign of God, lord!"

The prediction came true in 1517, when Yucatan was discovered by Hernández de Córdoba, who died of wounds inflicted by Maya warriors at Champoton. The year 1518 saw the exploratory expedition of Grijalva, and that of the great Hernán Cortés followed in 1519, but Yucatan was for a while spared, as the cupidity of the Spaniards drew them to the gold-rich Mexico. The Spanish Conquest of the northern Maya began only in 1528 under Francisco de Montejo, on whom the Crown bestowed the title of Adelantado, "one who goes before," an honorific dating to the time of the Crown's re-conquest of Iberia. In practice, that centuries-long conflict strongly influenced the Spanish assault on the New World. But the conquest of the Maya was no easy task, for unlike the mighty Aztecs, there was no overall native authority that could be toppled, bringing an empire down with it. Nor did the Maya fight in the accepted fashion. Attacking the Spaniards at night, plotting ambushes and traps, they were jungle guerrillas in a familiar modern tradition. Accordingly, it was not until 1542 that the hated foreigners managed to establish a capital, Mérida; even so revolt continued to plague the Spaniards throughout the sixteenth century. As historian Matthew Restall has shown, the process of "pacification" of the more recalcitrant Maya of the Yucatan Peninsula – who often fled to the forest when faced with defeat – could never have been carried out successfully without the active collaboration of some Maya lords, such as the Xiu family of Mani, or the Chontal Maya ruler Paxbolonacha. Like the turn-coats of World War II, these individuals risked all that they would benefit in the long run from siding with the invaders. And so they did, at least for a while. In many places, as in Lamanai and Tipu, Belize, the Spanish imprint was lightly felt, in the form of so-called "visita" churches that were only periodically visited by Catholic friars or priests [147].

The conquest and "pacification" of the Southern Area has traditionally been ascribed to the military prowess of several hundred Spanish *conquistadores*, led by the ruthless and cruel Alvarado brothers, Pedro and Jorge. But a recent study by the University of Leiden researcher Florine Asselbergs of a large painted cloth map depicting the conquest of Guatemala has revealed the all-important role played by many thousands of indigenous allies from central and southern Mexico in the various Spanish campaigns – a role barely acknowledged by the victorious Spaniards. By 1541, the year of Pedro de Alvarado's death, the K'iche' and Kaqchikel kingdoms had fallen under the Spanish yoke, and native resistance was largely at an end. As for the "indigenous conquistadores",

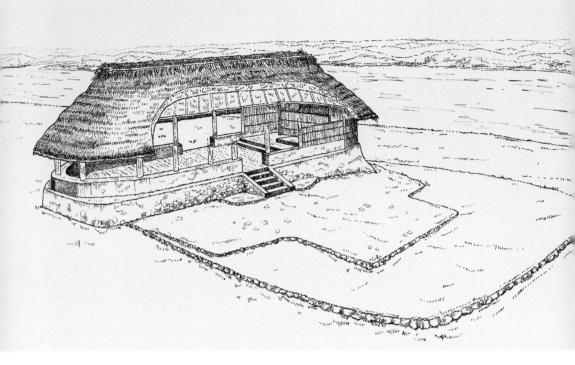

147 Franciscan church at Lamanai, Belize, *c.* 1568.

most of them were settled across the highlands and along the Pacific coast; possible testimony to their presence can be found in the many place names of Nahuatl origin still to be found throughout southern Guatemala, although these might also come from the Pipil migrants who arrived in the area a few centuries earlier.

But the Maya are, for all their apparent docility, a remarkably resilient set of peoples, and the struggle against European civilization has never once halted. In 1847 and again in 1860 the Yukateko Maya rose against their white oppressors, coming very close the first time to taking the entire peninsula. As late as 1910 the independent chiefs of Quintana Roo were in rebellion against the dictatorial regime of Porfirio Díaz, and only in the last few decades have these remote Maya villagers begun to accept the rule of Mexico. Likewise the Tseltal of highland Chiapas have repeatedly risen, most notably in 1712 and 1868, and both they and the Tsotsil Maya form the backbone of the Zapatista National Liberation Army which has challenged the Mexican authorities since the initial uprising of 1994. The Ch'olan-speaking regions west of Lake Izabal in Guatemala were long feared by missionaries and soldiers alike as "The Land of War," and the pacification of these Maya took centuries. The survival of the Itza on their island Tayasal is a case in point; another is that of the Lakandon, still vibrant into the twentieth century. No, the Maya were never completely conquered, but their civilization and spirit were seemingly broken – and went underground. As a poem from one of the books of Chilam Balam puts it:

Eat, eat, thou hast bread;
Drink, drink, thou hast water;
On that day, dust possesses the earth;
On that day, a blight is on the face of the earth,
On that day, a cloud rises,
On that day, a mountain rises,
On that day, a strong man seizes the land,
On that day, things fall to ruin,
On that day, the tender leaf is destroyed,
On that day, the dying eyes are closed,
On that day, three signs are on the tree,
On that day, three generations hang there,
On that day, the battle flag is raised,
And they are scattered afar in the forests.
On that day, the battle flag is raised,
And they are scattered afar in the forests.

8

MAYA LIFE ON THE EVE OF THE CONQUEST

We have until this moment been dealing mainly with the pots, jades, and ruins of a once great people. We actually know a good deal more about the daily life of the Maya, particularly the natives of Yucatan, on the eve of the Conquest. For it is our good fortune that the early Spanish missionaries were accomplished scholars, and that owing to their eagerness to understand the nations they wished to convert to the Cross they have left us with first-class accounts of native culture as it was as they arrived. So it is upon this foundation that we must interpret the archaeological remains of the Postclassic Maya – and the Maya of the Classic as well.

THE FARM AND THE CHASE

Maya agriculture (described in some detail in Chapter 1) was the foundation of their civilization. Maize, beans, squashes, chile peppers, cotton, and various kinds of root crops and fruit trees were cultivated. That the pre-Conquest lowlanders usually prepared their plots by the slash-and-burn method is certain, but exactly how large trees were felled prior to the adoption of copper axes in the Postclassic (and of steel ones in Colonial days) is unclear; perhaps they were merely ringed and left to die, or hacked with polished stone axes. The times of planting were determined by a kind of farmer's almanac of which we apparently have examples in two of the codices. According to Landa, fields were communally owned and jointly worked by groups of twenty men, a pattern of collective action roughly documented in early Colonial times.

In Yucatan, the Maya stored their crops in above-ground cribs of wood, but also in "fine underground places" which might well be the *chultunob* so common in Classic sites. The Spanish sources consistently fail to mention tortillas or flat cakes (*pek wah*) for the lowland Maya; while a few clay griddles have been found in Postclassic occupations in sites like Lamanai, these may have been used to toast cacao beans rather than tortillas. However, other ways of preparing maize

148 Woman grinding maize on a *metate*, from a Late Classic figurine from Lubaantun, Belize.

are mentioned in the sources. These include *saka'*, a cornmeal gruel which was taken with chile pepper as the first meal of the day; *k'eyen*, a mixture of water and sour dough carried in gourds to the fields for sustenance during the day; and the well-known *tamales* (*keehel wah*), painted among food offerings on Late Classic ceramics. The peasant cuisine (we know little of that current among the elites) was largely confined to such simple foods and to stews of meat and vegetables, to which squash seeds and peppers were added [148].

"Cash crops" were of prime importance to Yucatan. Cotton was widely grown; the province was famed for its textiles, which were exported over a very large area. Along river drainages in southern Campeche, Tabasco, and Belize, and on the Pacific slope of Guatemala, groves of cacao trees were planted. In the north these were restricted to the bottoms of filled-in *cenotes* and other natural depressions. The cacao bean from this tree provided chocolate, the preferred drink of the Mesoamerican ruling classes, but well into Colonial times the beans also served as a form of money in regional markets; so precious were they that the Maya traders encountered off the coast of Honduras by Columbus were said to have snatched up any that had dropped as though it was their own eyes that had fallen to the canoe bottom.

Every Maya household had its own kitchen garden in which vegetables and fruit trees were raised, and fruit groves were scattered near settlements as well. Papaya, avocado, custard apple, sapodilla, and the breadnut tree were all cultivated, but many kinds of wild fruits were also eaten, especially in times of famine.

Several breeds of dog were domesticated by the Maya, each with its own name. One such strain was barkless; males were castrated and fattened on corn, and either eaten or sacrificed. Another was used in the hunt. Both wild and domestic turkeys were known, but only the former used as sacrificial victims in ceremonies. As he still does today, the Maya farmer raised the native stingless bees, which are kept in small, hollow logs closed with mud plaster at either end and stacked up in A-frames, but wild honey was also much appreciated.

The larger mammals, such as deer and peccary, were hunted with the bow-and-arrow in drives (though in Classic times the atlatl-and-dart must have been the principal weapon), aided by packs of dogs [149]. Birds like the wild turkey, partridge, wild pigeon, quail, and wild duck were taken with pellets shot from blowguns. A variety of snares and deadfalls are shown in the Madrid Codex, especially a specialized trap for armadillo.

In Yucatan, fishing was generally of the offshore kind, by means of sweep and drag nets and hook-and-line, but fish were

149 Hunter slaying deer, on a Late Classic figurine from Lubaantun, Belize.

also shot with bow-and-arrow in lagoons. Inland, especially in the highland streams, stupefying drugs were pounded in the water, and the fish taken by hand once they had floated into artificial dams; one of the expertly incised bones from Late Classic Tikal shows that this was also the practice in the Peten. Along the coasts the catch was salted and dried or roasted over a fire for use in commerce.

Among wild lowland forest products of great cultural importance to the Maya was *pom*, the resin of the copal tree, which (along with rubber and chewing gum!) was used as incense – so holy was this that one native source describes it as the "odor of the center of heaven." Another tree produced a bark for flavoring *balche'*, a "strong and stinking" mead imbibed in vast amounts during festivals. Curiously, *balche'* is apparently not much mentioned in Classic texts, other than on a few depictions of vessels marked with the term *kab*, "honey"; what is mentioned is *chih*, a fermented beverage made from agaves, well known in modern Mexico by its Colonial-period name, *pulque*.

INDUSTRY AND COMMERCE

Yucatan was the greatest producer of salt in Mesoamerica. The beds extended along the coast from Campeche, along the lagoons on the north side of the peninsula, and over to Isla Mujeres on the east. The salt, which Landa praised as the "best . . . which I have ever seen in my life," was collected at the end of the dry season by the coastal peoples who held a virtual monopoly over the industry, although at one time it was entirely in the hands of the overlord of Mayapan. A few localities inland also had salt wells, such as the Chixoy Valley of Guatemala, but it was sea salt that was in most demand and this was carried widely all over the Maya area. Other valuable Yucatecan exports were honey, cotton mantles, and slaves, and one suspects that it was such industrial specialization which supported the economy, not maize agriculture.

Further regional products involved in native trade were cacao, which could only be raised in a few well-watered places (especially, as we have seen, the perpetually damp bottoms of waterless *cenotes*), quetzal feathers from the Alta Verapaz, flint and chert from deposits in the Central Area, obsidian from the highlands northeast of Guatemala City, and colored shells (particularly the thorny oyster, *Spondylus*) from both coasts. Jade and a host of lesser stones of green color were also traded, most originating in the beds of the Río Motagua, but some which appeared on the market could well have been looted from ancient graves.

The great majority of goods traveled by sea, since roads were but poor trails and cargoes heavy. This kind of commerce was cornered by the Chontal Maya, or Putun, such good seafarers that Eric Thompson called them "the Phoenicians of Middle America." Their route skirted the coast from the Aztec port of trade in Campeche, Xicallanco, around the peninsula and down to Nito, where their great canoes put in to exchange goods with the inland Maya. (Zachary Hruby of Northern Kentucky University has identified this spot as Miramar, at the opening of the Río Dulce in Guatemala, fronting a bay leading out into the Bay of Amatique and Gulf of Honduras.) However, one special group of traders did travel the perilous overland trails, under the protection of their own deity, Ek' Chuwah, the Black God. Markets (*k'iwik*) were common in Yucatan, and are known archaeologically in Classic cities such as Calakmul. Ethnohistorian Ralph Roys felt no doubt that there was a great market at Chichen Itza, "where pilgrims came from foreign parts to trade as well as to worship"; according to one source, the lords of Chichen carried on a trade in feathers and cacao with Honduras. Yet another source tells us that highland Guatemalan markets were "great and celebrated and very rich," and many have persisted to this very day.

It was this trade that linked Mexico and the Maya, for the Maya had much to offer; it was probably the smooth business operations conducted by the Chontal that spared the Maya from the Aztec onslaught that had overwhelmed less cooperative peoples in Mesoamerica.

THE LIFE CYCLE

Immediately after birth, Yukateko mothers washed their infants and then fastened them to a cradle, their little heads compressed between two boards in such a way that after two days a permanent fore-and-aft flattening had taken place, which the Maya considered a mark of beauty. As soon as possible, the anxious parents went to consult with a priest so as to learn the destiny of their offspring, and the name which he or she was to bear until baptism.

The Spanish Fathers were quite astounded that the Maya had a baptismal rite, which took place at an auspicious time when there were a number of boys and girls between the ages of three and twelve in the settlement. The ceremony took place in the house of a town elder, in the presence of their parents who had observed various abstinences in honor of the occasion. The children and their fathers remained inside a cord held by four old and venerable men representing the Chahks or Rain Gods, while the priest performed various acts of purification and blessed the candidates with incense, tobacco, and holy water. From that time on the elder girls, at least, were marriageable.

In both highlands and lowlands, boys and young men stayed apart from their families in special communal houses where they presumably learned the arts of war (and other things as well, for Landa says that prostitutes were frequent visitors). Other youthful diversions were gambling and the ball game. A double standard was present among the Maya, for girls were strictly brought up by their mothers and suffered grievous punishments for lapses of chastity. Marriage was arranged by go-betweens and, as among all peoples with exogamous clans or lineages, there were strict rules about those with whom alliances could or could not be made – particularly taboo was marriage with those of the same paternal name. Monogamy was the general custom, but important men who could afford it took more wives. Adultery was punished by death, as among the Mexicans.

Ideas of personal comeliness were quite different from ours, although the friars were much impressed with the beauty of the Maya women. Both sexes had their frontal teeth filed in various patterns, and we have many ancient Maya skulls – probably from elite individuals – in which the incisors have been inlaid with small plaques of jade. Until marriage, young men painted themselves black (and so did warriors at all times); tattooing and decorative scarification began after wedlock, both men and women being richly elaborated from the waist up by these means. Slightly crossed eyes were held in great esteem, and parents attempted to induce the condition by hanging small beads over the noses of their children.

Death was greatly dreaded by all, the more so since the deceased did not automatically go to any paradise. Ordinary folk were buried beneath the floors of their houses, their mouths filled with food and a jade bead, accompanied by idols and the things that they had used while alive. Into the graves of priests the mourners are said to have placed books. Great nobles, however, were cremated, a practice probably of Mexican origin, and funerary temples were constructed above their urns; in earlier days, of course, inhumation in sepulchers beneath such mausoleums was the rule. The Kokom dynasty of Mayapan was unique in mummifying the heads of their defunct lords, these being kept in the family oratories and fed at regular intervals – a practice which, if even more ancient, may explain why some early royal burials at Tikal are missing their heads.

SOCIETY AND POLITICS

The ancient Maya realm was no theocracy or primitive democracy, but a class society with political power strongly concentrated in the hands of an hereditary elite. To understand the basis of the state in sixteenth-century Yucatan, we have to go right to the heart of the matter, to the people themselves.

In Yucatan, every adult Maya had two names. The first came to him or her from the mother, but could only be transmitted from women to their offspring, that is, in the female line. The second derived from the father, and similarly was exclusively passed on in the male line. There is now abundant evidence that these two kinds of name represented two different kinds of cross-cutting and coexistent descent groups: the matrilineage and the patrilineage. There were approximately 250 patrilineages in Yucatan at the time of the Conquest, and we know from Landa how important they were. For instance, they were strictly exogamous, all inheritance of property was patrilineal, and they were self-preserving; all members had an obligation to help each other. Titles deriving from early Colonial times show that they

150, 151 (*Left*) Person of high rank in a palanquin, from a graffito incised on a wall at Tikal. (*Right*) Standing captive, possibly from Calakmul, incised on a bone from the Temple I tomb (Burial 116), Tikal. Late Classic period.

had their own lands as well, which is probably what Landa meant when he said that all fields were held "in common." As for the matrilineage, it probably acted principally within the marriage regulation system, in which matrimony with the father's sister's, or mother's brother's, daughter was encouraged, but certain other kinds forbidden.

Now, while among some other peoples such kin groups are theoretically equal, among the Maya this was not so, and both kinds of lineage were strictly ranked; to be able to trace one's genealogy in both lines to an ancient ancestry was an important matter, for there were strongly demarcated classes. At the top were the nobles (*almehen*, meaning "he whose descent is known on both sides"), who had private lands and held the more important political offices, as well as filling the roles of high-ranking warriors, wealthy farmers and merchants, and clergy [150]. The commoners were the free workers of the population, probably, like their Aztec cousins, holding in usufruct from their patrilineage a stretch of forest in which to make their *milpas*; but in all likelihood even these persons were graded into rich and poor. There is some indication of a class of serfs, who worked the private lands of the nobles. And at the bottom were the slaves who were mostly plebeians taken in war, prisoners of higher rank being subject to the knife [151]. Slavery was hereditary, but these menials could be redeemed by payments made by fellow members of one's patrilineage.

By the time the Spaniards arrived, political power over much of the inhabited Maya area was in the hands of ruling castes of Mexican or Mexican-influenced origin. Yukateko politics was controlled by such a group, which of course claimed to have come from Tula and Zuywa, a legendary home in the west. In fact, any candidate for high office had to pass an occult catechism known as the "Language of Zuywa." At the head of each statelet in Yucatan was the *halach winik* ("real man"), the territorial ruler who had inherited his post in the male line, although in an earlier epoch and among the highland Maya there were real kings (*ajawob*) who held sway over wider areas. The *halach winik* resided in a capital town and was supported by the products of his own lands, such as cacao groves worked by slaves, and by tribute.

The minor provincial towns were headed by the *batabob*, appointed by the *halach winik* from a noble patrilineage related to his own. These ruled through local town councils made up of rich, old men, led by an important commoner chosen anew each year among the four quarters which made up the settlement. Besides his administrative and magisterial duties, the *batab* was a war leader, but his command was shared by a *nakom*, a highly feared individual who held office for three years.

The Maya were obsessed with war. The Annals of the Kaqchikels and the Popol Vuh speak of little but intertribal conflict among the highlanders, while the sixteen states of Yucatan were constantly battling with each other over boundaries and lineage honor. To this sanguinary record we must add the testimony of the Classic monuments and their inscriptions. From these and from the eyewitness descriptions of the *conquistadores* we can see how Maya warfare was waged. The *holkanob*, or "braves," were the footsoldiers; they wore cuirasses of quilted cotton or tapir hide and carried thrusting spears with flint points, darts-with-spearthrower, and in late Postclassic times, the bow-and-arrow. Hostilities typically began with an unannounced guerrilla raid into the enemy camp to take captives, but more formal battle opened with the dreadful din of drums, whistles, shell trumpets, and war cries. On either side of the war, leaders and the idols carried into combat under the care of priests flanked the infantry, from which rained darts, arrows, and stones flung from slings. Once the enemy had penetrated into home territory, however, irregular warfare was substituted, with ambuscades and all kinds of traps. Lesser captives ended up as slaves, but the nobles and war leaders either had their hearts torn out on the sacrificial stone, or else were beheaded, a form of sacrifice favored by the Classic Maya.

9

MAYA THOUGHT AND CULTURE

In Yucatan, ritualists still erect ceremonial tables with food and drink for spirits. Miles away, among the K'iche' of Highland Guatemala, calendar priests make offerings at altars or visit water and mountain shrines. Such beliefs and practices have evolved in great variety; many, indeed, have not endured. In some places, native spirituality has given way to evangelical Christianity or other faiths. Yet, more often than not, deep traditions and shared principles inform Maya views of the world. Mayan texts of the Colonial period, recorded by early friars wishing to introduce Christianity, highlight similar themes, if strongly affected by European ideas. Various esoteric works such as the Books of Chilam Balam and the Popol Vuh, written in Mayan tongues but transcribed into Spanish letters, offer us indigenous perspectives mixed with outside views. Court cases, too, show Colonial enthusiasm for stamping out local beliefs, but equally clear evidence of resilience.

For pre-Conquest times, information is plentiful and, thanks to recent advances in decipherment of the Maya script, more accessible than ever before. There are physical remains – city layouts, burials, ceremonial paths, caches placed underground, deposits in caves – along with now-decoded images and texts. At least 15,000 examples of Maya writing have survived, supplemented by an immense range of ceramic figurines, shell and stone carvings, modeled stucco, and paintings on walls and pots. These reveal a tightly controlled canon of ideas, expressed in rigid styles of representation. Aberrant depictions occur only in a few, lumpish figurines, cave daubs and scribbles, and graffiti scored into palace or temple walls. The remainder are remarkably consistent, even if their subjects vary according to locally prominent gods or rituals.

Nonetheless, our knowledge of ancient Maya thought must represent a tiny fraction of the whole picture. Much is lost, and images on painted ceramics imply how much has disappeared. Wood abounds in Maya forests, but the few wooden objects that survive come only from unusual water-logged deposits and dry caves, or as lintels in well-aired doorways. However, wooden carvings, some of deities, must have existed in countless number; vestiges of several occur in a tomb at Tikal. Similarly rare gourds, stuccoed, painted, and inserted into tombs, also exhibit legible glyphs and ritual images. A few paintings display sophisticated texts and pictures on textiles, almost all now rotted away. Even more heartbreaking is the loss of thousands of books, in which the full extent of learning and ritual was recorded.

152 (*Above*) Trickster rabbit writing in a folding-screen codex with jaguar-skin covers. Detail from a Late Classic cylindrical vase in codex style, northern Peten or southern Campeche. Eighth century AD.

153 (*Left*) The Dresden Codex is the finest of the surviving folding-screen books of the Maya. Written on a long strip of bark paper, each page coated with fine stucco, much of it is concerned with 260-day ritual counts divided up in various ways, the divisions being associated with specific gods. The texts immediately above each deity contain their names and epithets. Ht 8 in. (20.3 cm).

The discovery of careful, codex-like incisions and paintings on a room wall at Xultun, Guatemala, indicates a rare form of "back-up," or perhaps the first stages of composition for a long-gone book.

Only four codices have survived to modern times (imagine if all that posterity knew of ourselves were to be based upon three prayer books and *Pilgrim's Progress*). These are written on long strips of bark paper, taken from the inner bark of wild figs, scraped of its latex, arranged into at least three layers, and pounded with grooved mallets. An unknown adhesive, perhaps tree sap or orchid juice, glued separate sections together, which were then folded into screens. Such paper might have come as tribute, a taxation known for the Aztecs who used such paper mostly for ritual vestments. Working fast, a craftsman then covered the surface with white calcite and smoothed it with a polished stone. Pictorial representations on Classic Maya funerary pottery show that in Classic times the codices had jaguar-skin covers, and were painted by scribes using brush or quill pens dipped in black or red paint contained in cut conch shell inkpots [152]. A few probable coffers exist for books, including the recent find of a lidded limestone box from Hun Nal Ye cave in Guatemala [154].

According to the early sources, the Maya books contained histories, prophecies, maps, tribute accounts, songs, "sciences," and genealogies, but our four examples are completely ritual, or ritual-astronomical, works compiled in the Northern Area during the Postclassic. The Dresden Codex is the most carefully painted, and measures 8 in. high and 11 ft 9 in. long (20.3 by 358.2 cm) [153]; while much of its content was certainly copied

154 The Hun Nal Ye box, carved in two phases, *c.* AD 600 and 800. L. 15 in. (38 cm).

155 Pages from the Grolier Codex, a Toltec-Maya book dealing with the planet Venus.

from Late Classic sources, some of the iconography of the Dresden has been shown by Karl Taube to be Aztec-influenced, so that it must date in its present form to just before the Conquest. The Madrid and the very fragmentary Paris codices are more poorly executed than the Dresden, but probably similar in date, though their precise provenance is disputed; Eric Thompson suggested that a Spanish priest might have obtained the Madrid Codex at Tayasal while others, identifying a patch with Spanish letters, perhaps from a papal document, think it came from the area of Chancenote, Yucatan. As for the Paris, Taube believes its imagery points to Mayapan.

In 1971 a fourth Maya book was exhibited at the Grolier Club in New York, which has since been labeled the "Grolier Codex." It once belonged to a private collector in Mexico and based on circumstantial evidence seems to have been found with a wooden box in a cave in Chiapas or Tabasco. Unfortunately in very bad condition, it comprises about one half of a twenty-page table concerned with the Venus cycle [155]. Although its authenticity was vigorously disputed by Thompson and others, its paper has been radiocarbon dated to *c*. AD 1230, fully consistent with the Toltec-Maya style in which the glyphs and associated deities are drawn. As a hybrid work, the codex has a gypsum rather than a calcite covering, and is thus more like a Mexican codex. The Grolier is now considered genuine by knowledgeable epigraphers, making it the earliest of the four pre-Conquest Maya manuscripts.

BEING RELIGIOUS

The Maya did not easily separate everyday life from ritual. Stories surrounding everyday activities linked humans to larger, primeval events. Planting a maize seed, a seasonal act, invoked a mythic journey of the Maize God. Sweat-bathing, probably common at Maya settlements, did more than renew the human body; at Palenque it alluded to the birth of gods, an early reference to the current practice of burying placenta in the steam baths. Humans existed within a larger set of expectations. The virtuous person was *toj*, "right" and "straight," at times a literal term that Colonial Mayan languages tied to cleaning, confession, and prophecy. The Classic Maya applied the word to political duty: *tojil* was the tribute payment owed to a lord. Processional routes, the "white roads" or *sakbih* described earlier, carved straight paths across broken landscapes. To walk along them was to move in acceptable, ritually decorous ways. To lay out a house was to place four corner posts and a central hearth, a cosmic pattern recognizable to the earlier Olmec. Whatever the scale, to define boundaries, directions, and centers was to create orderly space, whether of a house, field or universe.

Ultimately, humans were obligated to abide by covenants. A covenant, as defined by the ethnographer John Monaghan, is a binding contract that explains how one should behave. Gods were usually involved, as in the case of maize production. This crop is so fundamental today that its cultivation and consumption define what it means to be Maya. To dine together is to form a social bond, simulating kinship. The Popol Vuh recounts, in what must have been an ancient story, how an earlier people were like artifacts shaped from mud and sticks. Heedless of the gods' wishes, they were replaced by humans created out of maize dough. Humans could now enjoy life, yet, as part of their covenant, they had to reciprocate by praising the gods or offering their own bodies as divine food. At death, humans would repay their debt, returning to the ravenous earth from which their flesh had come. But payment could be deferred by ritual substitutes, known in some Mayan languages as *k'ex*. Incense, animals, and even elegant prayer did the job temporarily. The most dramatic offering, however, came from the human body, by bloodletting from the mouth, penis, ears, or the surrogate flesh of captives or slaves. For the Maya, the world moved by appetites large and small.

To be religious was also to entreat the gods. If ethnographic evidence is any guide, such communication involved special places, tones of voice or figures of speech. Whether the prayer was heartfelt was apparently irrelevant – more important were proper form, respectful address, and sacrificial enticements. In fact, some gods, especially malign ones, come across as dim-witted and easily fooled. Specialists took charge of these prayers or acts of divination in brisk, almost lawyerly fashion, the better to discern messages from the gods and to understand the imbalances leading to disease, drought, and other problems. Birds were considered messengers, too. Most likely, those in charge of entreaties ranged from small-scale practitioners, accessible to most Maya, to the kings themselves.

For some reason, the calendar priests active in Highland Guatemala today are almost undetectable in earlier times, other than the occasional find of crystals used by such specialists. But similar figures must have existed. At Classic-era Comalcalco, Tabasco, Ricardo Armijo recovered the remains of a priest buried in an urn, equipped for the afterlife with glyphically incised stingray spines and small plaques deciphered by epigrapher Marc Zender. On these, mention of "drought" and various avatars of the rain god, Chahk, suggest a role in weather prediction and control. In other respects, the distinction between priestly and political roles may have been blurred in the Classic period. Enigmatic figures known as the *Aj K'uhu'n* served as courtiers, ritual attendants, and perhaps keepers of sacred books.

Far more is known of later Maya priests. In contrast to their Aztec counterparts, they were not celibate. Sons acquired their fathers' offices, although some were second sons of lords. Their title in Yukateko Maya, *Ah K'in* ("He of the Sun/Day"), suggests a close connection with the calendar and astronomy, and the list of duties outlined by Landa makes it clear that Maya learning as well as ritual was in their hands. Among them were "computation of the years, months, and days, the festivals and ceremonies, the administration of the sacraments, the fateful days and seasons, their methods of divination and their prophecies, events and the cures for diseases, and their antiquities and how to read and write with the letters and characters," but they also kept the all-important genealogies. During the prosperity of Mayapan, a hereditary Chief Priest resided in that city whose main function seems to have been the overseeing of an academy training candidates for the priesthood, but in no source do we find his authority or that of the priests superseding civil power. The priest was assisted in human sacrifices by four old men, called Chahks in honor of the Rain God, who held the arms and legs of the victim, while the breast was opened up by another individual who bore the title of Nakom (like the war leader). Another religious functionary was the Chilam, a kind of visionary shaman who received messages from the gods while in a state of trance, his prophecies being interpreted by an assembly of priests. Before and during rituals food taboos and sexual abstinence were rigidly observed, and self-mutilation was carried out by jabbing needles and stingray spines through ears, cheeks, lips, tongue, and the penis [156], the blood being spattered on paper or used to anoint the idols. On the eve of the Conquest such idols were censed with copal and rubber as well as ritually fed. Other censers took the form of richly painted effigies in many parts of the Yucatan Peninsula. Presumably, these depicted the divine recipient of the incense they held. Human sacrifice was

156 Modern rendering of a mural depicting the bloodletting and deer sacrifice ritually undertaken by the Hero Twin Hunahpu (Huun Ajaw). San Bartolo, Guatemala, *c.* 100 BC.

perpetrated on prisoners, slaves, and children (bastards or orphans bought for the occasion). Wild turkeys, deer, dogs, squirrels, quail, and iguanas, too, were considered fit offerings for the Maya gods.

ORDERING THE UNIVERSE

The Maya had several models of the universe. The world was imagined as either a giant turtle or crocodile floating on a sea. Plants, especially maize and cacao, sprouted from the backs or bodies of these creatures. Perhaps as in ancient India, the shifting of these immense beasts explained earthquakes, known to the Classic Maya as *yuklaj kab*, "the shaking earth." In the primordial sea were monstrous sharks that, when speared by gods, issued great spouts of blood. A variant tale from Palenque may ascribe such fluid and perhaps the sea itself to the decapitation of a mythic crocodile, and a similar scene may appear on one of the largest bowls from the Early Classic period, from Becan, Mexico [157]. It is difficult to know whether these alternative accounts were mutually exclusive, tied to the beliefs of different cities, or if they represented equally acceptable stories. Curiously, among all regions, the saline nature of the sea was of little interest to the great cities of the Maya. The sea, known as the *K'ahk' Nahb*, or "fiery pool," was not clearly distinguished from bodies of fresh water, and both could be portrayed with the salt-averse waterlily. Present-day Maya, especially the Ch'orti' of Guatemala, believe that lakes, rivers, and springs contain supernatural snakes that cause earthquakes and hurricanes. These are probably the figures depicted in Classic imagery as serpents with water-lily headdresses and sinuous and bubbly bodies.

Earth, *kab*, was soft, marked in depictions with signs for musk or excrement to underscore its pungent smell. Firmament itself consisted of stone and earth. Stone, *tuun* in the language of the Classic inscriptions, took two forms. It was either a material shaped by humans or, when marked by crevices, signaled the idea of a *witz* or "hill". Within were caves or rocky irregularities known as *ch'e'n*, a term applied in the Classic to any settlement. James Brady of California State University, Los Angeles, has discovered a good reason for this. In the karstic limestone terrain of the Maya lowlands, occupants often took care to situate their communities atop cave systems. A dramatic example is the pyramid of El Duende at Dos Pilas, Guatemala, which has a cave running right under it; similar finds have been made at other cities. And when there was no natural cave, the Maya

157 Scene of primordial bloodletting around a hybrid beast with iguana and mammalian features. Becan, Mexico, *c.* AD 450.

created them. The cities of Oxkintok, Tonina, and Yaxchilan, Mexico, have elaborate labyrinths that appear to replicate such subterranean passages.

It does not take an overactive imagination to see another feature of caves. Their openings resemble mouths, their stalagmites and stalactites a set of chomping teeth. The Preclassic murals from San Bartolo, Guatemala, display such a cave. From its recesses, the Maize God gingerly extracts water in a gourd. This act was embodied by later Maya, who took "virgin water" from caves for certain ceremonies. The flowery yet wild nature of this cave – orioles are eaten by a jaguar on top – has led Karl Taube to liken it to a flowery mountain found in myths across the region and into North America. Another denizen of caves was the rain god, Chahk. There, according to some scenes, he bellowed and made music – one can only imagine the deafening echoes. To this day, mist gathers in humid weather around outcrops and cave entrances, a likely basis for sensing his presence within. Caves can sometimes be detected, even with small openings, by the rush and pulsation of air. This results from changes in air pressure; the Maya, however, would have understood it as breath, both from Chahk and the cave itself.

That stone could live introduces a radically different view of material. Europeans cherish distinctions between the animate and the inanimate, the living and the non-living. The Maya carved up the world in different ways, as we saw for their views of water as a being, not just a fluid. Stone could appear with eyes, mouth, nose, and ears, as could flint and obsidian, if far bonier to indicate their brittle nature. Cavities dug in the ground were more than just holes. They were perceived as the voracious jaws of the centipedes, a poisonous arthropod that crept along the ground to scavenge food. One iconic image from the Classic period illustrates this creature. The sarcophagus lid of Pakal the Great at Palenque depicts him after death (not as an alien astronaut, a ludicrous misreading of some fantasists), growing as a newborn Maize God from centipede jaws. Like a maize kernel, he has been inserted into a cavity, watered, and reborn, in this case to become a majestic jeweled plant. The sides of the sarcophagus underscore this aspect of royal death and rebirth: his predecessors sprout as plants from a surface embellished with the sign for earth. The earth has taken their bodies, as clear example of debt payment, but given them back as sustenance for the living.

Another pervasive idea was the division of the world into sectors associated with a color value: red for east, white for north, black for west, and yellow for south, with blue-green at the center. Most have a logical basis. Red corresponds to the rising sun in the east, coming out of the Caribbean each morning, and black to the sun as it sets in the Gulf of Mexico. Blue-green, *yax*, stands for a great tree, the ceiba, *yaxte'* in the glyphs, at the center of the world or, by another model, for the new maize growth that would be cultivated for food. Yet another view, geared to elites and thoroughly studied by Simon Martin, fused maize with chocolate trees, a source of wealth among all Mesoamerican peoples. In the Classic period, eagles were thought to perch in each of the four directions, tied to celestial features such as the sun, moon,

158 Mythic mountain, North Wall, Tomb 25, Río Azul, Guatemala, *c.* AD 450.

Venus, and darkest night. Such themes date back to the Preclassic period; the murals of San Bartolo show directional eagles and world trees, along with the animal and self-sacrifices necessary for their sustenance. Mythic mountains appear in the sectors, too. The four walls of spectacular, now heavily damaged royal tombs at Río Azul, Guatemala, display distinct hills, known as *witz* in some Mayan languages [158]. Placed in the middle, the deceased became the center of the universe. One interment at Río Azul even identifies sub-quadrants of the directions. The idea of spatially organized mountains with associated colors, creatures, and plants may be one of the oldest attested ideas in the world. Found around the Pacific Rim and into Asia, it likely dates to when the Bering land bridge last connected these regions.

Away from light pollution, the Milky Way and other stars blaze brightly. This nightly show clearly captivated the Maya. In the Classic period, the sky was represented in two ways, appearing either as the body of a crocodile or as a "sky band," a sequence of signs for the sun, moon, stars, or comets. These sky bands sometimes terminated in an eagle head, its body luminous and polished. This might have been the ecliptic, the apparent path of the sun, moon, Venus, and other celestial bodies. In part, the sky was the habitual place of the gods. The royal names of the Classic Maya tend to describe kings as aspects of deities, with the added feature that most relate to certain actions by gods in the sky. The rain god, Chahk, was "born from the sun" – because clouds usually came from the east where the sun rises? – or "made fire" in the sky. Fierce tropical storms and lightning strikes probably led to this analogy.

159 Nobles impersonating Atlantean beings supporting a hill, a wall panel likely from Guatemala, AD 799.

The sky needed help to stay aloft. Colonial sources speak of *bakab*, a set of four beings supporting the sky, sometimes fused with the rain god in its directional manifestations. But this term had a very different sense in Classic times. A *bakab*, from *baah-kab*, "head of the earth," served as a title of the most exalted Maya kings and a few queens. As David Stuart has argued, the supporter of the sky and the earth in Classic times was an elderly god known as an Itzam, an Atlantean being of great age and strength, fused in some cases with rock itself [159]. Other supernatural supporters included wind gods, some with duck beaks to show their aerial home, others merged with the identities of high nobles. The latter was a political metaphor. Just as an Itzam held up heaven and earth, the Classic-era nobleman sustained the king. In the ideal, he was the perfect aristocrat, strong but subservient, eager to steady the throne. The hopeful image suggests that reality could be far different.

Time played a large role in the lives of the Maya, from the humblest farmer to the highest lord. Most basic was the agricultural cycle and the solar year that shaped it. We will speak of these cycles in more detail later.

What is important here is that time had a spatial dimension to the Maya. In Postclassic Yucatan the greatest ceremonies apparently had to do with the inauguration of the New Year. These took place in every community within the Wayeb, the five unnamed and unlucky days at the close of the previous year, and involved the construction of a special road (perhaps like the Classic "causeways") to idols placed at a certain cardinal point just outside the town limits; a new direction was chosen each year in a four-year counterclockwise circuit. The tradition had a long history: a map of world directions, adorned with gods and sacrifices appropriate to each quarter, appears in the Late Postclassic Madrid Codex. Paths marked by footsteps lead to the center from the four corners, and a continuous set of days in the 260-day calendar leads around the page. Nonetheless, the layout is so similar to a Mexican codex, the Fejérváry-Mayer, that its Maya origins are uncertain; the calendar, too, differs from that of the New Year. Far clearer confirmation comes from a text at Naranjo, Guatemala, studied by David Stuart. Much like in later Yucatan, the Classic-period New Year celebrations here involved the erection of monuments, evidently presided over by a set of four young gods, a nod to the four directions. One of the Early Classic tombs at Río Azul clinches the link between space and time. Where legible, each wall of the crypt presents a New Year day sign above a directional mountain.

How the Maya believed the universe came into existence is still unclear. The idea of cyclical creations and destructions is a typical feature of all Mesoamerican religions. The Aztecs, for instance, thought that the universe had passed through four such ages, and that we were now in the fifth, which would be destroyed by earthquakes. Earlier peoples transformed into monkeys, turkeys, and fish. According to our post-Conquest Maya sources, the last Creation prior to our own ended with a great flood (a belief also found among the Aztecs) at the end of which the sky fell on the earth, extinguishing light. A kind of interregnum ensued, a time of magic and heroism celebrated in the early chapters of the Popol Vuh, which tell of the doings of the Hero Twins (Chapter 3) – before a new and more perfect world could be formed, the imperfections of the old one had to be expunged. It is a challenge, however, to find such cycles in earlier evidence. Much hinges on the meaning of a date mentioned in several sources, 4 Ajaw 8 Kumk'u 13.0.0.0.0 (14 August 3114 BC). Some scholars describe this as a moment of creation. When a similar cycle comes to an end, as indeed happened on 24 December AD 2012, it was thought to anticipate another cycle of destruction and creation.

The problem is that the events of 4 Ajaw 8 Kumk'u, although esoteric and difficult to interpret, seem benign rather than cataclysmic. Texts referring to the occasion, which vary somewhat, concern a "new hearth place," depicted as three stones wreathed in flame, a feature of all traditional Maya homes but here heaped at "the edge of the sky." They also mention the arrival, descent or marshaling of gods, and the placement of three mythic stones, surely part of a cosmic hearth. It is mostly at Palenque where several opaque inscriptions spell out the circumstances before and after the 4 Ajaw

8 Kumk'u date. As interpreted by David Stuart, a set of three gods, presided over by a probable variant of the Maize deity, are born around this time. One, known to specialists by the arbitrary name of "G1" (for God 1), ascended to a heavenly throne, followed by the birth of the Maize god and a series of mysterious events, one involving the sea. Strangely enough, this culminated in the rebirth of G1, succeeded by the birth of what may been two of his siblings. These gods loomed large in the iconography and theology of Palenque. Other cities seem to have emphasized other gods and perhaps alternative origin stories. These are momentous yet hardly horrific events. The few Classic-period citations of 24 December AD 2012, tend, if anything, to be rather dull. They note the expected completion of a cycle but nothing like the prophecies found in Colonial Maya books or among the Aztec.

There are hints, however, of darker periods in the past. Some Mesoamerican peoples allude to a wholly black world or one lit by a wan sun quite different from ours. Two Classic pots, painted by the same artist and commissioned for the court of Naranjo, Guatemala, may portray that setting on 4 Ajaw 8 Kumk'u [160]. A trading god, seated on a throne within a stony house, perhaps a cave, assembles a set of night-time gods; he, too, has

160 Rollout of a Late Classic vase, likely from Naranjo. This scene takes place in darkness in the palace of God L (right), at the beginning of our present era on 4 Ajaw 8 Kumk'u. Several deities face him, including the Jaguar God of the Underworld and the yet-enigmatic G1.

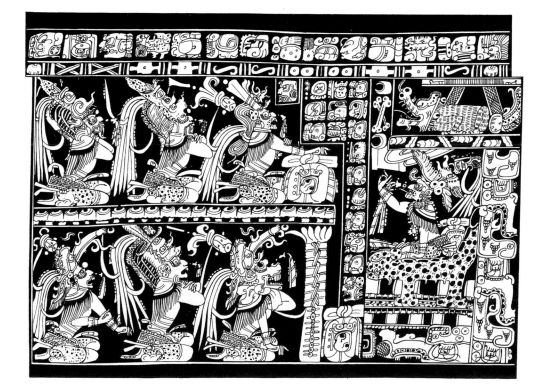

the jaguar-like features of a nocturnal deity. A jaunty cigarette in his mouth cues the gloomy scene – the Maya must have delighted in the dramatic prop of red-tipped, burning tobacco. The black and deep red backgrounds heighten the effect. In a gesture of submission, the summoned gods fold and grasp their arms. Clearly, the trading god is in charge. The longer version of this conference, which is illustrated here, tells us that the assembly will soon be brighter. It takes places at *K'inchil*, the "Great Sun Place," perhaps the realm of the Sun God. Endless night will soon give way to daily cycles, a new celestial machinery in motion.

A relevant Maya term from these ceramics is *tz'ak*, the idea of ordering. A key part of creation was the establishment of opposites. These are presented in alternative spellings for the *tz'ak* glyph, of which the most revealing examples come from Palenque. The exquisite Tablet of the 96 Glyphs, the seat of a late throne, lays out a long series of such opposed pairs [161, 169]. It begins with sun and night, followed by possibly life and death, then Venus and moon, wind and water. Each sign introduces a set of elapsed days in the dynastic succession of Palenque. Spellings at other cities supplement the list by contrasting, as variants of the *tz'ak* glyph, green growth and

161 *Tz'ak* or "ordering" glyphs at Palenque, Tablet of the 96 Glyphs. The signs juxtapose opposite but complementary features of the natural world: star with moon (*above*); wind and water (*below*). For the complete tablet, see fig. 169.

harvested crops – distinguished by their color, green-blue and yellow – sky and earth, cloud and rain, stingray spine and blood, lady and lord. These are oppositions to be sure, but they also suggest deeper ideas. The first element indicates cause and effect. It defines or leads to the second. Clouds drop rain, and green growth leads to ripe, harvestable food. The cadences, too, hint at creation itself as laid out in the Popol Vuh, a world ordered and made complete by gods in primeval time.

GODS AND SPIRITS

The Maya universe was filled with spirits. For earlier periods, the basic concept was *k'uh*, a vitalizing essence that clustered in royal blood. When used as an adjective, *k'uhul*, it meant "holy" and among humans was generally restricted to the rulers themselves or to deceased women. But its main application was to gods. In the Colonial-era Ritual of the Bacabs, 166 were mentioned by name, and over 30 distinct deities appear in the pre-Conquest codices. There must have been many at any given period. Classic texts refer to 8,000 in "earth" and "heaven," although this could have been a figure of speech, to emphasize their large number, identifiable only to a few specialists. Maya theology probably had various levels of understanding, with most people able only to recognize major gods in the imagery; the esotericism in some texts seems purposeful, a method of reserving knowledge to elites. A challenge in Maya scholarship is tying earlier deities with the great number known from later sources. For a few gods, such as Chahk, this is relatively easy. For many others, however, the divide is vast.

Gods had several supernatural features. Those associated with directions, like Chahk, the rain god, appeared in multiples; one for the east, west, north, and south. Others occurred singly and then fused with other beings in a process described by Simon Martin as "theosynthesis," a blurring together of gods. For example, the eagle-like supernatural known to scholars as the Principal Bird Deity merged with an elderly god, Itzam, to become a high god, "God D," who presides over throne scenes. In Classic times, that bird was a messenger whose presence sanctified important events like royal enthronement and, in some accounts, as explained in Chapter 3, was a precursor to Wuqub Kaquix of the Popol Vuh. That one wing was marked with the sign for "sun" and the other for "night" suggests the bird was liminal, perhaps linked to transitions like the dawn or twilight.

Several gods worked in pairs. The epitome were the Hero Twins (see pp. 70-1), among the longest-attested of Maya deities [xxv, xxvi]. The Popol Vuh calls them Hunahpu and Xbalanque – the former recognizable by the black spots on his face and body, perhaps a mark of his deceased state, the latter by patches of jaguar skin. In one scene they assist the Maize God while he emerges anew from a world turtle. In other images, Hunahpu, named Huun Ajaw in the Classic period, is an especially adept hunter with his favorite weapon, a blowgun. Karl Taube has suggested that the Hero Twins define two different realms, one of humans, the domain of Huun Ajaw, the other of animals, a more disorderly, chaotic world outside of human control. The two deities known as the "paddlers," one with jaguar-like features, the other with a stingray through the septum of his nose, often joined to row the Maize God on his watery journey into death and rebirth. Some gods had consorts, as with the wizened Itzam and his evident spouse, an aged goddess of healing and midwifery; these were likely to have been Maya creator gods. And a final attribute of divinity was the transformation of the gods as they went on their daily journeys. The Sun God acquired jaguar attributes as he descended into dark zones underground – the Santo Domingo cave in Guatemala contains a reference to his emergence from his subterranean haunts. Rising each morning from the eastern sea, he became shark-like with fish fins and, in place of an incisor, a single shark tooth. Recall that most Maya never saw the actual predator – but they might have handled his impressive dentition, traded from the coast along with stingray spines and other maritime exotics that found their way into burials and caches.

Many gods arose from Maya perceptions of nature. The central figure was the Maize God, the epitome of a near-androgynous beauty, a dancer, laden with jewelry and surrounded by females. He embodied a high aesthetic ideal for the Maya. His story, recounted in Classic Maya ceramics, involved watery journeys, dressing and undressing, and emergence as the main Maya food, to be reborn again as seed. The Sun God, dominant in the sky, punishing in the dry season, provided an obvious model for kings. But Chahk, who brought rain, was the most necessary. Brandishing a lightning axe or snake, he was revered even in Olmec times, as Karl Taube has demonstrated. The axe in turn corresponded to an enigmatic deity of lightning and vegetation known as K'awiil. So important was this god that rulership itself in the Classic period came about when kings received the god at their time of accession. Another crucial being, although ambivalent to the Maya, was God L, a deity of merchants. A nocturnal god – the better to transport goods through hostile territory? – he was also somewhat oversexed, as were other older gods. A vessel at the Princeton Art Museum shows him with five maidens or courtesans, a theme which recurs in ceramic figurines highlighting such liaisons. On one, a trickster rabbit takes notes in a Maya book while the *real* scribe, a monkey god, is decapitated nearby. Probably the rabbit has been up to some mischief. Beliefs among Maya today about wealthy earth lords may derive from this figure, as does Maximon, a greedy, alcohol-swilling, cigar-loving "saint" celebrated in several communities of Highland Guatemala.

Goddesses are generally less well understood. An unusually vivid image of them occurs on a Classic-period pot studied by Karl Taube [162]. The aged goddess of midwives, often depicted with the feline skin of night deities, presides over a supernatural birth. By miracle, the umbilicus of a young goddess splits into two serpents. From them come a set of gods who were born already old. Massaging the abdomen of the pregnant woman – she stands to facilitate birth – is one form of this goddess (a good example

162 Square vase with scene of mythic birth. A young goddess stands on a hill, the pull of gravity assisting in childbirth. For support, she clutches ropes in the shape of snakes, lashed to glyphs above. An elderly goddess with jaguar paws massages her belly from behind; another midwife goddess holds a bowl to receive the placenta. A split umbilicus, criss-crossed with veins, loops out below. Ht. 9.66 in. (24.5 cm).

of multiplicity – her identical sisters assist her by lifting out the newborns, cutting the umbilicus with sharp blades, and collecting the placenta in a bowl). The experience of older women in healing and life passages may explain their presence at beginnings and endings. On one pot this goddess attends the emergence of humans from a cave, though she plays a more destructive role in the Dresden Codex. The place is sinister indeed, a "black sky" and "black earth." Against the red background typical of pre-dawn tableaux, a celestial crocodile disgorges a flood of water, and signs for eclipses release torrents. The world itself is coming undone, drowning. War is afoot, too: the god of trading has switched his backpack for spears. In the middle, the aged goddess, labeled Chak Chel, the "great" or "red rainbow" (an unpleasant augury for the Maya), upends a water vessel and releases yet more water.

Yet the goddess has younger counterparts that are more sexualized. Easy with her virtue, a goddess in the Dresden copulates with many male gods. Another, the Moon Goddess, often cuddles an emblem of fecundity, a rabbit. She may have been the consort of the Sun God; when merged with the identity of Maya queens, her spouse is the king in solar guise. The natural cycle of the Moon Goddess accords roughly with human menstruation, so the tie to procreation is logical.

Hieroglyphic texts from the Classic period tell us a great deal about human interactions with gods. Deities were often summoned to witness events or, as local patrons, were said to pertain to particular lords. The few effigies of gods that have survived from earlier periods may well have been housed in temples from which they were taken long ago. A sample of such small representations of Chahk, from the Preclassic to the Late Classic, serves as a stunning reminder of what is so often lost [163]. As proved by Simon Martin, other effigies were dynastic gods transported around cities, much like the statues of saints carried in Maya processions today. Evidently of large size – some tower over humans – these also became the target of enemy ire. Not a few were captured, recalling the Aztec practice of incarcerating enemy gods in a special temple. But not all gods' homes were literal: deity dwellings called *wahyib*, "places for sleeping," occur at Copan in the form of solid house models. Mostly dormant, these gods were presumably "awakened" by sacrifice or incense-burning. The late Andrea Stone developed the plausible argument that such dwellings, on hilltops and in caves, were concentrated under royal control by being replicated in

163 Chahk effigy of fuchsite, Early Classic period. Ht 5.25 in. (13.3 cm).

pyramids and temples. In a sense, then, a Maya city is a domesticated version of a preexisting, pre-human landscape.

Yet, the most direct way of accessing gods was through impersonation. Rulers and queens donned masks of deities, through this ritual becoming one with the spirits. One such mask was found by Takeshi Inomata and Daniela Triadan at Aguateca, Guatemala, made of lightweight material; a textile soaked in clay slip and molded into a face. This was theater of the most sacred sort, in that ritual dances invited the gods themselves to appear. The actual ancient dances cannot be reconstructed but, by analogy with the vibrant tradition of Maya theater in Highland Guatemala, they surely enacted stories of the sort that adorn Maya ceramics. Plazas were the location for most dances. The stelae that now fill some of them petrify kings in perpetual dance, as we can tell by their pose, dress, and explanatory glyphs. While many such dances were solemn, there must also have been, as among Maya today, buffoonery, social commentary, and other theatrical effects intended to entertain. History was re-enacted as well: a stairway at Dos Pilas, Guatemala, records events from the founding of the local dynasty and then, on a step added later, depicts the commemoration of the whole with a dance.

Gods were not the only spirits in the Maya universe. Ethnographic sources describe many, several of which live in the human body. For earlier periods, the most puzzling are the *wahy*, from a term for "sleep." Shown on many Maya ceramics, they seldom seem very pleasant [164]. To mention a few, there are prancing skeletons, seated men who rather casually cut off their own heads, fire-snorting peccaries, and odd composites like tapir-jaguars or monkey-deer, along with a supernatural associated with inebriation. Most are said to belong to the lords of particular dynasties, perhaps as inherited spirits; indeed, *wahy* is a label in some Mayan languages for certain aspects of human souls – Maya concepts of such religious matters are quite complex and varied, allowing multiple forces within a single body. The *wahy* are those that leave the body at night. Several academic theories explain these beings. One is that they account for the surreal experience of dreams, or refer to diseases controlled by kings in an elevated, almost dynastic form of sorcery. Another is that they express royal self-knowledge beyond the ability of other mortals. A cautious view is that we simply do not know, nor are there cogent reasons why they should appear together on what mostly are pots for chocolate drink.

The *wahy* may be connected to important ritual sites for the Maya: caves. Such unsettling places, widely thought among descendants to lead down to Xibalba (a grim underworld smelling of decay and urine), may have been tied to these disquieting spirits. The most spectacular may be Naj Tunich, discovered in 1979 by local residents in karst terrain near Poptun in the southeastern Peten. The cave is huge, measuring 2,790 ft (850 m) deep along its longest passage. It has ancient walls, Late Classic burials, and terminal Late Preclassic pottery, but it was apparently thoroughly looted

164 Maya *wahy* spirits, the dread aspects of royal souls. Most take hybrid forms. (*Above*) A seated spider monkey features traits of a deer. (*Below*) A fire- or smoke-breathing bat carries a bowl crammed with human body parts. Eyeballs, tokens of death and night, powder his wings.

before archaeologists could get to it. The importance of Naj Tunich lies in its extensive hieroglyphic texts (altogether comprising about 400 glyphs) and scenes, all executed in carbon black on the cave walls. The latter include depictions of the ball game, amorous activities that are probably of a homosexual nature, and Maya deities, including the Hero Twins, Hunahpu and Xbalanque [165]. The style of the writing and painting is closely related to Late Classic vases in "codex style," and must have been carried out by one or more artists or scribes skilled in the production of Maya books. One was the prince of a royal house. A key text mentions that someone "sees a *wahy*," hinting at visionary experiences in such spaces. The abundance of references, visual and textual, to young men in caves raises the prospect that the cave was somehow involved in rites of passage. The events recorded in Naj Tunich speak largely of arrivals and various acts of "seeing" by lords from varying dynasties.

165 The Hero Twins, Hunahpu (Huun Ajaw) and Xbalanque, in the Naj Tunich cave, Guatemala. Ht 9.5 in. (24 cm).

NUMBERS AND THE CALENDAR

Otto Neugebauer, the historian of science, considered positional, or place value, numeration as "one of the most fertile inventions of humanity," comparable in a way with the invention of the alphabet. Instead of the clumsy, additive numbers used by the Romans and so many other cultures of the world, a few peoples have adopted "a system whereby the position of a number symbol determines its value and consequently a limited number of symbols suffices to express numbers, however large, without the need for repetitions or creation of higher new symbols."

The Maya usually operated with only three such symbols: the dot for one, the bar for five and a stylized element for nought [166]. There is a concrete quality to these signs, as though they began with actual objects, perhaps pebbles and tally sticks. Unlike our system, adopted from the Hindus, which is decimal and increases in value from right to left, the Maya system was vigesimal and increased from bottom to top in vertical columns. Thus, the first and lowest place has a value of one; the next above it the value of twenty; then 400; and so on. It is immediately apparent that "twenty" would be written with a nought in the lowest place and a dot in the second. The very concept of a vigesimal system probably stemmed from the full set of human digits: the term for "person," *winik*, is indistinguishable from that for a unit of "twenty."

What kinds of calculations were made, and for what purposes? Landa says that the purely vigesimal notation was used by merchants, especially those dealing in cacao, and he mentions that computations were performed "on the ground or on a flat surface" by means of counters, presumably cacao beans, maize grains and the like. But the major use to which Maya arithmetic was put was calendrical, for which a modification was introduced: when days were counted, the values of the places were those of the Long Count,

166 Examples of Maya vigesimal numeration.

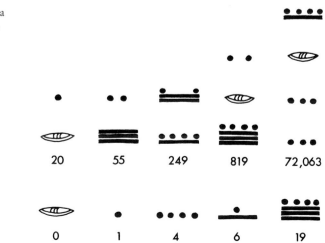

| 20 | 55 | 249 | 819 | 72,063 |

| 0 | 1 | 4 | 6 | 19 |

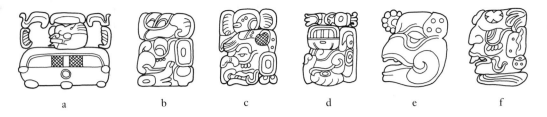

a   b   c   d   e   f

167 Glyphs for the cycles of the Long Count. *a*, Introductory Glyph; *b*, bak'tun (*pih*); *c*, k'atun (*winik-ha'b*); *d*, tun (*ha'b*); *e*, winal; *f*, k'in. Note that, for the first three signs, the Classic-period names were different, here in parentheses.

so that while the first two places had values of one and twenty respectively, the third was thought of as a tun or, in Classic times, *ha'b*, of 360 days (18 x 20), and so on up the line [167]. The tun is the heart of the Long Count, a cycle of special interest for the erection of stone monuments. For operating within their incredibly involved calendar, which among other things included the permutation of the Long Count with the 52-year Calendar Round, the Maya scribes found it necessary to construct tables of multiples; in the Dresden Codex, such tables include multiples of 13, 52, 65, 78, and 91 (the nearest whole number approximating one quarter of a year). Fractions find no place in their system – they were always trying to reach equations of cycles in which all numbers are integers, e.g. 73 x 260 days equals 52 x 365 days. The recent finds from Xultun exemplify this practice. As pointed out by Barbara MacLeod and Hutch Kinsman, drawing on an earlier discovery at Palenque by Floyd Lounsbury, one date combines multiples of cycles, including that for the so-called 819-count, the product of 7, 13, and 9, all of ritual importance to the Maya.

There are several kinds of dates expressed on Classic Maya monuments and in the Dresden manuscript. Leading off a typical Classic inscription is the Initial Series, a Long Count date preceded by an Introductory Glyph with one of the nineteen month-gods infixed. Notionally, this indicated the time elapsed from the 4 Ajaw 8 Kumk'u date mentioned before. This is immediately followed by the day reached in the 260-day count, and, after an interval filled by several other glyphs, the day of the month (365-day count). The intervening glyphs indicate which of the nine gods of the Underworld is ruling over that day (in a cycle of nine days), and lunar calculations which will be considered later.

However, this is not the whole story, for there are usually a number of other dates on the same monument. These are reached by Distance Numbers, which tell one to count forwards or backwards by so many days from the base date, and while the intervals are usually of modest length, in a few examples these span millions of years. And then there are Period Ending dates in the inscriptions, which commemorate the completion of a k'atun, half-k'atun ("lahuntun," that is, ten tuns), quarter-k'atun ("hotun"), or tun. According to David Stuart, time was a presiding force, often an embodiment of the king, and an ethereal concept transformed into the concrete form of a stela: the very word k'atun comes from a word for "wrapping" or dedicating a stone, *k'al-tuun*. "Anniversaries" also dot the Classic inscriptions; these are Calendar Round dates falling at intervals of so many k'atuns or tuns from some date other than the above-mentioned Period Ending Dates.

Why this apparent obsession with dating and the calendar? What do all the dates on the Classic monuments mean? They were formerly explained as the work of priests working out the positions of calendrical and celestial cycles in a religion which was essentially the worship of time itself. As we shall see, an utterly different explanation is not only possible, but certain.

THE SUN AND THE MOON

To the Maya the round of 365 days (18 months of 20 days plus the 5 extra days of the Wayeb) was close to the solar year, anniversaries of which do occur in certain inscriptions at Piedras Negras and elsewhere. The "Vague Year" of 365 days began among the Yucatec of Landa's time on 16 July (Julian calendar – the Gregorian was not to appear until 1582). Yet the earth actually takes about 365 1/4 days to complete its journey about the sun, so that the Vague Year must have continually advanced on the solar year, gradually putting the months out of phase with the seasons. We know that none of the Maya intercalated days on Leap Years or the like, as we do, and it has been shown that more sophisticated corrections thought to have been made by them were a figment of scholars' imagination. Yet their lunar inscriptions show that they must have had an unusually accurate idea of the real length of the Tropical Year [168].

168 Deceased parents at Yaxchilan shown in sun and moon cartouches, possibly Bird Jaguar IV to the right, Lady Great Skull to the left. Yaxchilan Stela 4, AD 775.

Curiously, the Maya went to far greater trouble with the erratic moon. In the inscriptions, Initial Series dates are followed by the so-called Lunar Series, which contains up to eight glyphs dealing with the cycles of that body. One of these records whether the current lunar month was of 29 or 30 days, and another tells the age of the moon from its first appearance on that particular Long Count date. Naturally, the Maya, like all civilized peoples, were faced with the problem of coordinating their lunar calendar with the solar, but there is no indication that they used the 19-year Metonic cycle (on which the "Golden Number" in the Book of Common Prayer is based). Instead, from the mid-fourth century AD each center made its own correction to correlate the two. However, in AD 682 the scribes of Copan began calculating with the formula 149 moons = 4,400 days, a system which was eventually adopted by almost all the Maya centers. In our terms, they figured a lunation to average 29.53020 days, remarkably close to the actual value 29.53059! The Xultun discovery, with its many wall graffiti of calendrical notations, shows even more precision, placing it within four minutes of current estimates.

Of great interest to Mayanists and astronomers alike have been the eclipse tables recorded in the Dresden Codex. These cover a cycle of 405 lunations, or 11,960 days, which equals 46 x 260 days – a kind of formula with which the Maya were deeply concerned, for such equations enabled them to coordinate the movements of the heavenly bodies with their most sacred ritual period. The ancients had realized, at least by the mid-eighth century AD (but possibly much earlier), that lunar and solar eclipses could only occur within plus or minus 18 days of the node, when the moon's path crosses the apparent path of the sun. This is what the tables are: a statement of when such events were likely. The Maya also seem to have been aware of the recession of the node (or at least of its effect over long periods of time), and Eric Thompson suggested that the tables were constructed anew every half-century or so.

THE CELESTIAL WANDERERS AND THE STARS

Venus is the only one of the planets for which we can be absolutely sure the Maya made extensive calculations. Unlike the Greeks of the Homeric age, they knew that with the Evening and Morning Stars they were dealing with the same object. For the apparent, or synodical, Venus year they used the figure of 584 days (the actual value is 583.92, but they were close enough!), divided into four periods of varying length – Venus as Morning Star, disappearance at superior conjunction, appearance as Evening Star, and disappearance at inferior conjunction. After five Venus "years" its cycle met with the solar round, for 5 x 584 = 8 x 365 = 2,920 days. One such eight-year table can be found in the Dresden Codex and in the Grolier Codex.

Some have questioned whether the movements of planets other than Venus were observed by the Maya, but it is hard to believe that one of the Dresden tables, listing multiples of 78, can be anything other than a table for Mars, which has a synodic year of 780 days; or that the Maya intellectuals could have overlooked the fact that 117, the product of the magic numbers 9 and 13, approximates the length of the Mercury "year" (116 days). The Maya savants were, of course, astrologers not astronomers, and all these bodies which were seen to wander against the background of the stars were thought to influence the destiny of prince and pauper alike. Venus itself, or at least an allusion to stars, figured in an expression for war or stormy tumult that included a sign for a flood of water. A martial text at Naranjo presses the metaphor by describing a conflict in terms of a whirlwind, perhaps a hurricane.

The astronomer Anthony Aveni and the architect Horst Hartung have determined that the ancient Maya used buildings and doorways and windows within them for astronomical sightings, especially of Venus. At Uxmal, for instance, all buildings are aligned in the same direction, except the House of the Governor. A perpendicular taken from the central doorway of this structure reaches a solitary mound about 3.5 miles (5.6 km) away; Venus would have risen precisely above the mound when the planet reached its southerly extreme in AD 750. In collaboration with Sharon Gibbs, they have shown that the Caracol at Chichen Itza was entirely aligned to the northerly extremes of Venus at about AD 1000, as is a diagonal sightline in one of the windows of the tower top; another diagonal sightline matched the planet's setting position when it attained its maximum southerly declination.

The Babylonian and Egyptian astrologers divided up the sky in various ways, each sector corresponding to a supposed figure of stars, so as to check the march of the sun as it retrogrades from sector to sector through the year, and to provide a star clock for the night hours. The zodiac of Mesopotamia is the best known of such systems. Did the Maya have anything like it? It has been recognized for years that two much-damaged pages of the Paris Codex show a scorpion, a peccary, and other beings pendant from the sky-serpent, and a similar series appears sculpted on the Nunnery at Chichen Itza. Earlier still, at Bonampak, Mexico, the summit of the second room in the murals building alludes to star formations clumped into constellations, a herd of stampeding "peccaries" (among the more frightening creatures of the forest), then what appear to be two men, one with a stick (a spear-thrower for meteors?), concluding with a turtle that Linda Schele identified as Orion. From Bishop Landa's account, we know that the Yukateko Maya called the zodiacal constellation Gemini ak, "peccary." Indeed, the entire scene in Bonampak may correspond to the sign for stormy tumult, stars above, a dark sky, and bloody violence below.

THE NATURE OF MAYA WRITING

Notable advances have been made in epigraphy, and in the decipherment of the Maya writing system, but if by "decipherment" we mean the matching of a sign or sign group to a specific sound or word in the ancient language,

169 Tablet of the 96 Glyphs, Palenque. A very long text of the Late Classic period, marking the first k'atun anniversary of the accession of K'inich K'uk' Bahlam II in AD 764. The text is completely historical, recounting the king's descent from Pakal the Great.

then probably only about 80% of the code has actually been "broken." Nonetheless, at this point in time we certainly understand the meaning of many of the remaining glyphs with some precision, even if we do not always know how they were pronounced in Maya. This means that the ancient Maya are now one of the few truly historical civilizations in the New World, with records going back to royal names in the Preclassic period.

Only half a century ago, however, it could honestly be said that few studies had made such little advancement with so much effort as the decipherment of the Maya script. This is not to say that a great deal was not understood, but there is a difference between unraveling a meaning for a sign, and matching it with a word in a Mayan tongue. Progress was most

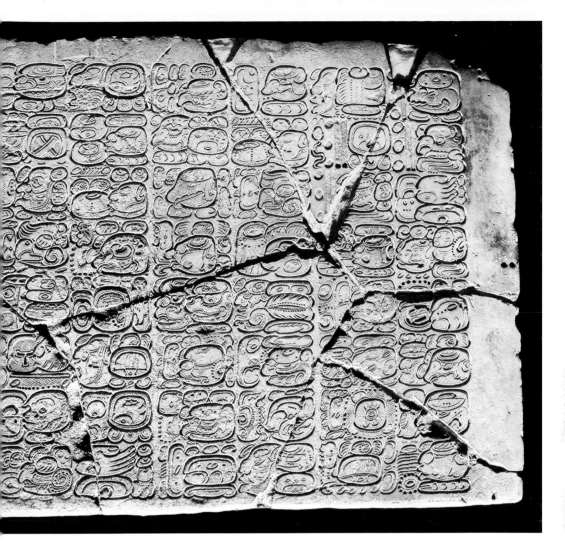

rapid on those glyphs that were of mainly calendrical or astronomical significance. For instance, by the mid-nineteenth century the Abbé Brasseur de Bourbourg had discovered Landa's *Relación*, from which he was able to recognize day glyphs and interpret the bar-and-dot numeration in the codices. It was quickly discovered that Maya writing was to be read in double columns from left to right, and top to bottom. At the turn of the century all of the following had been successfully deciphered by scholars in Europe and America: the zero and "twenty" signs, the world directions and the colors, Venus, the months (also in Landa), and the Long Count. In a remarkable collaboration between astronomers and epigraphers, the mysteries of the Lunar Series had been unveiled by the early 1930s. But after these intellectual triumphs, fewer and fewer successes were scored, leading a few pessimists such as Sylvanus Morley and Eric Thompson to the quite unfounded claim that there was little else in these texts but calendrical and astronomical mumbo-jumbo.

170 The glyph for *wi-WITZ*, "mountain," from Aguateca.

It is generally accepted among linguists that all true writing systems express the utterances of a particular language. Earlier generations of scholars once held that some early scripts, such as Chinese and Egyptian, were "ideographic" in that they expressed thoughts directly without the intervention of language, but this has proved to be a delusion. All, we now realize, have a strong phonetic component (they denote sounds), no matter how pictorial some of the signs may look. Yet even in heavily phonetic scripts, including our own alphabetic one, there are some signs (for instance, our mathematical notation) that are purely semantic and can be "read" in any tongue on earth.

True writing emerged simultaneously with the evolution of complex societies in various parts of the Old World. All these early scripts are both logographic and phonetic, especially after their initial period of development: that is, they have a large number of logograms, signs standing for parts of words or (less commonly) whole words, along with phonetic and semantic ("meaning") signs to help in their reading. In logophonetic writing, semantic and phonetic elements are often complexly intertwined, sometimes in a single hieroglyph or "character," and the logograms themselves require a certain degree of memorization. Such scripts were always easier to read than to write. In Chinese, ancient Egyptian, and Sumerian, the auxiliary semantic signs accompany logograms or phonetic signs to indicate the class of things the referred item belongs to (such as "wood," "water," and so on). These are not used in some scripts, but, after the time of origin and first experimentation, phonetic signs helped to indicate the pronunciation of a logogram. For example, in writing the Maya word *witz*, "mountain," the scribe prefixed the syllabic sign *wi* to the logogram [170]. This was a relatively late introduction, however, and each tradition of writing must be understood to have its own history. The earliest Maya writing, exceedingly difficult to decode, is quite different from its later versions. Presumably, the need to clarify sounds arose because of a perceived problem. Languages might change, leading to ambiguities and uncertainty of reading, or alternative values of a sign needing to be eliminated.

Behind the phonetic signs in all logophonetic systems is the principle of the rebus. While many logograms may have originated as pictures of actual objects, as in Egypt and China, most of the nouns and verbs in a language are more abstract and thus not so easily visualized. But here the scribe could take a pictorial logogram and exploit it for its sound value alone, as the sign for "fire" could be utilized in English as a sign meaning to "fire" or sack a subordinate. As children we have all run across examples of rebus or puzzle writing, such as "I saw Aunt Rose" expressed by pictures of an eye, a saw, an ant, and a rose flower. The Mixtecs and Aztecs used such writing to record personal and place names, and it was apparently the only kind of script they knew. One of the earliest Maya signs is *baah*, a term for the lowly pocket gopher, an unlikely denizen of a royal text. The actual reference was to "body" or "portrait," a term having the same sound but very different meaning.

In many ancient logophonetic scripts, the phonetic component takes the form of a syllabary, in which each sign represents a complete syllable (usually a consonant followed by a vowel), although each of the "pure" vowels will have its own sign. This is the case with the kana syllabary of Japanese, which gives the grammatical endings for Chinese-derived logograms expressing word roots. Some peoples have eschewed logograms altogether or relegated them to minor importance, and have constructed largely syllabic systems; the two most famous examples are the Linear B syllabary of Bronze Age Greece, and the Cherokee syllabary invented in the nineteenth century AD by Sequoyah.

The ultimate reduction to an almost (but never completely) phonetic script is the alphabet, perfected by the Greeks from a script handed to them by their Phoenician trading partners in the eastern Mediterranean. In the alphabet, most of the phonemes of the language – the smallest distinctive units of speech – become separately indicated, instead of appearing together as syllables.

With these preliminary remarks in mind, what kind of system do we then find in the Maya script? Bishop Landa has given to us his famous "alphabet" in which some 29 signs are presented [171]. Several extremely distinguished Maya scholars stumbled badly in trying to read the codices and the inscriptions with Landa's treacherous "ABC," while some went so

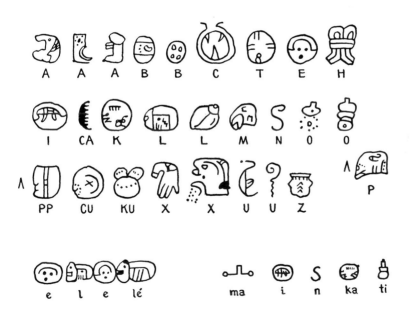

171 The Maya "alphabet" according to Bishop Landa. Below he gives words as written in this system, which we now know is syllabic rather than alphabetic.

far as to declare it a complete fraud. A more careful examination suggests that this is not really an alphabet in the usual sense. For instance, there are three signs for "A," two for "B," and two for "L." Secondly, several signs are quite clearly glossed as syllables of the consonant–vowel sort, i.e. *ma*, *ca*, and *cu* (*ka* and *ku* by present conventions). We shall consider this important point later.

After the almost complete failure of decipherments along the strictly phonetic lines suggested by the Landa "alphabet," a diametrically opposite line was taken by Eric Thompson and many others, namely that the script was purely "ideographic," with perhaps a few rebus signs embedded in the texts from time to time. That is to say, any one sign could have as many referents or associations as the priests could think up, and that only they could read the holy signs, which in general character were more ritualistic than linguistic. There is a striking resemblance between this position and that of the would-be decipherers of the Egyptian script before the great discoveries of Champollion.

This resemblance was not lost upon the Russian epigrapher Yuri Knorosov, a student of Egyptian hieroglyphic writing. In 1952, he began publishing a series of studies which re-examined the validity of the Landa "alphabet" and the possibility of phoneticism in the Maya script. About 287 signs, not including variants, appear in the codices [172]. If the system were completely alphabetic, then the language of the texts would have contained this many phonemes; if purely syllabic, then there would have been about

172 Phonetic-syllabic readings of Maya signs given by Yuri Knorosov, and amended by others.

ku-tz(u)
"turkey"

[bu]-lu-k(u)
"eleven"

tzu-l(u)
"dog"

ku-ch(u)
"burden"

chu-ka-h(a)
"to capture"

chi-k'in-n(i)
"West"

k'u-ch(i)
"culture"

k'u-k'(u)
"quetzal"

mu-t(i)
"omen"

mu-wa-n(i)
"Muwan" (month)

m(o)-o-o
"macaw"

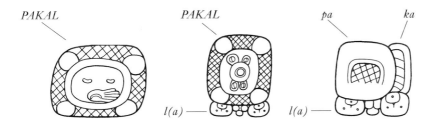

173 Variant spellings of Pakal the Great's second name. Logograms in upper case, phonetic signs in lower case. The middle sign also contains an added element reading *Janahb*.

half this number of phonemes. Both are linguistic impossibilities. On the other hand, if all signs were semantic – representing units of meaning only – then the script represented an incredibly small number of ideas, certainly not enough for civilized communication. With this in mind, Knorosov presented convincing evidence that the Maya were writing in a mixed, logophonetic system in which phonetic and semantic elements were combined as in Sumerian or Chinese, but that they also had a fairly complete syllabary.

Knorosov's starting point was Landa's "ABC." Thompson had already demonstrated that the bishop's native informant had mistaken his instructions, that is, he gave the Maya sign not for the letter itself, but for the names of the letters; see, for instance, the first "B," which shows a footprint on a road – "road" is *be* in Yucatec, and this is exactly what the Spaniards call that letter. But the point is that this is really a partial and much flawed syllabary, not an alphabet, and Knorosov was able to show that words of the very frequent consonant-vowel-consonant (CVC) sort were written with two syllabic signs standing for CV-CV, the final vowel (usually but not always the same as the first) not being pronounced. The proof of phonetic-syllabic writing is, of course, in the reading, and a number of Knorosov's readings have long been confirmed by the contexts in which the signs appear in the codices, especially by the pictures which accompany various passages of text.

If this were all that needed to be done, it would be a simple job to read the Maya hieroglyphs, but the semantic dimension is very much there. Phonetic complements were often attached to logograms to help in their reading, either prefixed as a representation of the initial sound of the sign, or post-fixed as the final consonant; the recognition of these has notably advanced the process of decipherment. Phonetic redundancy of this sort was already being practiced in the Classic; David Kelley was the first to notice that the second part of the name of the great Palenque ruler Pakal could be written either as a picture of a hand-shield (*pakal*, in Maya), or phonetically as *pa-kal-l(a)*, or both [173]. Epigraphers actively search for such substitutions, for that is the basic way that we learn how the logograms were actually pronounced.

Although ridiculed by Thompson and his followers, Knorosov's logo-syllabic approach is now universally utilized by Maya epigraphers: this is the way the script works. Since the initial work of Knorosov and Kelley, the recognition of phonetic construction in the script has proceeded at such a pace that epigraphers are now in general agreement on over 140 signs that have phonetic value (some of them, of course, variations on one and the same syllabic sign). It is also now recognized that in Mayan, as in many ancient scripts, a number of signs are polyvalent: a particular sign may have more than one phonetic reading, and it may also be read for its logographic value. For example, in English the compound sign *ch* has totally different sound values in the words *chart*, *chorus*, and *chivalry*.

Another discovery fills in a gap left by Knorosov. He could not explain why some syllabic spellings failed to have the same vowel, as in *mu-ti*, "bird" – *mu-tu* would have been the expected form. It now seems the Maya used this to show a different kind of vowel, yielding not *mut*, as Knorosov would have interpreted it, but *muut* with a long vowel (the doubled *u* denotes this phoneme). This is a highly archaic feature, from the earlier days of Mayan languages, and thus thought impossible by some linguists who believed it lost by Classic times. Indeed, the use of syllables may have started as a way of distinguishing different kinds of vowels. By detecting such nuances of sound, specialists can now reconstruct much of the grammar of hiero-glyphs, albeit with continuing disagreement about details. There are both active and passive verbs, along with positionals, distinct to Mayan lan-guages, that encode for position in space, along with ways of noting time and ongoing action. The linguistic sophistication is such that one suspects the presence of some great grammarian, like Pāṇini, who systematized the study of Sanskrit in ancient India. Several Maya texts even use first- and second-person pronouns ("I," "me," "you"), as though recording actual conversations. These often occur on "folkloric" scenes that show, for example, animals or gods in some now-lost story. Others appear, as David Stuart has shown, in the inner precincts of temples, their inscriptions seeming to murmur in a continuous address, no human audience necessary.

As each new phonetic decipherment has been made, we have been brought closer to identifying the language of the inscriptions and of the surviving books. As has been said in Chapter 1, this has turned out to be Ch'olti', a now extinct member of the Ch'olan branch of Mayan. This may well have served as a lingua franca among elites and surely evolved, as did Medieval Latin or Coptic, into an arcane, sacred language used by few. Even some of the inscriptions of Chichen Itza seem to be written in some form of this language. But what about Yukateko Maya? To the ancient scribes, this apparently lacked the literary prestige of Ch'olti', although some Yucatec spellings are found in the Dresden and Madrid codices.

All four codices deal exclusively with religious and astronomical matters, as is quite obvious from the pictures of gods associated with the texts, from the tables, and from the high frequency of passages geared to the 260-day count. Thus, we have in these texts little more than short phrases of esoteric significance, which often seem to match passages in the Books of Chilam Balam. When Maya writing disappeared is a matter of debate. The historian John Chuchiak argues, from court records of seized codices in Yucatan, that it continued into the 1600s and perhaps beyond, especially in areas not closely monitored by the Spaniards. But these captured books, if hieroglyphic, could simply have been heirlooms, hidden and preserved long after their composition. Aside from the rare exception, Maya writing probably died far earlier. Landa's syllabary is, for all its importance, rather inept. Much like Latin script, it spells out phrases in linear order. A fully-fledged scribe would have compacted them into glyphs blocks. These agglomerations of signs, organized as small squares, differ strongly from the linear, cursive writing used by Spaniards and Maya in the Colonial period.

HISTORY GRAVEN IN STONE

What, then, of the subject matter of the inscriptions? Until quite recently, the prevailing opinion was that it differed in no way to that of the books; and further, that all those dates recorded on the monuments were witnesses to some sort of cult in which the time periods themselves were deified. The great John Lloyd Stephens was of a different mind, writing about Copan:

> One thing I believe, that its history is graven on its monuments. No Champollion has yet brought to them the energies of his enquiring mind. Who shall read them?

The discovery within the last few decades of the historical nature of the monumental inscriptions has been one of the most exciting chapters in the story of New World archaeology.

It began in 1958, when Heinrich Berlin published evidence that there was a special kind of sign, the "Emblem Glyph," associated with specific archaeological sites, and recognizable from the same kind of glyphic elements which appear affixed to each [174]. Thus far, the Emblem Glyphs for over thirty Classic centers – including Tikal, Piedras Negras, Copan, Quirigua, Ceibal, Naranjo, Palenque, and Yaxchilan – have been securely identified. Berlin suggested that these were either the names of the cities themselves or of the dynasties that ruled over them, and proposed that on the stelae and other monuments of these sites their histories might be recorded. We now know what Emblem Glyphs really are: they are titles of Maya kings, describing each as the *k'uhul ajaw*, or "holy lord," of a kingdom whose name appears as the main sign of the glyph. It has since become clear that many of these kingdoms took their name from place names; an acute sense of sacred locations informed most Maya inscriptions. Where events took place was just as important as who was involved, and indeed the events themselves.

174 Some Emblem Glyphs from the Classic monuments. *a, b*, Palenque (*Baak*); *c, d*, Yaxchilan (*Pa'chan* or *Pa'kan*); *e*, Copan; *f*, Naranjo; *g*, Machaquila; *h*, Piedras Negras (*Yokib*); *i*, Ceibal; *j*, Tikal (*Mut*). Not all signs are fully deciphered. The affix attached to the left of the main signs spells *k'uhul*, "holy," that to the top, *ajaw*, "king [of]."

The next breakthrough was by Tatiana Proskouriakoff of the Carnegie Institution, who analyzed 35 dated monuments from Piedras Negras. The arrangement of stelae before structures she found was not random; rather, they fell into seven groups. Within a single such group, the time span covered by all the dates on the stelae is never longer than an average lifetime, which immediately raised the possibility that each group was the record of a single reign. This has now proved to be so. The first monument in a series shows a figure, usually a young man, seated in a niche above a platform or plinth; on this stela two important dates are inscribed. One is associated with a glyph like an animal's head with a toothache, and has been shown to record the accession to power of the young man; the other appears with the "upended frog" glyph, now known to read *sihyaj*, and is that same person's date of birth [175]. Later monuments in a particular group celebrate marriages and the birth of offspring, and Proskouriakoff was able to identify the signs for personal names and titles, particularly of women, who are quite prominent in Classic Maya sculpture. Military victories were also frequently marked, especially if an important enemy had been taken captive by the ruler.

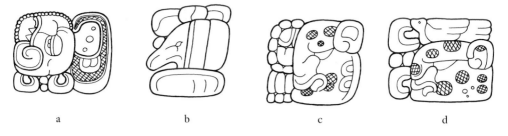

175 Historical glyphs in the monumenal texts. *a*, birth ("upended frog," *sihyaj*); *b*, accession ("toothache," *johyaj ti ajawlel*); *c*, "Shield Jaguar"; *d*, "Bird Jaguar."

Thus, virtually all the figures that appear in Classic reliefs are not gods and priests but dynastic autocrats and their spouses, children, and subordinates. As the records for one reign come to an end, the next begin with the usual accession motif. Among the more complete documents are the inscriptions carved on the many stone lintels of Yaxchilan; from these Proskouriakoff reconstructed the history of the extremely militant dynasty that ruled the site in the eighth century AD. The record begins with the exploits of a lord whom she called "Shield Jaguar"; he was succeeded in AD 752 by his son "Bird Jaguar" after a mysterious interregnum. Lintel 8 of Yaxchilan [176] exemplifies how much of the writing that accompanies the

176 Lintel 8, Yaxchilan. A record of the capture of "Jeweled Skull" and one other enemy by "Bird Jaguar" and a noble companion.

7 Imix

14 Sek

chuhkaj
(he captured)
"Jeweled
Skull"

2nd captive

u baak
(his captive)

"Bird Jaguar"

Yaxchilan Emblem Glyph

2nd captive   "Jeweled Skull"

reliefs celebrating the victories of this ruler can now be read, or at least interpreted. It begins with a Calendar Round date falling in AD 755. Below this is the *chuhkaj* or "capture" glyph, then a glyph resembling a jeweled skull, which names the prisoner on the right. Above right, the second glyph is that of "Bird Jaguar" himself (the spear-holding figure), beneath which is the Emblem Glyph of Yaxchilan.

Of special interest are those inscriptions that indicate the interference of some centers with the destinies of others. For instance, the Yaxchilan Emblem Glyph appears with one of the most prominent women in the Bonampak murals, and, thanks to a royal marriage, the glyph for Dos Pilas appears on monuments at Naranjo. Piedras Negras is not far downstream from Yaxchilan, and the famous Panel 3 from that site is now believed to show a royal visitor from Yaxchilan, perhaps a pretender to that throne – he is never mentioned at his home site! As we shall see, this interference took on major dimensions in the affairs of a number of cities in the southern lowlands. In 1973, building on work by Heinrich Berlin, Linda Schele and Peter Mathews worked out the dynastic record of all the Palenque rulers going back to AD 465; this record has since been extended as far back as AD 431, and shadowy figures go back to AD 252 and before. One seems even to correspond to the Olmec period. We can now place such important figures as Pakal the Great and Kan Bahlam in relation to the stupendous art and architecture that was created for them. Palenque, like Yaxchilan, had entered into the realm of history.

Important glyphs now known to relate to dynastic affairs include the signs for events such as battles (the "star-shell" and other glyphs), inauguration or "seating" in office, ritual bloodletting, and death and burial, in addition to the birth and accession glyphs. As one would expect with ruling families obsessed with noble lineage and marriage affiliation, there are a number of relationship glyphs which have now been recognized, such as "child of father," "child of mother," and "wife" (*atan* in Maya), as well as a sign expressing the relationship (unpleasant in the extreme) between a local dynast and an important captive whom he had taken.

THE GREAT GAME

As our understanding of the script has evolved, ideas about the nature of the Classic Maya political system in the Central Area have also been modified. Sylvanus Morley had thought that there was once a single great political entity, which he called the "Old Empire," but once the full significance of Emblem Glyphs had been recognized, it was clear that there had never been any such thing. In its stead, Mayanists proposed a more Balkanized model, in which each "city state" was essentially independent of all the others; the political power of even large entities like Tikal would have been confined to a relatively small area, the distance from the capital to the polity's borders seldom exceeding a day's march. When it became clear that warfare between polities was frequent, the main motivation behind these activities was not believed to be control and territorial aggrandizement, but the need to acquire royal captives destined for humiliation and sacrifice.

Based on a better understanding of Classic texts, and particularly verbs relating to royal actions, Simon Martin and Nikolai Grube have come up with a model that lies somewhere between an imperial and a Balkan one. We now know that not all Maya polities were equal: the kings of some lesser states were said to be "possessed" by the rulers of more powerful ones (the phrase *y-ajaw*, "his king," specifies this relationship). Royal investitures in such vassal states were sometimes witnessed and therefore validated by the foreign "divine ruler" to whom they owed allegiance. These dominance-dependence relationships can also be seen in royal visits, gift-giving, joint ritual activity, and marriage.

While city-states such as Palenque, Copan, and Piedras Negras exercised considerable political control over wide areas beyond their borders, the two major "players" were Tikal and Calakmul, the latter being the largest of all Maya cities [177]. Their conflict recalls the global Great Game of imperial powers in the nineteenth century, fighting wars through proxies, far away from their borders. It is hardly surprising that Tikal and Calakmul were bitter enemies through much of Classic history. Smaller sites, such as La

177 Calakmul's dominance of the Maya lowlands during the Classic period, as deduced from inscriptions recording forms of diplomatic exchange between the city and nearby kingdoms. With rivals Calakmul and Tikal, the relationship was one of armed conflict.

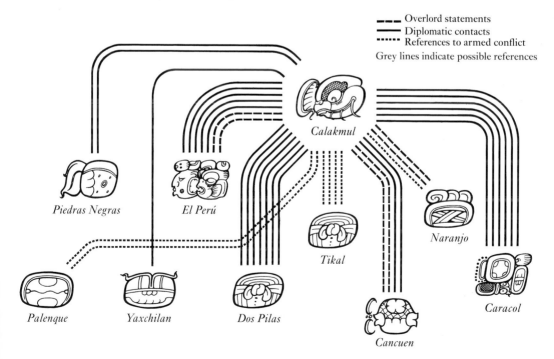

Overlord statements
Diplomatic contacts
References to armed conflict
Grey lines indicate possible references

Calakmul

Piedras Negras   El Perú   Naranjo

Tikal   Caracol

Palenque   Yaxchilan   Dos Pilas

Cancuen

Corona, studied by David Stuart, Marcelo Canuto, and Tomás Barrientos, have histories utterly dominated by Calakmul, with whose dynasty it intermarried and sent its sons as court pages and quasi-hostages. Tikal's influence was more hedged and reactive.

The dynasty of Calakmul probably originated not in that sprawling city, but to the east, in the southern part of what is now the Mexican state of Quintana Roo. Moving west, that family occupied Calakmul, a city with ancient roots, and took off as a dynastic power. As testified by diplomatic activities, it had extensive influence over Cancuen, Piedras Negras, Dos Pilas, El Perú, Naranjo, and Caracol, a large and fluctuating alliance directed against Tikal. Calakmul's ability to wage war was formidable, and it was plainly more aggressive than its main antagonist: in AD 599 it attacked Palenque, 150 miles (240 km) to the southwest, in 631 it conquered Naranjo, far to the southeast, and in the year 657, Tikal itself. It is not unreasonable to see one of its kings, Yuknoom the Great, as their Charlemagne, a figure of unusual energy and territorial ambition. Tikal finally had its revenge on 5 August AD 695, when forces under its king Jasaw Chan K'awiil defeated Calakmul and captured its king, Yich'aak K'ahk' ("Fiery Claw") – a triumph recorded on the wooden lintel of Tikal's Temple 1, under which Jasaw Kan K'awiil is interred. The enigma is why Calakmul did not go further and become a true imperial power. Sacred dynasties may been so entrenched that uprooting them proved impossible. Or perhaps Calakmul found it easier, as with so many other powers, to rule through local authorities.

By the eighth century, the age of such powers was over. No longer could a few powerful polities have hegemony over others. As the system broke down, an intense military rivalry among lesser states sprang up, and the Maya lowlands became truly Balkanized. Spiraling interregional warfare and its attendant miseries and disruptions (for which the Petexbatun sites give ample testimony) were surely factors in the ultimate breakdown of Classic Maya civilization.

A POSSESSED WORLD

If the writing of the Classic period has any theme it is its obsessive focus on ownership. Underlings belonged to higher-ranking rulers, wives to husbands, children to parents. But if Maya kings were anything, they were rich, or at least wanted to be: glyphic texts point to their possession of all manner of objects, many carefully labeled with the name of their owners. Even stone monuments, including stelae and altars, belonged to certain rulers or, if diminutive, to lower-ranking nobles or females – there appear to have been sumptuary codes dictating what certain people were permitted to own. Buildings, too, were said to belong to certain kings, and the history of construction at some cities can be elucidated through these records. The list of owned things includes portable items too. There are bones, *baak*, earspools, *tuup*, including a splendid pair of ground obsidian

178 Obsidian earspools from Altun Ha, Belize, *c.* AD 500. Made or incised in Peten, Guatemala, they belonged to a high-ranking lady. Her son, who probably gave her the ornaments, is named on the left earspool. Diam. 2 in. (4.4 cm).

from Altun Ha, Belize [**178**], and, above all, the large inventory of painted ceramics from the Classic period.

Many such pots have a text that is formulaic and repetitive, usually painted or carved around its rim. The person drinking from the vessel would have placed their lips on or close to that text, making its scrutiny inevitable; the formula named the type of vessel and identified its owner. Some were plates, *lak*, others drinking vessels, *uk'ib*. The contents of the plates seemed not to matter, but those for drinking were another story: decipherments have detected recipes for different kinds of liquid, ranging from *atole*, a potable maize gruel, to sundry recipes for chocolate. As we have seen, one unusual screw-top jar from an Early Classic tomb at Río Azul subjected to tests by the Hershey Company indeed contained chocolate [**53**]. Not all owners were humans: several objects were said to belong to *mam*, or ancestors, perhaps the grandparents of living lords. These were true heirlooms

179 Name of sculptor, Piedras Negras. Throne 1, AD 785.

and carried, as did all such objects, a social record of who first owned a piece. Yet a surprisingly large number belonged to royal youths, the *ch'ok*, or more usually, the "great youth," *chak ch'ok*, perhaps the heir-designate. Some of the most stunning ceramics of the Classic Maya may have served in rites of passage, as gifts to the rising generation.

Along with the owners, we also know the names of the craftsmen responsible for these products. Over 114 distinct sculptors have been identified, along with 17 painters – the initial work was done by David Stuart in a seminal set of papers. There is a highly regional pattern to their distribution, however, in that one site alone, Piedras Negras, hosted 42 of these sculptors, while most of the calligraphers inhabited a small part of northern Guatemala which had strong dynastic ties to a kingdom near Lake Peten Itza. The evidence for craftsmanship at Piedras Negras is particularly revealing [179]. It allows us to trace the careers of certain carvers, which lasted from 7 to 24 years. Generally, sculptors correlate with certain kings. Only a few continue into succeeding reigns, and with several, during the rule of the last well-known king, a break seems to occur about halfway through his time in office. The sculptors probably worked in ateliers, and one title, the "first" or "head-sculptor," hints at masters under whom apprentices learned their skill. Politics was unavoidable in this craft of royal representation: some carvers were labeled as lords, but most were not, and the vast majority operated within one kingdom. But there were exceptions that almost recall Renaissance Italy. A few sculptors were loaned to subordinate cities or came from them, some went to work with friendly dynasties, and a few sculptors – just like Leonardo in a very different time and place – must have displeased their masters by carving for enemies.

10

THE ENDURING MAYA

The approximately five million Maya alive in the world today are survivors: they have endured repeated cycles of conquest or oppression that continue unabated to our own time. What has kept the Maya people culturally and even physically viable is their hold on the land (and that land on them), a devotion to their community, and an all-pervading and meaningful belief system. It is small wonder that their oppressors have concentrated on these three areas in incessant attempts to exploit them as a politically helpless labor force. As the novelist and anthropologist Oliver La Farge put it over a half century ago, "from the Conquest until recently there has been a steady drive, with some reversals, to destroy the Indian ownership of large blocks of land which forms the physical and economic base of tribal solidarity and of freedom from the necessity to work for non-Indians."

La Farge, largely drawing on Guatemalan data, saw five broad stages in the history of the Maya since the initial invasion of their lands by the Spaniards. These continue to have validity. The first is the *Conquest Period*, from 1524 until the end of the sixteenth century. This was a violent era, in which Indian cultural structures were shattered – although some native polities, particularly in the Peten, were not subdued until the close of the following century. The next stage was the *Colonial Indian*, which lasted until 1724, at which time the Spanish Crown abolished the *encomienda* system, an oppressive institution which had given Spanish land barons total right to Indian forced labor in return for the supposed conversion of the natives to the Christian religion. (Another system, the *repartamiento*, strong-armed the Maya into supplying a labor quota; in Yucatan, this was finally abolished in 1783, under the more enlightened Bourbon monarchs.) It was a time when Spanish and Christian elements were absorbed wholesale into the fabric of Maya life and somewhat altered to fit the pattern of native culture; many features of Maya existence were destroyed or mutilated, while others were greatly changed. Although little noted in most histories, this was also a period in which African slaves were imported into Guatemala, Campeche, and, in subsequent years, into what is now Belize. Mass-deaths from imported diseases had compelled Spaniards to find replacement labor.

During the *Transition Period*, lasting until the colonies broke away from Spain about 1820, life became more tolerable for the Maya, as Spanish control slowly relaxed, and suppressed Maya cultural traits re-emerged. It was during this time that traditional Maya patterns took on the form that are preserved in part today. Yet the pattern was not the same across the Maya region: in Yucatan, by contrast, the later eighteenth century saw the growth of cattle ranches and the decline of Maya peasants. *Recent Indian I* was ushered in by the independence of Mexico and Guatemala, and persisted until the 1870s or 1880s; while La Farge saw this as an era of smooth integration between Spanish and Maya elements, with relative tranquility, this is true only for the Guatemalan highlands under the country's pro-Indian Conservative government. A different story could be told in Chiapas, with major Indian revolts, and in Yucatan, with the Caste Wars in which the Maya came close to crushing their white overlords.

From 1880 until today we are in *Recent Indian II*, marked by a new tide of intervention in Indian life, and with concerted efforts by governments to force the Maya to become laborers on cash crop plantations as part of the world market system. Travelers to Guatemala City may drive along the "Avenida de la Reforma," but they surely will not know what the "reform" was: the abolition by President Rufino Barrios of Indian communal lands, and the imposition of a system to supply forced labor from the Maya highlands to the newly-established coffee *fincas* of the Pacific Piedmont zone. Bitter revolts against this injustice took place, but they were put down by the Liberal government of Barrios with a ferocity that foreshadowed more modern developments. Such imposed seasonal migrations were absent in the Yucatan Peninsula, but on the great sisal (*henequén*) plantations which covered much of the north, rock-bottom wages and debt peonage were the rule.

This last period was marked by the emergence of a new cross to be borne by the Maya: the invasion of their lands, villages, and towns by a class of *ladinos*, Hispanic or hispanicized citizens who occupied all the lucrative and politically powerful positions in largely Maya territories; they were the shop keepers, the labor majordomos, the schoolteachers, the judiciary, the Catholic priests. Descendants of Maya or of mixed Maya background, they spoke Spanish rather than the Indian "dialects" (as the Maya languages were pejoratively thought of), they dressed in Western clothes, and they generally held themselves to be superior to the native peoples. It is a situation that persists.

XXI, XXII Lidded basal flange bowls of the Tzakol culture, from Burial 9, El Diablo Complex, El Zotz, Guatemala. Early Classic. (*Above*) Ht 8.5 in. (19.5 cm). (*Below*) Ht 11.5 in. (29 cm).

Overleaf
XXIII, XXIV Richly painted figurines from Burial 39, Structure O14-4, El Perú, Guatemala. *c.* AD 650–700. Part of a group of 23 clay figures, found arrayed in a concentric pattern on a bench near the royal skeleton. Most depict members of a royal court, others are mythological beings. Here, a king (*left*) wears an heirloom shell on his chest; the headdress may display his name. A queen (*right*), identified by her long skirt, holds a shield, an object linked to royal consorts at El Perú. See also figs. 65 and 66.

XXI

XXII

The Hero Twins

XXV (*Left*) A Hero Twin, Hunahpu (Huun Ajaw), in an act of bloodletting on the West Wall of the San Bartolo murals. *c.* 100 BC. A long spine, perhaps of maguey, slices through his penis, causing blood to gush out. Birds flutter behind his body, while, to upper left, glyphs may label him as the "Venus Person," a name spelled out on his headdress. Part of larger scene with turkey sacrifice and other offerings to the Principal Bird Deity.

XXVI (*Above*) Plate in codex style, from northern Guatemala or southern Campeche, *c.* AD 700–750. In the center, the Maize God (Huun Ixi'm) emerges from the split surface of the earth – depicted as a turtle carapace with firefly and torch. The Hero Twin Hunahpu (Huun Ajaw) stands in swirling water on the left, while his counterpart on the right, with jaguar-pelt markings, pours water to ensure the sprouting of the corn.

XXVII Mural depicting the serving and drinking of *ul* (maize gruel) in the Chiik Nahb market, Calakmul. A richly attired upper-class lady, perhaps even a courtesan, places or removes an olla filled with gruel from the head of a servant. Beginning of the Late Classic.

XXVIII Dance scene found on the walls of a late Colonial house, Chajul, Guatemala. Created by Ixil-speaking Maya, the scene highlights seated and bearded Spaniards, labeled by their official titles above. One plays a drum, an unusual task for a foreigner. To the right is a Maya dancer or lord in what may be a jaguar-skin costume.

THE NEW SPANISH ORDER

To understand the processes of conflict, accommodation, and integration that have gone on among the Maya since the Conquest, it is necessary to understand what the Spaniards introduced. First and foremost were epidemic diseases previously unknown in the New World, such as smallpox, influenza, and measles. It is generally agreed among scholars that these produced a holocaust unparalleled in the world's history: within a century, 90% of the native population had been killed off, including that of the Maya area. Smallpox, in fact, had reached the Guatemalan highlands even before the arrival of the Alvarado brothers, and it is a wonder that the weakened Maya put up the defense that they did. Still, there are always quislings. In part, the Alvarados succeeded because of their alliances with native groups, such as, at first, the Kaqchikel. Large numbers of indigenous warriors from central Mexico offered eager service too, for which they were rewarded with property in colonial cities.

Over the next two centuries, then, the Spaniards were able to impose their own cultural pattern on regions that had been devastated by disease. By order of Church and Crown, the scattered populations were "reduced," that is, concentrated into villages and towns on the Spanish pattern, where they could be better controlled and converted. These new settlements were laid out on the grid plan, with rectilinear streets, a central plaza, and a church, a settlement type still to be seen throughout the Maya area. Along with the church, the seat of religious power, there was usually a building housing the *Ayuntamiento*, the civil government run by, or under the thumb of, Spaniards or *ladinos*; and, later on, a *ladino*-run store.

Catholicism brought its priests, its rituals, and its saints, and was usually the principal agent of acculturation. One of its most successful institutions was the *cofradía* (confraternity or brotherhood), adopted enthusiastically throughout the highlands, each dedicated to the care and honor of a particular saint. There are twelve of these brotherhoods, for instance, among the Ixil of the Nebaj region, and they play a crucial role in the ritual life of these people. The Christian sacrament of baptism introduced another element into native social life, namely that of *compadrazgo* or co-godparenthood, which formalizes bonds of friendship between adult Maya.

There was, of course, a great deal of syncretism or blending between Spanish and Maya religious institutions and beliefs, since in many respects they were so similar. Both burned incense during rituals, both had images which they worshiped, both had priests, and both conducted elaborate pilgrimages and processions with effigies set by their respective calendars. Both, as Nikolai Grube reminds us, had a hero god who died and was resurrected – for the Spaniards, this was Jesus Christ, and for the Maya, the Maize God. Thus, when the Tsotsil Maya of Zinacantan make pilgrimages to crosses set up on holy mountains, it is irrelevant to ask if this is a Maya or Spanish custom: to the Tsotsil, both cross and ancestral mountain are a unity.

But the European invaders brought with them more than their civil and religious order: they imposed a new economic order as well. Iron and steel tools replaced chipped or ground stone ones, and the Maya took readily to the Spaniards' axes, machetes, and billhooks, which in the lowlands enabled them to cope with the forest as they never had before. Cattle, pigs, and chickens began to replace game as the main source of meat in the diet, although the Maya never took to the heavy use of lard and oil which was such a prominent feature of the Spanish cuisine. The invaders brought in citrus trees, watermelons, and other welcome crops, but the sugarcane and coffee (the latter largely supplanting the native cacao) introduced as cash crops were a mixed blessing as they led to the plantations that put economic shackles on the Maya.

Perhaps the most destructive of these introduced elements was distilled alcohol. The Maya had always used alcohol in their rituals – chicha or maize beer in the highlands, and *chih* (*pulque*) and *balche'* (a flavored mead) in the lowlands, but they were unprepared for the power of the Spaniards' *aguardiente* (a term meaning "fire water"), and many despondent Maya sought relief or oblivion in strong drink, a habit encouraged by the *ladino* majordomos and store owners.

On the plus side, though, was the Roman alphabet, initially used by the earlier missionaries to write down sermons and the like in the native languages. It was not long before educated Maya were using it to transcribe their own ritual and historical texts, which had previously existed in hieroglyphic form, an activity which was probably conducted in secret. To this we owe the preservation of the great K'iche' epic, the Popol Vuh, and the Yukateko Books of Chilam Balam, themselves a prime example of intellectual hybrids drawing on native and European thought. In Yucatan, there has always been a strong tradition of native literacy, still kept by men who occupy the office of *ah tz'ib*, "scribe." It was probably such specialists who produced the large body of surviving letters in Yukateko exchanged between leaders of the Caste Wars of the 1840s and 50s.

In all of this, the various Maya groups have clearly assimilated and altered many disparate foreign, and even threatening, elements to fit their own cultural patterns inherited from the pre-Conquest era. Take the marimba, a percussion instrument ultimately of African origin, but introduced to Guatemala in Colonial times. Today it appears as a typically "Maya" instrument in native performances, both religious and secular; so assimilated is it that many tourists believe that it must be pre-Columbian.

THE HIGHLAND MAYA, YESTERDAY AND TODAY

Anthropologists and other social scientists agree that about 20% of Guatemala's population of 15 million is Maya in the sense of speaking a native language; most of these live in the central and western highlands of the country, the eastern part having been subject to heavy Spanish migration

180 Tz'utujil Maya housewife weaving a trouser leg on a backstrap loom, Santiago Atitlan, Guatemala.

and consequent "ladinoization" over the centuries. Another 850,000 Maya, mainly Tsotsil and Tseltal, occupy the adjacent Chiapas highlands. All of these populations are rapidly growing and expanding, in spite of poverty, malnutrition, and Guatemala's recent history of terror and insecurity.

The highland Maya economy is both a part of, and separate from, the economies of the modern nation-states of Mexico and Guatemala. Most Maya households engage in corn farming and the production of crafts for local consumption or for sale in Indian-run markets, but in many areas the men must travel long distances to work in the lowlands for part of the year on coffee *fincas*, cotton or sugar plantations, and the like. Others grow fruits and vegetables to be shipped abroad. One of the most striking features of the Maya lands in Guatemala, apart from the magnificent landscape, is the vast network of markets and trade routes which link them, producing – as one anthropologist called it – a kind of "penny capitalism." These markets can be spectacular, like the ones at Solola and Santiago Atitlan, near Lake Atitlan, with row upon row of colorfully garbed Maya women selling produce of all kinds [180].

Typically in the Maya highlands each village will have its own distinctive style of dress. The skirts of the women are usually machine-made, *ikat* wrap-arounds, but their embroidered cotton blouses or *huipiles* mark them as members of a particular community. Studies by Walter "Chip" Morris have shown that the designs on them are not merely decorative, but rather illustrate a complex iconographic system based on native and sometimes

Christian cosmology: these are not static art forms but ones that change while also projecting a sense of tradition. The men, in contrast, wear clothing more or less based on Spanish modes of dress, but even this has been transformed into something distinctive to the community: Solola men, for example, wear short black-and-white jackets with frogging, but on the back of each is a great emblematic bat, while the Tsotsil men of Zinacantan are clad with broad-brimmed, beribboned straw hats, ponchos, and high-backed sandals recalling those of the Classic Maya. Such clothing, a delight to see, is, alas, beginning to disappear in many communities.

The old Maya Calendar Round has survived to an extraordinary degree in the highlands. Among peoples like the Ixil and the K'iche', the 260-day count is an integral part not only of native ritual, but of their everyday life, as it was among their distant ancestors. Wherever it is found, there are shaman-priests or "day-keepers" whose job it is to keep track of the round of days; an important function of all highland shamans is divination. Along with the mechanism of the 260-day count is the casting of certain red seeds or maize kernels, a practice deeply rooted in the pre-Spanish past; the cast maize kernels are separated into groups of four, the outcome depending upon whether the number of piles is odd or even, or the remainder odd or even. Shamans conduct rituals for both individuals and the whole community in accord with its dictates. The most dramatic of these is the great Eight Monkey, or *Wajxaqib Batz'*, ceremony, held in the K'iche' community of Momostenango every 260 days. On the day of that name, tens of thousands of Indians gather at dawn at altars formed of mounds of broken pottery, while over 200 shamans act as intermediaries between individual petitioners and the supreme deity Dios Mundo ("God World"). Prayers are made for forgiveness for past sins, and requests that some boon be granted, as each individual adds a potsherd to the pile. Other performances, especially of dances, have come to spectacular light, as painted on the walls of a building in Chajul, Guatemala, an Ixil Maya town. Dating to the later Colonial period, but only discovered in 2007, they show what may be the Dance of the Conquest, still performed in highland communities today [xxvIII].

THE TSOTSIL MAYA OF ZINACANTAN

The resilience of the contemporary highland Maya when left in relative peace to work out their own destinies in a changing world is well exemplified by the Tsotsil of Zinacantan, a community intensively studied over nearly two decades by a Harvard project directed by Evon Vogt, begun in 1957.

The approximately 36,000 Zinacantecos live in a landscape of rugged mountains; several thousand occupy the ceremonial center within a densely occupied valley, while the rest are scattered in outlying hamlets. The Zinacanteco world is conceived of as a large quincunx, with four corners and a "navel of the earth" in the middle – actually a low, rounded

181 A Tsotsil Maya shaman from Zinacantan prays for the soul of a patient at a mountain shrine; in the background is another sacred mountain resembling a Maya pyramid.

mound in the ceremonial center. This all rests on the shoulders of the *Vaxak-Men*, the four-corner gods; when one of these shifts his burden, there is an earthquake. The sky above is the domain of the sun, moon, and stars. The sun, "Our Holy Father," is associated in Zinacanteco cosmology with God the Father or Jesus Christ, and the moon is thought to be one with the Virgin Mary.

Mountains and hills located near settlements are the homes of ancestral deities, "fathers and mothers"; these supernaturals are pictured as elderly Zinacantecos, living eternally in their mountain abodes, and are referred to constantly in prayers and rituals conducted in their honor and sustained by offerings of black chickens, candles, incense, and liquor [181]. Many Mayanists, incidentally, are convinced that these holy, ancestral mountains are directly analogous to the temple-pyramids of the Classic Maya cities, which celebrated the cult of the dead and presumably deified royal ancestors. Almost of equal importance in Zinacanteco religious life is the Earth Lord – thought of as a fat, greedy *ladino*! – who dwells in caves, limestone sinks, and waterholes. He owns all the waterholes, and controls and produces lightning and rain.

The most sacred objects in Zinacantan are the wood or plaster images of the saints. These carry their own legends and associated beliefs (not always the same as those in official hagiographies), and most are kept in three churches in the village center. The Zinacanteco people, at their simplest level of social organization, live in patrilocal, extended families, which in turn are grouped into local patrilineages, or *sna*. Each *sna* maintains a series of cross shrines on nearby mountains, for communicating with the ancestral deities, and in caves, for communicating with the Earth Lord. Two to over a dozen patrilineages form a waterhole group (waterholes are highly sacred), and in turn keep up their own series of cross shrines; a particular hamlet will be made up of several waterhole groups.

It will be remembered that the Spaniards imposed a civil hierarchy on each Maya group, and this persists in the ceremonial center of Zinacantan, with strictly ranked officials elected to three-year terms. But the more important hierarchy, as can be seen in native communities throughout the New World, is religious. Some 250 of the people with religious power are shamans or "seers," almost all adult males. But also of overwhelming significance to the community is the system of ranked religious offices which functions on the cargo principle, in which each office is conceptualized as "bearing a burden" (or cargo, in Spanish). Within this hierarchy, which fulfills the function of the confraternities found elsewhere, there are 61 positions grouped into four levels of seniority. All cargo-holders must reside in the center for the duration of the office, and as they rise through the ranks, their expenses grow increasingly exorbitant. After occupying the most senior rank, a Zinacanteco can expect to retire as a poor but highly honored individual. This is a "burden" indeed!

Zinacanteco rituals involve formalized eating and drinking, and often large processions to sacred places. The abiding concern with rank is evident in how individuals are placed in these activities. There are many rituals for the curing and wellbeing of individuals, which involve a person's innate soul (*ch'ulel*), as well as their animal counterpart (every Zinacanteco has such an alter-ego, all of which live together in corrals within a 9,200-ft (2,800-m) high extinct volcano; the alter-ego is clearly cognate with the *mahy* of the Classic Maya).

There are waterhole and lineage rituals, as well as frequent ceremonies conducted in the ceremonial center by cargo-holders. But the greatest of all are the end-of-the-year/New Year cargo rites, which reach their culmination in the latter half of January in celebrations held in honor of St Sebastian. Like the myths which surround this Roman saint – themselves the result of four centuries of syncretism – these dramatic ceremonies show a heady mixture of Christian and Maya-pagan elements. Much of the action is pure theater, with actors ritually impersonating monkeys (animals left over from a previous Creation), jaguars, "Blackmen," and Spanish men and women. The entire religious drama is directed toward renewal of the universe and of the community, and ends with the transfer of the sacred objects of office to a new set of cargo-holders.

As Professor Vogt has said of these Zinacantan Maya, "they are a shrewd people, and have not retreated from the encroachment of *ladino* civilization. What is most valued and most vital to the culture has been reinforced, for the ritual life is, if anything, more intensified and elaborated than ever before."

THE YUKATEKO MAYA

The Spanish conquest of Yucatan was a protracted and by no means completely successful process, and it ended with Spanish control being confined to the northern third of the peninsula, along with portions of the west and east coasts. The foreign overlords lived in villas with European administrative machinery and the usual grid plan; around and between them were hundreds of Maya communities that were compelled to provide *encomienda* tribute and essentially forced labor, as well as to give up their "idolatry."

The ethnohistorian Grant Jones has documented that to the south and east lay a huge area inhabited by tens of thousands of Maya who had refused to submit to this oppression; this included most of the Peten and Belize, the east coast of the peninsula, and the region to the south of Campeche. At the heart of these defiant lands was Tah Itza (or Tayasal) which, as we have seen in Chapter 7, only surrendered to Spanish arms in 1697. Various attempts to colonize the region by the Spaniards failed time and time again, one reason being, as Professor Jones has found, that vast numbers of Yukateko Maya were arriving from the north, fleeing the terrible *encomienda* system. As a result, the eastern part of the peninsula – including most of what later became the Mexican Territory of Quintana Roo – remained a bastion of Maya independence until very recent times.

THE WAR OF THE CASTES

As in the highlands, the achievement of independence by the modern nation-states that control the Maya meant not a betterment of conditions for the latter, but a decline. The cruelty and misery of the sisal plantations and cattle ranches of Yucatan were amply documented in the books of John Lloyd Stephens, who saw them first hand. The storm that became known to rich whites in Yucatan as the "War of the Castes" broke out in 1847, not long after Stephens' visit. Almost all the Maya of the peninsula took up arms against the hated whites; eventually, the government troops held only Mérida, some towns along the coast, and the main road leading from Campeche. The Conquest had been reversed!

The dénouement of this story is well known: when the time came for the Indians to plant corn in their *milpas,* the native army disintegrated. Nonetheless, in 1850 the conflict was reignited, as in Chan Santa Cruz, a native village in central Quintana Roo, a miraculous "Talking Cross" began to prophesy a holy war against the whites. Bolstered by arms and other military equipment received from the British in Belize, the Maya of the region now formed into quasi-military companies and, inspired by messianic zeal, once more battled the armies of the oppressors. Fighting was not to end until 1901, when Federal forces under General Ignacio Bravo took Chan Santa Cruz. But Mexican government control gradually faded away during the ensuing decades, Talking Crosses proliferated, and the Maya of Quintana Roo went their own way (Coe saw a Talking Cross inside the Castillo at Tulum as late as 1948). Only the frantic development of tourism over the last thirty years has managed to spell the doom of Maya culture in this part of the peninsula.

THE MAYA OF CHAN KOM

Studied by the anthropologists Robert Redfield and Alfonso Villa Rojas in the 1930s, Chan Kom, located in just about the center of the Yucatan Peninsula, was the typical Yukateko Maya village. With its houses of white-washed walls and thatched roofs, and its women in spotlessly white *huipiles* edged with colorful embroidery, it offered a picture of rural tranquility belied by the turbulent history of victors and vanquished in the Maya lowlands. It has since been "modernized" considerably, with many of its people migrating to work in the tourist center of Cancun. But settlements like Chan Kom as it then was can yet be found throughout the peninsula.

Like their counterparts in Zinacantan, most of the Chan Kom Maya were and are maize farmers, but here they practice lowland slash-and-burn, shifting cultivation rather than the fixed-field systems of the highlands. There is the usual Spanish-style municipal government, but nothing like the religious hierarchy that is so striking among people like the Tsotsil. Two types of religious specialists practice here and in other traditional Yukateko settlements. One is the *Maestro Cantor* ("choirmaster"), a layman who nevertheless knows the Catholic prayers that may be used in Christian rituals like baptism, weddings, and funerals. The other is seemingly imbued with far greater spiritual and perhaps real power: this is the *hmeen,* "he who does or understands things" – that is, the shaman. *Hmeenob* are found all over the peninsula, even in large cities like Mérida, and are an integral part of the agricultural rituals so vital to rural life. Even though the traditional Maya 260-day calendar has disappeared in Yucatan, these specialists still play an important role in divination and prophecy, using their crystals to scry the future.

The supernatural world is ever-present in Chan Kom and in the outlying fields and forest. At the four entrances to the settlement are four pairs of crosses and four *balam* ("jaguar") spirits, watching to keep evil away from the villagers. The benevolent yet feared *balamob* also act as guardians of the cornfields. There are many *Chaakob*, rain gods descended from the Classic and Postclassic deity Chahk, visualized as old men on horseback, led by St Michael Archangel. Other supernaturals invoked in agricultural rites are deities of the forest in which the farmer must clear his plot, gods of the bees, and guardians of deer and cattle. Evil winds loose in the world can attack one and cause sickness; also to be avoided are the *aluxob*, leprechaun-like dwarves with large hats who bring misfortune.

Judging from the intensity of farming rituals in Yucatan, anxiety centered on subsistence must be far higher than in the highlands; as we have seen in Chapter 1, the peninsula has generally thin soils, and rainfall is far more sparse here than in the south. Underlying the ceremonies performed in the *milpas* of Chan Kom farmers is the idea that "what man wins from nature, he takes from the gods." The nature gods must be asked for favors, and duly repaid through prayers and offerings, including sacred foods and the first-fruits of the harvest.

The sacred foods are not consumed in everyday life: stacks of bean-smeared tortillas cooked in the *piib* or pit, *balche'* mead, *saka'* (sacred maize gruel), broth made from fowls, and sacrificed animals. About every fourth year, an individual farmer will sponsor an *u hanli kol* ("dinner of the *milpa*") rite, conducted by a *hmeen* at a rustic altar set with these holy foods and drink.

The largest and most dramatic of the Yukateko agricultural ceremonies is the *Ch'aa'-chaak*; its purpose is to request rain for a successful harvest, and thus it involves all members of a particular *ejido* (a unit of Mexican land distribution). The participants are exclusively men, who, in preparation for the ritual, withdraw for up to two days to the place on the village's outskirts where the *Ch'aa'-chaak* is to be held. The rite begins after the *hmeen* has consulted his *zaztun* or crystal. The altar is covered with fowl, venison, and the sacred breadstuffs and drink, all set out in predetermined order; under the altar, and tied to its legs, are four boys, who croak like the *wo* frogs which are harbingers of rain in the Maya lowlands. Off to one side is an older man, chosen to impersonate the *K'unk'u-chaak*, the chief of the rain gods, holding in one hand the calabash from which he unleashes rain on the cornfields, and in the other a wooden knife symbolizing the lightning that accompanies downpours.

The Maya *hmeenob* have other duties as well, most importantly to cure sickness, which the people of Chan Kom generally hold to come from evil winds and the evil eye; for this, curing rituals are held which include the usual offerings to the gods. As with their highland counterparts, these shamans also engage in divination, either by using their magic crystals, or by casting maize kernels. Witchcraft is an omnipresent danger; the witch takes the form of an animal alter-ego, and may be male or female. The witch visits sleeping individuals like the incubus of European folklore, and through illicit sex saps that person's strength.

THE LAKANDON

Visitors to the site of Palenque may well encounter near the entrance two or three Maya men, with long hair and wearing long, white robes, selling bows and arrows especially made to cater to the tourist trade. These are Lakandon, members of a stubbornly independent tribal group that some say number only 250, and others place at 500 or more. This discrepancy may arise from the fact that some of the Lakandon choose to live as *ladinos* for part of the year.

The Lakandon inhabit three small villages in what was once a vast rainforest in eastern Chiapas. Further archaeological vestiges of their communities, abandoned for a century or so, have been detected in Guatemala by Joel Palka of the University of Illinois, Chicago. Historically, the Lakandon originated as one of the Yukatekan refugee groups who chose to flee to the jungle fastnesses at the base of the peninsula rather than submit to Spanish rule. Other populations, perhaps speakers of Ch'olan languages, contributed to their numbers, as did descendants of Postclassic peoples in the Peten and Belize. While most Lakandon have been converted to fundamentalist Christianity, some have remained conservative, preserving many elements of the old Maya religion; until recently, these latter still made pilgrimages to the ruined temples of Yaxchilan, invoking the gods with their incense-filled pottery censers. At one time they hunted and farmed in an unbroken, high-canopied forest; this was set aside for them in the 1970s by presidential decree, an edict which was soon abrogated, releasing lumber companies to sack its valuable timber. The lumber trucks were followed by an army of landless peasants, largely impoverished Tseltal Maya from the highlands or Chol from Chiapas, who cut down much of what remained of the jungle. The final stage in the death of the Lakandon forest has been the conversion of peasant holdings to great cattle *fincas*, supplying beef to feed Americans' hunger for hamburgers.

UPRISING IN CHIAPAS

Most of the land, and all of the political life of the State of Chiapas, has been in the hands of *ladino* ranch owners and merchants for centuries. Closely allied with Mexico's powerful political party, the PRI, they have managed to keep the Maya majority disenfranchised and land-poor. The signing of the North American Free Trade Agreement (NAFTA) by Mexico and the United States threatened to further worsen the economic situation of the indigenous people in southeastern Mexico; the Maya seemed powerless. Then, on 1 January 1994, the Zapatista National Liberation Army (EZLN) – a guerrilla force of Tsotsil and Tseltal Maya, led by a *ladino* former university student calling himself "Subcomandante Marcos" – stormed San Cristóbal de las Casas, one of the major centers of *ladino* power in the state.

This was an unprecedented event in the history of Mexico, where the indigenous peoples have generally been mute and defenseless bystanders in whatever internal conflicts the country has gone through. In spite of the presence of tens of thousands of army troops brought in to control the situation, the Zapatistas managed for a time to maintain their armed resistance; and through a sophisticated use of the media (including the internet), they have won considerable sympathy for their cause from the rest of Mexico and the outside world. Their demands include economic, political, and cultural rights not only for the Maya of Chiapas, but also for all of Mexico's indigenous peoples. Whether Mexican governments, which have tended to pursue a policy of assimilation for Mexico's indigenous peoples, will ever accede to these demands remains to be seen. Nor can a certain irony be denied. At least some of the conflict arose from official attempts to set aside nature reserves and preserve traditional lands for the Lakandon. Similar conflicts are now playing out among the Q'eqchi' in southern Belize, relatively recent immigrants at times in conflict with the central government.

THE GREAT TERROR

The greatest and bloodiest episode in the "cycles of conquest" that have befallen the Maya since the arrival of the Spaniards began on 29 May 1978 in the Q'eqchi'-speaking town of Panzos in the Department of Alta Verapaz, Guatemala. There, a unit of the Guatemalan army opened fire on a group of Indians peacefully protesting the government's refusal to award them land titles. Over 100 men, women, and children were immediately killed.

Worse yet for the highland Maya, a second element had entered the picture: the Guerrilla Army of the Poor (later reorganized as the Guatemalan National Revolutionary Unity, or URNG), which had chosen to base its antigovernment operations in the western part of the highlands. Consisting largely of Marxist *ladinos*, at first led by ex-army officers, the guerrillas looked upon traditional Maya culture as an obstacle to the proletarian revolution which they intended to bring about. Nevertheless, the Indian villagers had little choice but to give them support in the way of food and shelter.

Retribution by the Guatemalan government, its army, and its police came swiftly: under a series of military regimes (some actively supported by the Reagan administration), the official security forces and governmental death squads unleashed a reign of terror against the Maya that was almost unprecedented in its ferocity. It is estimated by anthropologists such as George Lovell of Queen's University in Kingston (Ontario) that over one million Maya were displaced. According to a report by the National Academy of Sciences of the United States, approximately 150,000 people were killed, and an additional 40,000 "disappeared" – almost all of them Maya. By the end of the terrible decade of the 1980s, 35,000 Indian refugees were living in camps in Mexico, and thousands more had fled to the United States.

This was indeed ethnocide and genocide on a grand scale. Uprooted communities were forced into "model villages" (a move recommended by American military advisors), where able-bodied men were required to perform service in civil patrols. For hundreds of thousands of K'iche', Ixil, Mam, and other Maya, the traditional ties with the land had finally been shattered – or so the army leaders thought. As these immense disruptions took place, fundamentalist Christian missionaries from the United States, with government support (two recent presidents have been evangelical Protestants), began to make vast numbers of converts among Guatemala's Maya. This was accentuated by the steady reduction in Catholic priests, unable to serve larger communities, as well as a desire for new identities and the message of material prosperity promised by certain sects. With whole villages undergoing mass baptism, the effect on the traditional structure of Maya life (the confraternities and cargo system, for instance) may well be imagined.

THE MAYA FUTURE

Will the Maya survive? Like all peoples anywhere, they will surely change. And, to be sure, they have been under attack from every side: from the army and death squads in Guatemala, mass tourism and the destruction of the tropical forest in Mexico, and *ladino* encroachments onto their lands. These almost intolerable pressures have resulted in vast dislocations and migrations throughout the Maya area, further intensified by burgeoning populations and diminishing land for agriculturalists. Opportunities have proved better elsewhere. As of 2010 – though such tallies are difficult to specify with any precision – Guatemalans in the US are estimated to number close to 1.32 million. A good percentage of these were Maya. Some 10,000 speakers of Yukateko live and work in California alone, and rural communities in the Yucatan Peninsula have been nearly halved by this migration. A new, transnational identity will surely affect what it means to be Maya in the coming century. There has been another response too. In Guatemala, Maya intellectuals have realized that to survive, various Maya linguistic groups, heretofore separate, must come together to save their language and culture. And many more Maya now know that they can stand up to terror by speaking out: Rigoberta Menchú, a K'iche' Maya woman who lost most of her family to the death squads, did so – for which she was awarded the Nobel Peace Prize for 1992.

A turning point in the fortunes of the Maya may have been reached in Guatemala. In December 1995, with a new and less anti-Maya government in power (and a Democratic President in the White House), the regime signed a series of peace accords with the main guerrilla group, the URNG. Among the provisions (negotiated under United Nations auspices) were an accountability for all of the human rights violations perpetrated by the armed forces over the years, a resettlement of an estimated one million displaced persons (many of them, of course, Maya), and an affirmation of the cultural identity and rights of the indigenous Maya population. In fact, in Guatemala there is now bilingual instruction in several hundred schools, and active teaching of local Maya languages. Maya shamans have been granted permission to conduct their ceremonies in designated areas within major Maya sites such as Iximche, Utatlan, and Tikal. Yet the sad reality is that conditions of insecurity have only increased in recent years. Across the region, a present scourge is an unprecedented wave of gang- and drug-related violence, along with disputes over mining and land rights.

There is now a pan-Maya movement in eastern Mesoamerica, and a profound sense among these people of their glorious past. This has sometimes taken a millenarian form. For instance, the Yukateko of the Talking Cross villages in Quintana Roo prophesy a coming Great War, an Armageddon when (as they told Paul Sullivan) a new king will awaken in Chichen Itza, along with thousands of petrified beings from a past creation, and a stony Feathered Serpent will come to life and inflict havoc on the creatures of this creation. Messianic predictions like this will doubtless crop up again and again as pressures on the Maya intensify. Yet the Maya are actually increasing, not dwindling. They possess a heightened awareness of their proud history, as attested by the stunning works and cities their ancestors left behind. This great people will adapt but also, most surely, they will endure.

VISITING THE MAYA AREA

GENERAL INFORMATION

There are literally hundreds of Maya sites, of varying size and importance, distributed among five nation states: Mexico, Guatemala, Belize, Honduras, and El Salvador. It would take decades, perhaps a lifetime, to visit all of them. The interested traveler will have to make a balance between budget and available time before deciding on which ones to explore. Those with only a few weeks at their disposal should probably concentrate on the largest and most accessible sites; and it is these that usually have the best local accommodation. For more adventurous travelers, however, willing to put up with less-than-luxurious lodging – which might consist of a hammock slung in a thatched hut – there is the opportunity to explore jungle-shrouded ruins which few other tourists ever see.

When is the best time to go? Although one can travel at any time of the year in the Maya area, it should be remembered that in eastern Mesoamerica there are two strongly marked seasons. Depending on area, the dry season begins in late November and lasts until the coming of the rains in late May, and it is during that time that most organized archaeological tours take place. Some travel agencies believe that the optimal time is from November through January into early February, when daytime temperatures are relatively cool. But potential visitors should be aware that during those months, cold *nortes* (northers) may occasionally sweep down from Texas, bringing gray skies and often rain to the Yucatan Peninsula. As the dry season progresses, daytime temperatures increase; for many veteran visitors to the Maya cities, the least attractive months are April and May, when the thermometer reaches a maximum, smoke and haze from burning *milpas* obscure the sun, many trees lose their leaves, and (at least in Yucatan) the countryside is brown and sere.

Actually, the rainy season – in spite of the prevailing high humidity – has its advantages. There are far fewer fellow tourists, seed-ticks (a plague in off-the-beaten-track Yucatecan sites during the dry months) are almost totally absent, and there is a fresh greenness of vegetation that enhances the beauty of the ancient ruins. Except in the southeastern part of the lowlands, the rain itself usually lasts for only a few hours each day, generally in the afternoon or at night, so the mornings can be bright and sunny. But there is a downside here, too: backcountry roads and trails can become impossibly muddy and often impassable, even to four-wheeled vehicles, and biting insects, especially mosquitoes, require constant application of repellent. Dengue and malaria are still a problem in some areas.

Even though these are the tropics, and light clothing is recommended for daytime wear, nights can be chilly at any time of year (above all in the highlands of Guatemala and Chiapas, where freezing temperatures are not unknown in the winter months and, of late, even some snow in the highest reaches), so the traveler should always be armed with a sweater. Superior-quality hiking shoes, preferably waterproof, are recommended, and hats and other sun protection should be the rule – the sun's rays can be extremely strong and even dangerous at midday in most ruins. And keep in mind that even in the dry months it can rain at unexpected moments.

Medical advice can be found in any good travel guide to Mexico and Central America. The most common complaint afflicting not only tyros but also seasoned archaeologists, is the ubiquitous *turista* – travelers' diarrhea – which can make an otherwise enjoyable trip a misery. Prevention is imperative here. Under no circumstances should one drink any water other than what comes in sealed bottles or which has been boiled for at least twenty minutes; ice is equally treacherous. And the wary should avoid salads, uncooked vegetables and garnishes, and the skins of unpeeled fruits. The good news is that most cases of *turista* clear themselves up in a few days. Less predictable is security in a region that has, in places, deteriorating protection against criminals. Sectors of Guatemala and Belize City are visited at some risk: gang activity is on the rise, and transport on urban buses can be highly unsafe.

Transportation is remarkably good over most of the Maya area. Mexico in particular has good, all-weather roads, with excellent bus services between major cities. For those visitors with ample pocketbooks, car rental gives a great deal of flexibility and the ability to cover many more sites than would be possible by public transportation. Driving at night is ill-advised in all places. Some parts of the lowlands – in particular the Petexbatun area – lack road access, and the travel may be by more primitive means, such as mules or horses, dugout canoes, or by foot. Visitors should always put their feet and hands in places they can see clearly, as noxious creatures may be present.

Should one hire a guide? An advantage of an organized tour is that one's group is almost always accompanied by a professional archaeologist or art historian, well-versed in Maya culture history and (optimally) even in Maya hieroglyphic writing. Some local guides are excellent, particularly at Copan, Honduras, or Tikal, Guatemala, but many have little or no training, and may well relay information that has no basis in fact. The true aficionado of Maya culture would do best by reading as much as possible about the ancient Maya beforehand, and by attending one of the Maya hieroglyphic weekends or week-long seminars at the University of Texas in Austin or Tulane University; European visitors would benefit greatly from the Wayeb meetings held annually on that continent, shifting location by year.

Good site maps for the major Maya cities are available in various publications, including final reports. It is always a good idea to have Xerox copies of these in hand when exploring a particular ruin. In the more remote ruins, which may not be kept open by clearing, it may be wise to carry a pocket compass along with the map, as well as a bottle of purified water – this activity is only recommended, however, for the seasoned bush-whacker. It carries many dangers. A harbinger of the future of do-it-yourself archaeological tourism may well be the iPhone and iPad app now available for the small site of Tulum: http://goo.gl/oW9B3L.

THE "MUST-SEE" SITES

Every professional Mayanist – and every seasoned Maya traveler – has his or her own favorite Maya ruins. Those most favored not only are bigger than most of the others, but also possess outstanding architecture and/or a wealth of well-preserved sculpture. Six appear on almost everyone's list. These are Palenque, Yaxchilan, Uxmal, and Chichen Itza in Mexico; Tikal in Guatemala; and Copan in Honduras. No one who has failed to see all of these can really be said to know the Maya area. A determined traveler could probably visit all within a three-week period, although each requires at least three days to know well. The museums at Copan – soon, it seems, to be replaced by a larger one – are among the best in the Maya world.

There are, of course, dozens of "lesser" sites, a number of which may be even larger than some of the above giants – Calakmul in Campeche and El Mirador in northern Guatemala come to mind – but these are sometimes so hard to get to or so lacking in above-ground attractions that only the most dedicated "Maya buffs" would find it worth the difficulties which must be overcome to visit them. This is still true of El Mirador, but Calakmul is now reachable by an all-weather road, leading southwest from the Classic site at Xpujil on the Chetumal-Escárcega highway.

THE PUUC SITES

The jumping off point for Uxmal and other sites in the Puuc is Mérida, one of Mexico's more pleasant provincial capitals, with good hotels and a most interesting archaeological museum. Uxmal, with its magnificent Terminal Classic architecture, lies about an hour south of Mérida, along the main highway to Campeche; buildings like its wonderful Governor's Palace and Nunnery Quadrangle inspired Frank Lloyd Wright and other architects of our own age, and are not to be missed. Those wishing to explore not only Uxmal but Kabah, Sayil, and Labna can visit these sites easily by car, but many more remote Puuc sites require a four-wheeled vehicle. While in the area, no Maya enthusiast should overlook Loltun Cave, which now has electric illumination; in this case, a local guide familiar with the cavern is a good idea. The well-preserved colonial city of Campeche and its light-filled museums are well worth visiting, too.

CHICHEN ITZA AND THE EASTERN PENINSULA

At least three days are required to do justice to Chichen Itza, an enormous and complex city which is still poorly understood. Easily reached from Mérida via a virtual superhighway, and equally accessible to tourists from Yucatan's so-called "Riviera Maya" – the resort of Cancun – it sometimes seems inundated with tourists, yet its sheer size makes it possible to get away from the crowds. Here is a site which has sculptures and reliefs in enormous profusion, all belonging to the Terminal Classic and Postclassic periods; its ball court is the largest in Mesoamerica, and the austere Castillo pyramid and the Sacred Cenote, rich in history, are very impressive indeed. Visitors should also not miss Ek' Balam and its remarkable stuccoes, some 33 miles (55 km) northeast of Chichen.

There are Late Postclassic sites all along the east coast, some of them almost minuscule. One of the most visited (perhaps too much so) is little Tulum, spectacularly perched on a cliff above the blue Caribbean. Sadly, it is now being "loved to death" by tour and cruise groups. Less thronged with tourists is the inland city of Coba, set among a series of beautiful lakes.

Crossing the base of the Yucatan Peninsula is an all-weather highway which gives access to several impressive Río Bec sites such as Xpuhil, Becan, and Chicanna, as well as a very early (Late Preclassic or beginning Early Classic) pyramid at Kohunlich, with large stucco masks of Maya gods. Dzibanche, probable seat of a dynasty ending up at Calakmul, is well worth a visit. These can all be seen in a single day, although if one wishes to venture further afield, such as to Río Bec itself, more time and a degree of stamina are necessary.

PALENQUE AND TONINA

If one could see only one Maya site, many are convinced that Palenque should be it: the lush forest setting, with views out over the coastal plain, the delicate architecture, and the beauty of its bas-reliefs and stuccoes are all enhanced by the detailed historical background that modern scholars have provided for this great city. At least two to four days are required to appreciate it, although one could easily spend a week here. One should not miss the beautiful Cross Group, the Palace, and a visit to Pakal the Great's tomb. There are a number of good hotels in the vicinity, and there is a superb and up-to-date museum at the site.

The acropolis-like ruins of Tonina, currently under excavation, are accessible by car over a paved road from Ocosingo, a town reached from the highway between Palenque and Tuxtla Gutierrez (the capital of Chiapas). Rich in Late Classic three-dimensional sculpture, Tonina has a recently-discovered stucco relief illustrating episodes in the Maya epic, the Popol

Vuh. Prepare to be puzzled: there is an excellent but eccentric local museum, with fine objects placed in often arbitrary, poorly labelled arrangements.

YAXCHILAN AND BONAMPAK

The easiest way to visit Yaxchilan and Bonampak is by renting a light plane in Palenque and Villahermosa, although some visitors now travel overland by a road which is promised to be passable even during the wet season. Yaxchilan is much the largest of the two, a Late Classic city arranged on a group of low hills and ridges above the Usumacinta River; there is much sculpture still left at the site. Bonampak is famed for the wonderful wall paintings contained in one small building, although inept cleaning and restoration, and deterioration due to the elements, have tragically rendered these to but a shadow of what they once were. Yaxchilan, incidentally, is one of several Usumacinta sites which can be visited through a trip down the river on inflatable rafts, but since the river forms the border between Mexico and Guatemala, much depends on the political situation in these countries. As of 2015, it is still a dangerous region, made even more so by an upsurge in drug- and human-trafficking through Guatemala north to Mexico and, ultimately, to the United States.

GUATEMALA: THE HIGHLANDS AND PACIFIC COAST

The largest museum in Guatemala City is the Museo Nacional de Arqueología y Etnología, in which many of the treasures excavated at the country's Maya sites are housed. The visitor should not, however, miss the far more up-to-date museums at the Universidad Francisco Marroquín: the Museo Ixchel, which concentrates on indigenous costume and textiles, and the Museo Popol Vuh, which has splendid and well-exhibited pre-Conquest objects. On the western outskirts of the city, in its own park, is what remains of the once-huge site of Kaminaljuyu, but there is little to see other than mounds. However, in the part of the site near the Tikal Futuro skyscraper there is the Museo Miraflores, which provides an excellent introduction to the Preclassic and Classic history of the site. Apart from the breathtaking Lake Atitlan, fringed with Maya towns and villages, the highland traveler should see one or all of the great Late Postclassic capitals: Iximche, Utatlan (Q'umarkaj), and Mixco Viejo, all three quite accessible by car.

A day trip down to Escuintla and the compact Cotzumalhuapa area is a highly advised side trip. The more important sites are located on coffee and/or cotton *fincas*, and the headquarters of each *finca* usually has a collection of sculptures. If one visits the Finca El Baúl on Sunday morning, one may see Maya shamans conducting ceremonies before the ancient carvings. While on the Pacific Coast plain, be prepared for torrid daytime temperatures.

THE PETEN

Tikal is reached by air from Guatemala City, most visitors staying in or near the Peten capital, Flores (site of the Itza island capital of Tayasal); they are then bussed up to the ruins. During the dry season, one can also drive to Flores from the Belize border. To appreciate properly this great and ancient city, with its towering temple-pyramids, one should budget at least three days. Not the least of its attractions is the surrounding tropical forest, with its wealth of birds and animals. The traveler should also not miss the local Museo Sylvanus G. Morley, which has on display many fine objects excavated at Tikal over the past decades, as well as the stela museum across from the now-abandoned airstrip at the ruins. A new conservation center has other objects on display, but access is limited.

There are around ten other major Classic sites in the northern Peten, such as Uaxactun, but other than Uaxactun these are usually difficult to reach and may require travel by jeep, mule, or foot over trails which can be extremely muddy at times. Only the most determined enthusiasts should attempt the journey.

Somewhat more accessible are Maya ruins in the southwestern Peten. The base for their exploration is Sayaxche, a frontier town with very basic accommodation and an active contraband culture that warrants caution. To reach these, one must hire an outboard-powered dugout in Sayaxche; there is a certain amount of overland hiking from wherever the boat puts in to shore. Ceibal is a very large ruined city on the Río Pasión, upriver from Sayaxche, which was excavated and partly restored by Harvard University, and studied more recently by Takeshi Inomata and Daniela Triadan of the University of Arizona; there are still several important stelae there in situ. One can gain access to the Petexbatun sites to the south and southwest of Sayaxche by boat, but it is a considerable hike over an often muddy trail to reach Dos Pilas, the largest of these sites. Potential visitors should also be warned that one has to bring in camping gear, and that many hundreds of landless peasants have illegally moved into this supposedly protected park area following the signing of the Guatemalan peace accords in 1995.

BELIZE

Reached in the dry season by a long dirt road, Caracol – the largest site in Belize – lies on the western edge of the Maya Mountains. It has twenty major plazas surrounded by temples, a few of which have been restored. Most of its carved monuments have been removed to the University Museum in Philadelphia, and to the Archaeology Museum in Belmopan, Belize's capital. Other visitors may wish to visit the Museum of Belize (a former prison from colonial days) in Belize City, an atmospheric reminder that Belize belongs to the English-speaking Caribbean. Nonetheless, both there and in parts of Guatemala and Honduras, visitors should be aware of high levels of crime.

So far as its environment and its historical heritage are concerned, Belize is in some ways the most progressive country in the region, with a farsighted, ongoing archaeological program. The two main sites to see here are Altun Ha, a modest-sized Classic center 35 miles (55 km) north of Belize City along a paved highway; and Xunantunich, a far larger center on the Guatemalan border, near the modern town of Benque Viejo. Neither has noteworthy stone monuments, but Xunantunich is distinguished by some important, ornate stucco facades embellishing the summit of a large temple-pyramid. Lamanai is also of note, with a small museum and a handsome location on a river.

RECOMMENDED READING

COE, ANDREW. *Archaeological Mexico: A Traveler's Guide to Ancient Cities and Sacred Sites.* Second edition. Emeryville (California) 2001.

KELLY, JOYCE. *An Archaeological Guide to Mexico's Yucatan Peninsula.* Norman (Oklahoma) 1993.

—, *An Archaeological Guide to Northern Central America: Belize, Guatemala, Honduras, and El Salvador.* Norman (Oklahoma) 1996.

—, *An Archaeological Guide to Central and Southern Mexico.* Norman (Oklahoma) 2001.

WRIGHT, RONALD. *Time Among the Maya: Travels in Belize, Guatemala and Mexico.* Grove Press (New York) 2000.

DYNASTIC RULERS
OF CLASSIC MAYA CITIES

Thanks to epigraphic research which has been going on since the early 1950s, a great deal is known about the kings and queens who ruled the Classic Maya cities in the Central Area. In some cases we are sure about their actual Maya names, but in cases where we are not, scholars refer to them by modern nicknames (indicated by inverted commas). The purpose of these nicknames is purely mnemonic – they may have little relation to linguistic reality. One may reasonably ask, why is it that *all* of these personal names have not been "cracked"?

The answer is that most of the glyphs standing for them are the hardest of all to decipher, for they generally are logograms for which phonetic substitutions or complements have not yet been – and may never be – discovered; fantastic animal heads and parts of animals are particularly common in these nominals.

In several cities, above all in Palenque, a number of kings prefaced their names with the title *K'inich*, meaning "Sun-faced," "Sun-eyed," or "Great Sun," probably because those rulers claimed descent from K'inich Ajaw, the Sun God.

In the following lists, compiled by Simon Martin and Nikolai Grube, the first date represents accession to the throne, while the second date is that of the ruler's death. A single date indicates that the ruler is known to be in power at that time. All dates are AD.

Tikal

c. 90	Yax Ehb Xook
? – ?	"Foliated Jaguar"
?	"Animal Headdress"
c. 307	Sihyaj Chan K'awiil I
c. 317	Unen Bahlam
? – 359	K'inich Muwaan Jol
360 – 378	Chak Tok Ich'aak I
379 – 404?	Yax Nuun Ahiin I
411 – 456	Sihyaj Chan K'awiil II
458 – 486?	K'an Chitam
c. 486 – 508	Chak Tok Ich'aak II
511 – c. 527	"Lady of Tikal"
c. 511 – c. 527	Kaloomte' Bahlam
?	"Bird Claw"
537 – 562	Wak Chan K'awiil

c. 593	"Animal Skull"
? – ?	"23rd and 24th Rulers"
c. 657 – c. 679	Nuun Ujol Chahk
682 – 734	Jasaw Chan K'awiil I ("Ruler A")
734 – c. 746	Yik'in Chan K'awiil ("Ruler B")
c. 766 – 768	"28th Ruler"
768 – c. 794	Yax Nuun Ahiin II ("Ruler C")
c. 800?	Nuun Ujol K'inich
c. 810	"Dark Sun"
c. 849	"Jewel K'awiil"
c. 869	Jasaw Chan K'awiil II

Calakmul

? – ?	Yuknoom Ch'een I
c. 520 – c. 546	K'altuun Hix
c. 561 – 572	"Sky Witness"
572 – 579	Yax Yopaat
579 – c. 611	"Scroll Serpent"
c. 619	Yuknoom Ti' Chan
622 – 630	Tajoom Uk'ab K'ahk'
630 – 636	Yuknoom "Head"
636 – 686	Yuknoom Ch'een II ("the Great")
686 – c. 695	Yuknoom Yich'aak K'ahk' ("Fiery Claw")
c. 702 – c. 731	Yuknoom Took' K'awiil
c. 736	Wamaw K'awiil
c. 741	"Ruler Y"
c. 751	"Great Serpent"
c. 771 – 789?	Bolon K'awiil
c. 849	Chan Pet
c. 909	Aj Took'

Naranjo

?	Tsik'in Bahlam
?	Naatz Chan Ahk
? – ?	Tajal Chahk
546 – c. 615	Aj Wosaaj Chan K'inich
c. 629 – 631?	K'uxaj
c. 644 – 680	K'ahk' "Skull" Chan Chahk
682 – 741	"Lady Six Sky"
693 – c. 728	K'ahk' Tiliw Chan Chahk ("Smoking Squirrel")
? – 744	Yax Mayuy Chan Chahk
746 – ?	K'ahk' Yipiiy Chan Chahk
755 – c. 780	K'ahk' Ukalaw Chan Chahk ("Smoking Batab")

?	Bat K'awiil
784 – c. 810	Itzamnaaj K'awiil ("Shield God K")
814 – ?	Waxaklahun Unbah K'awiil

Yaxchilan

359 – ?	Yopaat Bahlam I
?	Itzamnaaj Bahlam I
378 – 389	"Bird Jaguar I"
389 – 402?	"Yax Deer-antler Skull"
402 – ?	"Ruler 5"
?	K'inich Tatbu "Skull" I
c. 454 – 467	"Moon Skull"
467 – ?	"Bird Jaguar II"
c. 508 – c. 518	"Knot-eye Jaguar I"
526 – c. 537	K'inich Tatbu "Skull" II
c. 564	"Knot-eye Jaguar II"
c. 599	Itzamnaaj Bahlam II
?	K'inich Tatbu "Skull" III
629 – c. 669	"Bird Jaguar III"
681 – 742	Itzamnaaj Bahlam III ("Shield Jaguar the Great")
c. 749	Yopaat Bahlam II
752 – 768	"Bird Jaguar IV" ("Bird Jaguar the Great")
c. 769 – c. 800	Itzamnaaj Bahlam IV
c. 808	K'inich Tatbu "Skull" IV

Piedras Negras

c. 460	"Ruler A"
c. 460	"Ruler B"
c. 508 – c. 510	"Turtle Tooth"
c. 514 – c. 518	"Ruler C"
603 – 639	K'inich Yo'nal Ahk I
639 – 686	"Ruler 2"
687 – 729	K'inich Yo'nal Ahk II
729 – 757	"Ruler 4"
758 – 767	Yo'nal Ahk III
767 – 781	Ha K'in Xook
781 – 808?	"Ruler 7"

Dos Pilas

c. 648 – c. 692	Bailaj Chan K'awiil ("Ruler 1")
698 – 726	Itzamnaaj K'awiil ("Ruler 2")
727 – 741	"Ruler 3"
741 – c. 761	K'awiil Chan K'inich ("Ruler 4")

Palenque

431 – 435	K'uk' Bahlam I
435 – 487	"Casper"
487 – 501	Butz'aj Sak Chiik
501 – 524	Ahkal Mo' Nahb I
529 – 565	K'an Joy Chitam I
565 – 570	Ahkal Mo' Nahb II
572 – 583	Kan Bahlam I
583 – 604	Lady Yohl Ik'nal
605 – 612	Ajen Yohl Mat
612 – 615	Muwaan Mat
615 – 683	K'inich Janaab Pakal I ("the Great")
684 – 702	K'inich Kan Bahlam II ("Chan Bahlum")
702 – c. 720	K'inich K'an Joy Chitam II
721 – c. 736	K'inich Ahkal Mo' Nahb III
c. 742	K'inich Janaab Pakal II
c. 751	K'inich Kan Bahlam III
764 – c. 783	K'inich K'uk' Bahlam II
799 – ?	Janaab Pakal III

Caracol

331 – c. 349	Te' K'ab Chahk
c. 470	K'ahk' Ujol K'inich I
484 – c. 514	Yajaw Te' K'inich I
531 – c. 534	K'an I
553 – 599	Yajaw Te' K'inich II
599 – 618?	"Knot Ajaw"
618 – 658	K'an II
658 – c. 680	K'ahk' Ujol K'inich II
c. 702	"Ruler VII"
c. 793?	Tum Yol K'inich
799 – c. 803	K'inich Joy K'awiil
c. 810 – c. 830	K'inich Toobil Yopaat
c. 835 – c. 849	K'an III
c. 859	"Ruler XIII"

Copan

426 – c. 437	K'inich Yax K'uk' Mo'
c. 437 – ?	K'inich Popol Hol
?	"Ruler 3"
?	K'altuun Hix
?	"Ruler 5"
?	"Ruler 6"
524 – 532	Bahlam Nehn
532 – 551	Wi' Yohl K'inich
551 – 553	"Ruler 9"
553 – 578	"Moon Jaguar"
578 – 628	Butz' Chan
628 – 695	"Smoke Imix God K"
695 – 738	Waxaklahun Ubah K'awiil
738 – 749	K'ahk' Joplaj Chan K'awiil
749 – c. 761	K'ahk' Yipyaj Kan K'awiil
763 – c. 810	Yax Pahsaj Chan Yopaat
822	Ukit Tok'

Quirigua

426 – ?	Tok "Casper"
c. 455	Tutuum Yohl K'inich
c. 480	"Ruler 3"
c. 652	K'awiil Yopaat
724 – 785	K'ahk' Tiliw Chan Yopaat ("Kawak Sky")
785 – c. 795	"Sky Xul"
c. 800 – c. 810	"Jade Sky"

FURTHER READING

An up-to-date, comprehensive bibliography on the ancient, Colonial, and contemporary Maya would number in the many thousands of entries. The closest is an online, searchable source on the remarkable FAMSI website, http://research.famsi.org/mesobib.php; yet other treasures await those perusing http://www.mesoweb.com/. Here we have tried to concentrate on those articles and volumes that have proved most useful in the preparation of this book, and which might be of interest to those wishing to follow certain topics further. Three important series specializing in Maya culture should be consulted: *Estudios de Cultura Maya*, published since 1961 by the Centro de Estudios Mayas, Universidad Nacional Autónoma de México, *Research Reports on Ancient Maya Writing*, issued since 1985 by the Center for Maya Research, Washington, D.C., but now concluded as a series, and *The PARI Journal*, published by the Pre-Columbian Art Research Institute, San Francisco. Justin Kerr's Maya Vase Database contains over 1,850 photographic roll-outs of painted or carved Classic Maya vases, and is available at http://www.mayavase.com/. Specialist articles also appear in *Ancient Mesoamerica, Latin American Antiquity*, and *Mexicon. Arqueología Mexicana* publishes high-quality articles, in color, of finds from the Maya region as well as other parts of Mexico. An exceptionally useful series of annual proceedings from Guatemala may be consulted at: http://www.asociacion-tikal.com/. A reliable and active blog is moderated by David Stuart at: http://decipherment.wordpress.com/.

ABRAMS, ELLIOT M. *How the Maya Built Their World: Energetics and Ancient Architecture.* Austin 1994.

ANDREWS, ANTHONY P. *Maya Salt Production and Trade.* Tucson 1983. (Thorough study of an important Maya industry.)

ANDREWS, E. WYLLYS IV, and E. WYLLYS ANDREWS V. *Excavations at Dzibilchaltun, Yucatán, Mexico.* Middle American Research Institute, Tulane University, Publication 48. New Orleans 1980.

ASHMORE, WENDY. *Settlement Archaeology at Quirigua.* University Museum Monograph 126. Philadelphia 2007.

ASSELBERGS, FLORINE. *Conquered Conquistadors: The* Lienzo de Quauhquechollan, *A Nahua Vision of the Conquest of Guatemala.* Boulder 2004. (An amazing pictorial document detailing the role of indigenous allies from central Mexico in the subjugation of the Mayas of Guatemala.)

AVENI, ANTHONY F. *Skywatchers of Ancient Mexico.* Austin 1980. (The clearest introduction to Maya astronomy.)

BELL, ELLEN E., MARCELLO CANUTO, and ROBERT J. SHARER (eds). *Understanding Early Classic Copan.* Philadelphia 2004. (Among seventeen essays are descriptions and analyses of the spectacular finds at the base of the city's state temple.)

BENSON, ELIZABETH P., and GILLETT G. GRIFFIN (eds). *Maya Iconography.* Princeton 1988. (Pioneering essays on Maya art and epigraphy.)

BERLIN, HEINRICH. "El glifo emblema en las inscripciones mayas," *Journal de la Société des Américanistes*, vol. 47 (1958):111–119. (Article that presaged the historical approach to the inscriptions.)

BRENNER, MARK, *et al.* "Paleolimnology of the Maya lowlands: long-term perspectives on interactions among climate, environment, and humans," *Ancient Mesoamerica*, vol. 13 (2002):141–157.

BRICKER, HARVEY M., and VICTORIA R. BRICKER. *Astronomy in the Maya Codices.* Memoirs of the American Philosophical Society 265. Philadelphia 2011. (Numerically focused report on astronomy in Maya books.)

CARMACK, ROBERT M. *Quichean Civilization.* Berkeley and Los Angeles 1973. (Overview of the Postclassic K'iche' Maya of Guatemala.)

—, *The Quiché Maya of Utatlán.* Norman 1981.

—, *Rebels of Highland Guatemala: The Quiche-Mayas of Momostenango.* Norman 1995. Carr, Robert F., and James E. Hazard. "Map of the Ruins of Tikal, El Peten, Guatemala," in *Tikal Reports* no. 11. Philadelphia 1961.

CARRASCO VARGAS, RAMÓN, and MARÍA CORDEIRO BAQUEIRO. "The murals of Chiik Nahb Structure Subt 1–4, Calakmul, Mexico," in *Maya Archaeology 2*, eds C. Golden, S. Houston, and J. Skidmore, 8–59. San Francisco 2012. (Description of spectacular murals at Calakmul.)

CHAMBERLAIN, ROBERT S. *The Conquest and colonization of Yucatán.* Carnegie Institution of Washington, publ. 582. Washington 1948.

CHASE, ARLEN F., and PRUDENCE M. RICE (eds). *The Lowland Maya Postclassic.* Austin 1985. (Nineteen essays covering all aspects of the subject, up to the fall of Tayasal in 1697.)

CHEETHAM, DAVID. "Cunil: a pre-Mamom horizon in the southern Maya lowlands," in *New Perspectives on Formative Mesoamerican Cultures*, ed. T. G. Powis, 27–37. Oxford 2005.

CHINCHILLA MAZARIEGOS, OSWALDO. *Cotzumalguapa: la ciudad arqueológica, El Baúl-Bilbao-El Castillo.* Guatemala 2012. (Important, non-Maya cities in coastal and piedmont Guatemala, touching on relations to the Pipil.)

CHRISTENSEN, ALLEN J. (trans. and ed.). *Popol Vuh. The Sacred Book of the Maya.* New York 2003. (A scholarly edition of the great K'iche' Maya epic, a masterpiece of Native American literature.)

CLARK, JOHN E., and DAVID CHEETHAM. "Mesoamerica's tribal foundations," in *The Archaeology of Tribal Societies*, ed. W. A. Parkinson. Ann Arbor 2002. (Complete overview of Mesoamerica from Archaic times through the Middle Preclassic.)

COE, MICHAEL D. *The Maya Scribe and His World.* New York 1973. (Iconographic and epigraphic study of Maya vases, with description of the Grolier Codex.)

—, *Breaking the Maya Code.* Third edition. London and New York 2011. (History of the Maya decipherment.)

COE, MICHAEL D., and KENT V. FLANNERY. *Early Cultures and Human Ecology in South Coastal Guatemala.* Washington 1967. (Early Preclassic investigations.)

COE, MICHAEL D., and JUSTIN KERR. *The Art of the Maya Scribe*. London 1997, New York 1998. (A study of Maya calligraphy, and of the scribes and artists who produced it.)

COE, MICHAEL D., and MARK VAN STONE. *Reading the Maya Glyphs*. Revised edition. London and New York 2005. (An epigraphic handbook for beginning students.)

COE, SOPHIE D. *America's First Cuisines*. Austin 1994. (Maya foodstuffs and cooking are described in Chapters 7–11.)

COE, WILLIAM. *Tikal: A Handbook of the Ancient Maya Ruins*. Philadelphia 1967.

—, *Excavations in the Great Plaza, North Terrace and North Acropolis, of Tikal*. 6 vols. Tikal Report No. 14 The University Museum. Philadelphia 1990.

COGGINS, CLEMENCY C., and ORRIN C. SHANK (eds). *Cenote of Sacrifice: Maya Treasures from the Sacred Well at Chichen Itza*. Austin 1984. (Catalogue of objects recovered from the *cenote* at the beginning of the twentieth century.)

CULBERT, T. PATRICK. *The Ceramics of Tikal*. Philadelphia 1993. (Useful visual source on whole vessels from Tikal.)

CURTIS, JASON H., DAVID A. HODELL, and MARK BRENNER. "Climate variability on the Yucatan Peninsula (Mexico) during the past 3500 years, and implications for Maya cultural evolution," *Quaternary Research*, 46 (1996):37–47.

DEMAREST, ARTHUR, PRUDENCE M. RICE, and DON S. RICE (eds). *The Terminal Classic in the Maya Lowlands: Collapse, Transition, and Transformation*. Boulder 2004. (Essays on the end of the Classic period.)

DIEHL, RICHARD A. *The Olmecs: America's First Civilization*. London and New York 2004. (A readable, up-to-date introduction to the "mother culture" of Mesoamerica.)

DOYLE, JAMES A. "Re-Group on 'E-Groups': monumentality and early centers in the Middle Preclassic Maya lowlands," *Latin American Antiquity*, vol. 23 (2012):355–379. (Review of early Maya architectural plans and their meaning.)

EMERY, KITTY F. (ED.). *Maya Zooarchaeology: New Directions in Method and Theory*. Los Angeles, 2004. (Essays on fauna among the ancient Maya.)

ESTRADA-BELLI, FRANCISCO. *The First Maya Civilization: Ritual and Power Before the Classic Period*. New York 2011. (Synthesis of research on the Preclassic period.)

—, et al. "Two Early Classic Maya murals: new texts and images in Maya and Teotihuacan style from La Sufricaya, Petén, Guatemala." http://antiquity.ac.uk/projgall/estrada-bellio6/

EVANS, SUSAN. *Ancient Meixico and Central America: Archaeology and Culture History*. Third edition. London and New York 2001. (A thorough and up-to-date textbook covering all of Pre-Columbian Mesoamerica.)

FASH, WILLIAM L. *Scribes, Warriors and Kings: The City of Copán and the Ancient Maya*. Revised edition. London and New York 2001. (Authoritative introduction to this important city, combining archaeology, iconography, and dynastic analysis.)

FEDICK, SCOTT L. (ED.). *The Managed Mosaic: Ancient Maya Agriculture and Resource Use*. Salt Lake City 1996.

FINAMORE, DANIEL, and STEPHEN HOUSTON. *Fiery Pool: The Maya and the Mythic Sea*. New Haven 2010. (Catalogue of exhibit on the maritime orientation of Maya civilization.)

FIZSIMMONS, JAMES L. *Death and the Classic Kings*. Austin 2009. (Synthesis of research about royal death-practices and beliefs.)

FOX, JOHN W. *Quiché Conquest: Centralism and Regionalism in Highland Guatemalan State Development*. Albuquerque 1978.

(Argues for the Gulf Coast origin of the Postclassic highland elites.)

FREIDEL, DAVID, LINDA SCHELE, and JOY PARKER. *Maya Cosmos: Three Thousand Years on the Shaman's Path*. New York 1993. (Interpretation of the Creation Myth and cosmology in the lives of the ancient and modern Maya.)

GONZÁLEZ CRUZ, ARNOLD. *La reina roja: una tumba real de Palenque*. Mexico City 2011. (Lavish publication of queen's tomb.)

GRAHAM, ELIZABETH. *Maya Christians and Their Churches in Sixteenth-Century Belize*. Gainesville 2011. (Archaeology of religious encounters in the early Colonial period.)

GRAHAM, IAN. *Alfred Maudslay and the Maya*. Norman 2002. (Biography of a pioneering Maya archaeologist.)

GRUBE, NIKOLAI (ED.). *Maya: Divine Kings of the Rain Forest*. Köln 2001. (Lavishly and beautifully illustrated collection of essays on all aspects of Maya civilization.)

GRUBE, NIKOLAI. *Der Dresdender Maya-Kalender: Der vollständige Codex*. Freiburg 2012.

GRUBE, NIKOLAI, and WERNER NAHM. "A census of Xibalbá: a complete inventory of Way characters on Maya ceramics," in *The Maya Vase Book*, No. 4. New York 1994:686–715,

GUERNSEY, JULIA. *Sculpture and Social Dynamics in Preclassic Mesoamerica*. Cambridge 2012. (Early sculptures in coastal and piedmont Guatemala and adjacent zones.)

HANKS, WILLIAM F. *Referential Practice: Language and Lived Space among the Maya*. Chicago 1990. (Sophisticated description of Maya ritual practice and daily use of language.)

—, *Converting Words: Maya in the Age of the Cross*. Berkeley 2010. (Language and religious conversion in Yucatan.)

HANSEN, RICHARD D. "The Maya rediscovered: the road to Nakbé," *Natural History*, May 1991, pp. 8–14. New York. (Investigations at a great, Late Preclassic city.)

—, "El Mirador, Guatemala, y el apogeo del Preclásico en el area maya," *Arqueología Mexicana* 11, 66 (2004):26–33.

HARRISON, PETER D. *The Lords of Tikal*. London and New York 1999. (Up-to-date history of the city for the general reader and student.)

HARRISON, PETER D., and B. L. TURNER H. (eds). *Pre-Hispanic Maya Agriculture*. Albuquerque 1978.

HAY, CLARENCE L., et al. (eds). *The Maya and their Neighbors*. New York 1940. (A now-classic festschrift dedicated to the great Mayanist Alfred M. Tozzer.)

HOUSTON, STEPHEN D. *Hieroglyphs and History at Dos Pilas: Dynastic Politics of the Classic Maya*. Austin 1993. (Study of micro-history in one region of Peten, Guatemala.)

—, *The Life Within: Classic Maya and the Matter of Permanence*. New Haven 2014. (Maya concepts about materials.)

HOUSTON, STEPHEN D., and TAKESHI INOMATA. *The Classic Maya*. Cambridge 2009.

HOUSTON, STEPHEN D., KARL A. TAUBE, and DAVID STUART. *The Memory of Bones: Body, Being, and Experience among the Classic Maya*. Austin 2006. (Emotions and the human senses as expressed in iconography and hieroglyphs.)

HOUSTON, STEPHEN D., et al. *Veiled Brightness: A History of Ancient Maya Color*. Austin 2009. (Study of color use and meaning over time.)

HUTSON, SCOTT. *Dwelling, Identity, and the Maya: Relational Archaeology at Chunchucmil*. Lanham 2010. (Ways of life in ancient Yucatan.)

IANNONE, GYLES (ED.). *The Great Maya Droughts in Cultural Context*. Boulder 2014. (Discussion of droughts and their effects on Maya civilization.)

INOMATA, TAKESHI, et al. "Early ceremonial constructions at Ceibal, Guatemala, and the origins of lowland Maya civilization," *Science*, vol. 340 (2013):467–471.

INOMATA, TAKESHI, and DANIELA TRIADAN (eds). *Burned Palaces and Elite Residences of Aguateca: Excavations and Ceramics*. Salt Lake City 2010. (Report on the Classic Maya "Pompeii" in a first-rate monograph.)

INOMATA, TAKESHI, and STEPHEN D. HOUSTON (eds). *Royal Courts of the Ancient Maya*. 2 vols. Boulder, Colorado, and Oxford 2001.

JOHNSTON, KEVIN J. "The 'invisible' Maya: minimally mounded residential settlement at Itzan, Peten, Guatemala," *Latin American Antiquity* 15(2004):145–175. (Discovery of "invisible" house mounds, suggesting that the estimates of Classic Maya population have been far too low.)

JONES, GRANT D. *Maya Resistance to Spanish Rule: Time and History on a Colonial Frontier*. Albuquerque 1989. (Documentary history of the independent Maya of southern Yucatan and the Peten.)

JUST, BRYAN. *Dancing into Dreams: Maya Vase Painting of the Ik' Kingdom*. Princeton 2012. (Best monograph on a single class of fine Classic-era pottery.)

KENNETT, DOUGLAS S., et al. "Development and disintegration of Maya political systems in response to climate change," *Science*, vol. 338 (2012):788–791. (Study of cave deposits in Belize as indicators of climate change.)

KERR, JUSTIN. *The Maya Vase Book*. Vols. 1–5. New York 1989–1997. (A series presenting rollouts of Maya vases, accompanied by important essays on ceramic iconography and epigraphy.)

KIDDER, ALFRED V., JESSE L. JENNINGS, and EDWIN M. SHOOK. *Excavations at Kaminaljuyu, Guatemala*. Carnegie Institution of Washington, publ. 561. Washington 1946. (Excavation of Early Classic Esperanza tombs.)

KNOROSOV, YURI V. "The problem of the study of the Maya hieroglyphic writing," *American Antiquity*, vol. 23, no. 3 (1958):284–291. (First American publication of Knorosov's revolutionary approach to the glyphs.)

KOWALSKI, JEFF K. *The House of the Governor: A Maya Palace at Uxmal, Yucatan, Mexico*. Norman 1987. (Important architectural and iconographic study of a major administrative building of the Puuc.)

KRISTAN-GRAHAM, CYNTHIA, and JEFF KOWALSKI (eds). *Twin Tollans: Chichén Itzá, Tula, and the Epiclassic to Early Postclassic Mesoamerican World*. Washington 2007. (Essays from a Dumbarton Oaks conference on one of Mesoamerica's thorniest problems.)

LAPORTE, JUAN PEDRO, and JUAN ANTONIO VALDÉS. *Tikal y Uaxactún en el Preclásico*. Mexico 1993. (Important study of Guatemalan research at two crucial cities.)

LAW, DANNY. "Mayan historical linguistics in a new age," *Language and Linguistics Compass*, vol. 7 (2013): 141–156. (Recent developments in Mayan linguistics.)

LEE, THOMAS A. (ED.). *Los códices mayas*. Tuxtla Gutiérrez 1985. (Facsimile edition of all four codices.)

LITTLE, WALTER E. *Mayas in the Marketplace: Tourism, Globalization, and Cultural Identity*. Austin 2004. (Maya economic relations with the outside world, especially in tourist centers of Guatemala.)

LOHSE, JON C. "Archaic origins of the lowland Maya," *Latin American Antiquity*, vol. 21, no. 3 (2010):312–352.

LOOPER, MATTHEW G. *To Be Like Gods: Dance in Ancient Maya Civilization*. Austin 2009. (A study of ritual dance among the Maya elite, and its many levels of meaning.)

LOTHROP, SAMUEL K. *Tulum, An Archaeological Study of the East Coast of Yucatan*. Carnegie Institution of Washington, publ. 335. Washington 1924.

LOUNSBURY, FLOYD G. "Maya numeration, computation, and calendrical astronomy," in *Dictionary of Scientific Biography*, vol. 15, supplement I (1978):759 818. (Full account of these subjects, written for the advanced student.)

LOWE, GARETH W., THOMAS E. LEE, and EDUARDO E. MARTÍNEZ. *Izapa: An Introduction to the Ruins and Monuments*. Papers of the New World Archaeological Foundation, no. 31. Provo 1973. (Definitive study of the type site of the Izapan civilization.)

LUZZADDER-BEACH, SHERYL, et al. "Maya models and distant mirrors: wetland fields, drought, and the Maya abandonment," *Proceedings of the National Academy of Science*, vol. 109 (2012):3646–3651.

MARTIN, SIMON. "Hieroglyphs from the painted pyramid: the epigraphy of Chiik Nahb Structure Sub 1–4, Calakmul, Mexico," in *Maya Archaeology 2*, eds C. Golden, S. Houston, and J. Skidmore, 60–81. San Francisco 2012. (Study of hieroglyphs in murals at Calakmul.)

MARTIN, SIMON, and NIKOLAI GRUBE. *Chronicle of the Maya Kings and Queens*. Second edition. London and New York 2008. (Complete guide to the dynasties that ruled Classic cities, based upon the latest epigraphic and archaeological research. A must for every Mayanist library.)

MASSON, MARILYN A. A., and CARLOS PERAZA LOPE. *Kukulcan's Realm: Urban Life at Ancient Mayapán*. Boulder 2014. (Excavations in urban settlement at important Postclassic city in Yucatan.)

MATHENY, RAY T. (ED.). *El Mirador, Petén, Guatemala: An Interim Report*. Papers of the New World Archaeological Foundation, no. 45. Provo 1980. (Investigations at the largest Late Preclassic city.)

MATHENY, RAY, et al. *Investigations at Edzná, Campeche, Mexico*. Papers of the New World Archaeological Foundation, no. 46. Provo 1980 and 1983.

MAUDSLAY, ALFRED P. *Biologia Centrali-Americana, Archaeology*. Text and 4 vols. of plates. London 1889 1902. (Magnificent photographs and drawings of Maya monuments and cities; a milestone in the history of Maya research.)

MAXWELL, JUDITH M., and ROBERT M. HILL II. *Kaqchikel Chronicles: The Definitive Edition*. Austin 2006. (English translation of highland Maya historical documents.)

MCANANY, PATRICIA. *Living with the Ancestors: Kinship and Kingship in Ancient Maya Society*. Second edition. Austin 2014. (Sophisticated study of relations with the ancestors in Preclassic and Classic periods.)

—, *Ancestral Maya Economies in Archaeological Perspective*. Cambridge 2010. (Comprehensive view of Pre-Columbian Maya economics.)

MCGEE, R. JON. LIFE, *Ritual and Religion Among the Lacandón Maya*. Belmont 1990.

MENCHÚ, RIGOBERTA. *I, Rigoberta Menchú*. London 1984. (Firsthand account of the terror inflicted on the Maya of Guatemala, by the winner of the 1992 Nobel Prize for Peace.)

MILLER, ARTHUR G. *On the Edge of the Sea: Mural Painting at Tancah-Tulum, Quintana Roo*. Washington 1982. (Postclassic art in the eastern Yucatan Peninsula.)

MILLER, MARY. *The Art of Mesoamerica from Olmec to Aztec*. Fifth edition. London and New York 2012. (Excellent introduction to Mesoamerican culture as a whole.)

MILLER, MARY, and CLAUDIA BRITTENHAM. *The Spectacle of the Late Maya Court: Reflections on the Murals of Bonampak*. Austin 2013. (Thorough study of the greatest Maya murals.)

MILLER, MARY, and SIMON MARTIN. *Courtly Art of the Ancient Maya*. London and New York 2004. (Superb exhibition catalogue concentrating on the royal palace art of the Late Classic period.)

MILLER, MARY, and MEGAN E. O'NEIL. *Maya Art and Architecture*. Second edition. London and New York 2014. (Strong overview of Maya visual production.)

MILLER, MARY, and KARL TAUBE. *The Gods and Symbols of Ancient Mexico and the Maya: An Illustrated Dictionary of Mesoamerican Religion*. London and New York 1993. (Indispensable for understanding the mental world of the ancient Maya.)

MORLEY, SYLVANUS G. *The Inscriptions of Petén*. Carnegie Institution of Washington, publ. 437, 5 vols. Washington 1937–1938. (A basic resource on Maya inscriptions.)

MORRIS, EARL H., *et al. The Temple of the Warriors at Chichen Itzá, Yucatan*. Carnegie Institution of Washington, publ. 406, 2 vols. Washington 1931.

MORRIS, WALTER F., JR. *Living Maya*. New York 1987. (The text emphasizes the weaver's art, and has photographs of the contemporary Maya of Chiapas.)

PALKA, JOEL. *Unconquered Lacandon Maya: Ethnohistory and Archaeology of Indigenous Culture Change*. Gainesville 2005. (Archaeological vestiges of the Lakandon Maya.)

PARSONS, LEE A. *The Origins of Monumental Stone Sculpture of Kaminaljuyu, Guatemala, and the Southern Pacific Coast*. Dumbarton Oaks Studies in Pre-Columbian Art and Archaeology, no. 28. Washington 1986. (Study of a major body of Late Preclassic sculpture.)

PENDERGAST, DAVID M. *Excavations at Altun Ha, Belize, 1964–1970*. Toronto: Vol. 1, 1979; Vol. 2, 1982.

—, "Lamanai, Belize: summary of excavation results 1974–1980," *Journal of Field Archaeology*, vol. 8, no. 1 (1981):29–53.

PILLSBURY, JOANNE, *et al.* (eds). *Ancient Maya Art at Dumbarton Oaks*. Washington, DC, 2012. (Finest museum catalogue yet produced of Maya art.)

POLLOCK, H. E. D. *The Puuc: An Architectural Survey of the Hill Country of Yucatan and Northern Campeche, Mexico*. Memoirs of the Peabody Museum of Archaeology and Ethnology, Harvard University, vol. 19. Cambridge, Mass. 1980.

POLLOCK, H. E. D., *et al. Mayapán, Yucatan, Mexico*. Carnegie Institution of Washington, publ. 619. Washington 1962. (The account of Itza history in Chapter 7 is largely based upon the Roys essay.)

PREM, HANNS J. (ED.). *Hidden Among the Hills: Maya Archaeology of the Northwest Yucatan Peninsula*. Acta Mesoamericana 7. Möckmühl 1994. (Seventeen essays present recent thinking about cultural developments in the Northern Area, including Chichen Itza. Especially important is Karl Taube's study of Toltec iconography as it appears at Chichen.)

PROSKOURIAKOFF, TATIANA. *An Album of Maya Architecture*. Carnegie Institution of Washington, publ. 558. Washington 1946. (Reconstructions of Maya cities.)

—, *A Study of Classic Maya Sculpture*. Carnegie Institution of Washington, publ. 593. Washington 1950. (Stylistic dating of Maya monuments.)

—, "Historical implication of a pattern of dates at Piedras Negras, Guatemala," *American Antiquity*, vol. 25, no. 4 (1960):454–475. (A now-classic paper which established the historical nature of the Maya inscriptions.)

—, "The lords of the Maya realm," *Expedition*, vol. 4, no. 1 (1961):14–21. (A less technical treatment of the 1960 paper.)

REDFIELD, ROBERT, and ALFONSO VILLA ROJAS. *Chan Kom, A Maya Village*. Chicago 1962. (Classic anthropological study of a Yucatec Maya community.)

REED, NELSON. *The Caste War of Yucatán*. Stanford 1964. (Documentary history of the great nineteenth-century uprising by the Yucatec Maya.)

REENTS-BUDET, DORIE. *Painting the Maya Universe*. Durham and London 1994. (Beautiful exposition of Maya vase painting.)

RESTALL, MATTHEW. *Maya Conquistador*. Boston 1998. (Documentary study of the conquest of Yucatan, a complex history of collaboration, resistance, and adjustment.)

ROBERTSON, JOHN S., DANNY LAW, and ROBBIE A. HAERTEL. *Colonial Ch'olti': The Seventeenth-Century Morán Manuscript*. Oklahoma 2010. (Authoritative analysis of language most closely linked to the Classic-period inscriptions.)

RICE, PRUDENCE M., and DON S. RICE (eds). *The Kowoj: Identity, Migration, and Geopolitics in Late Postclassic Petén, Guatemala*. Boulder 2009. (Postclassic and Colonial history and archaeology in northern Guatemala.)

RINGLE, WILLIAM M. "The art of war: imagery of the Upper Temple of the Jaguars, Chichen Itza," *Ancient Mesoamerica*, vol. 20, no. 1 (2009):15–44. (Analysis of now-disappeared polychrome murals depicting battle scenes.)

ROBERTSON, MERLE GREENE. *The Sculpture of Palenque*. 4 vols. Princeton 1983–1991. (The most complete survey of the sculpture of any Maya city, magnificently illustrated.)

—, *Palenque Round Table Series* (Mesa Redonda de Palenque). (gen. ed.). Nos. 1–2, Pebble Beach, California 1974–1976. No. 3, Palenque 1979. Nos. 4–5, San Francisco 1985. No. 6, Norman 1991. No. 7, San Francisco 1994. (Much information on Maya iconography and epigraphy has appeared in this indispensable series.)

ROBIN, CYNTHIA. *Everyday Life Matters: Maya Farmers at Chan*. Gainesville 2014. (Study of peasant life in Belize.)

ROSENSWIG, ROBERT M., *et al.* "Archaic period settlement and subsistence in the Maya lowlands: new starch grain and lithic data from Freshwater Creek, Belize," *Journal of Archaeological Science*, vol. 41 (2014):308–321. (Important synthesis of the Maya Archaic.)

ROYS, RALPH L. *The Book of Chilam Balam of Chumayel*. Carnegie Institution of Washington, publ. 438. Washington 1933. (Annotated translation of the most important native Colonial-period text from the Maya lowlands.)

—, *The Indian Background of Colonial Yucatán*. Carnegie Institution of Washington, publ. 548. Washington 1943. (Documentary study of Late Postclassic Yucatan.)

—, *The Political Geography of the Yucatán Maya*. Carnegie Institution of Washington, publ. 613. Washington 1957. (Should be read in conjunction with the above.)

RUPPERT, KARL, J. E. S. THOMPSON, and TATIANA PROSKOURIAKOFF. *Bonampak, Chiapas, Mexico*. Carnegie Institution of

Washington, publ. 602. Washington 1955. (Reproduces Antonio Tejeda's copies of the murals.)

RUZ LHUILLIER, ALBERTO. *El Templo de las Inscripciones, Palenque.* Mexico City 1973. (Report on Pakal the Great's tomb, by its excavator.)

SABLOFF, JEREMY A. (ED.). *Tikal: Dynasties, Foreigners & Affairs of State.* Santa Fe 2003.

SATURNO, WILLIAM A., *et al.* "Ancient Maya astronomical tables from Xultun, Guatemala," *Science* 336 (2012):714–717.

SATURNO, WILLIAM A., DAVID STUART, and BORIS BELTRÁN. "Early Maya writing at San Bartolo, Guatemala," *Science* 311(2006):1281–1293.

SATURNO, WILLIAM A., KARL A. TAUBE, and DAVID STUART. *The Murals of San Bartolo, El Petén, Guatemala.* Ancient America 7. Barnardsville 2006.

SCARBOROUGH, VERNON L. "Ecology and ritual: water management and the Maya," *Latin American Antiquity*, vol. 9 (1998):135–159.

SCARBOROUGH, VERNON L., and DAVID R. WILCOX (eds). *The Mesoamerican Ballgame.* Tucson 1991.

SCHELE, LINDA, and PETER MATHEWS. *The Code of Kings: The Language of Seven Sacred Maya Temples and Tombs.* New York 1998. (Study of seven Classic and Postclassic sites.)

SCHELE, LINDA, and MARY E. MILLER. *The Blood of Kings: Dynasty and Ritual in Maya Art.* Fort Worth 1986, London 1992. (Catalogue of a ground-breaking exhibition of Maya art.)

SCHORTMAN, EDWARD M. *Archaeological Investigations in the Lower Motagua Valley, Izabal, Guatemala.* University Museum Monograph 80. Philadelphia 1993.

SEVER, THOMAS L., and DANIEL E. IRWIN. "Remote-sensing investigation of the ancient Maya in the Peten rainforest of northern Guatemala," *Ancient Mesoamerica*, vol. 14 (2003):113–122. (Research on the puzzle of the *bajos*.)

SHARER, ROBERT J. "Quiriguá Project 1974–1979," *Expedition*, vol. 23, no. 1 (1980):5–10.

SHARER, ROBERT J., with LOA TRAXLER. *The Ancient Maya.* Sixth edition. Stanford 2005. (A comprehensively rewritten edition of Sylvanus Morley's classic general book on the Maya, with extensive bibliography.)

SHEETS, PAYSON (ed.). *Before the Volcano Erupted: The Ancient Cerén Village in Central America.* Austin 2002.

SHOOK, EDWIN M., and ALFRED V. KIDDER. *Mound E III-3, Kaminaljuyu, Guatemala.* Carnegie Institution of Washington, Contributions to American Anthropology and History, no. 53. Washington 1952. (Excavation of rich Miraflores-period tombs.)

SMITH, A. LEDYARD. *Uaxactún, Guatemala: Excavations of 1931–1937.* Carnegie Institution of Washington, publ. 588. Washington 1950.

SMITH, ROBERT E. *Ceramic Sequence at Uaxactun, Guatemala.* Middle American Research Institute, publ. 20, 2 vols. New Orleans 1955. (Established the archaeological chronology of the southern Maya lowlands.)

SOLER-ARECHALDE, ANA MARÍA, *et al.* "Archaeomagnetic investigation of oriented pre-Columbian lime-plasters from Teotihuacan, Mesoamerica," *Earth, Planets, and Space*, vol. 58 (2006):1433–1439. (More precise dating of Teotihuacan's destruction.)

STEPHENS, JOHN L. *Incidents of Travel in Central America, Chiapas, and Yucatan,* 2 vols. New York 1841. (With the 1843 work, both illustrated by Frederick Catherwood, brought the Maya civilization to the attention of the outside world; still eminently readable.)

—, *Incidents of Travel in Yucatan,* 2 vols. New York 1843.

STONE, ANDREA. *Images from the Underworld: Naj Tunich and the Tradition of Maya Cave Painting.* Austin 1995. (Complete publication of the Naj Tunich paintings and texts, along with a perceptive treatment of the role played by caves in the Maya psyche.)

STONE, ANDREA, and MARC ZENDER. *Reading Maya Art: A Hieroglyphic Guide to Ancient Maya Painting and Sculpture.* London and New York 2011. (Insightful integration of Maya imagery and writing.)

STUART, DAVID. *Ten Phonetic Syllables.* Research Reports on Ancient Maya Writing, no. 14. Washington 1987. (A major epigraphic advance, building on the methodology pioneered by Knorosov.)

—, "The arrival of strangers: Teotihuacan and Tollan in Classic Maya History," in *Mesoamerica's Classic Heritage*, eds D. Carrasco, L. Jones, and S. Sessions, 465–513. Boulder, Colorado 2000.

—, *The Inscriptions from Temple XIX at Palenque.* San Francisco 2005. (The hieroglyphic record of one of Palenque's greatest kings, K'inich Ahkal Mo' Nahb.)

—, *The Order of Days: Unlocking the Secrets of the Ancient Maya.* New York 2012. (Thorough account of the function and meaning of the Maya calendar, with critical comment on the "2012" phenomenon.)

STUART, DAVID, and STEPHEN HOUSTON. *Classic Maya Place Names.* Washington 1994. (Discovery of glyphs for ancient Maya geography.)

STUART, DAVID, and GEORGE E. STUART. *Palenque: Eternal City of the Maya.* London and New York 2008. (An immensely readable and well-illustrated history of this beautiful Maya city.)

STUART, GEORGE E. "Quest for decipherment: a historical and biographical survey of Maya hieroglyphic investigation," in *New Theories on the Ancient Maya*, eds E. C. Danien and R. J. Sharer, 1–63. Philadelphia 1992. (Compact study of Maya decipherment, especially in the nineteenth century.)

—, "The royal crypts of Copan," *National Geographic*, December 1997, 68–93. (Reports the very early and spectacular tombs and structures found deeply buried in Copan's Acropolis.)

SULLIVAN, PAUL. *Unfinished Conversations: Mayas and Foreigners Between Two Wars.* New York 1989. (Perceptive account of the extraordinary dialogue in the 1930s between the Maya of Quintana Roo and the Carnegie archaeologists based at Chichen Itza.)

TATE, CAROLYN E. *Yaxchilan: The Design of a Maya Ceremonial Center.* Austin 1992.

TAUBE, KARL A. *The Major Gods of Ancient Yucatan.* Dumbarton Oaks Studies in Pre-Columbian Art and Archaeology, no. 32. Washington 1992. (Definitive study of Maya religious iconography.)

—, *Aztec and Maya Myths.* London 1993.

TEDLOCK, BARBARA. *Time and the Highland Maya.* Albuquerque 1982. (Herself an initiated day-keeper, the author shows how the ancient calendar functions in K'iche' life and society.)

THOMPSON, J. ERIC S. *Maya Hieroglyphic Writing: Introduction.* Carnegie Institution of Washington publ. 589. Washington 1950. (A monumental survey of Maya calendrics, religion, and astronomy, but written before the adoption of the historical and phonetic approaches to the glyphs.)

—, *A Catalog of Maya Hieroglyphs*. Norman 1962. (Covers glyphs of both the monuments and codices. While now in universal use, in bad need of revision.)

—, *Maya History and Religion*. Norman 1970. (Contains first-class studies of Maya ethnohistory. Especially important for its treatment of the Putun Maya.)

TOZZER, ALFRED M. *Chichen Itzá and its Cenote of Sacrifice*. Memoirs of the Peabody Museum of Archaeology and Ethnology, Harvard University, vols. 11, 12. Cambridge, Mass. 1957.

—, (ed.). *Landa's Relación de las Cosas de Yucatan*. Papers of the Peabody Museum of Archaeology and Ethnology, Harvard University, vol. 18. Cambridge, M ass. 1941. (Thanks to the extensive notes which accompany Landa's text, this is virtually an encyclopedia of Maya life.)

VILLACORTA, J. ANTONIO and CARLOS A VILLACORTA. *Códices Mayas*. Guatemala 1930. (Three of the four Maya hieroglyphic books reproduced by line drawings in a useful edition.)

VOGT, EVON Z. *Zinacantan: A Maya Community in the Highlands of Chiapas*. Cambridge, Mass. 1969. (A classic study of the contemporary Tsotsil Maya.)

VOLTA, BENJAMINO and GEOFFREY E. BRASWELL. "Alternative narratives and missing data: Refining the chronology of Chichen Itza," in *The Maya and Their Central American Neighbors: Settlement Patterns, Architecture, Hieroglyphic Texts and Ceramics*, ed. G. F. Braswell, 402–356. New York 2014. (Useful study of Chichen Itza's difficult chronology.)

WEBSTER, DAVID. *The Fall of the Ancient Maya*. London and New York 2002. (The definitive treatment of the Maya Collapse, with up-to-date evidence from sites like Copan and Piedras Negras.)

WILLEY, GORDON R. *The Altar de Sacrificios Excavations: General Summary and Conclusions*. Papers of the Peabody Museum of Archaeology and Ethnology, vol. 74, no. 3. Cambridge, Mass. 1973.

—, "General summary and conclusions," in *Excavations at Seibal*. Memoirs of the Peabody Museum of Archaeology, Harvard University, vol. 17, no. 4. Cambridge, Mass. 1990. (Ceibal – "Seibal" – was a huge Classic city on the Pasión, with important Preclassic and Terminal Classic components.)

—, *et al. Prehistoric Maya Settlements in the Belize Valley*. Papers of the Peabody Museum of Archaeology and Ethnology, Harvard University, vol. 54. Cambridge, Mass. 1965. (A pioneering work on Maya settlement pattern.)

WILLEY, GORDON R., and PETER MATHEWS (eds). *A Consideration of the Early Classic Period in the Maya Lowlands*. Institute for Mesoamerican Studies, publ. 10. Albany 1985. (Combines archaeological and epigraphic evidence.)

ZIMMERMAN, GÜNTER. *Die Hieroglyphen der Maya Handschriften*. Hamburg 1956. (A catalog of the glyphs in the codices, still useful.)

▼▼▼▼▼▼▼▼▼▼

SOURCES OF ILLUSTRATIONS

INDEX

Numerals in *italic* refer to
illustration numbers.

Acanceh 9, 123, 126; *61*
Actun Halal 45, 48
Adams, Richard 112
agriculture 16, 19–22, 49, 70,
 73–74, 84, 107, 174, 176,
 201, 230, 232, 248, 296; *62*;
 see also raised fields; terraces
aguadas 17
Aguateca 96, 150–51, 175,
 256; *170*
Agurcia, Ricardo 120
Ah Kauil Chel 199
Ah Xupan 199
Ahkal Mo' Nahb 7, 157, 160,
 164; *91, 99*; V
alcohol 290, 293; *see also*
 named alcoholic beverages
Almendáriz, Ricardo 25
alphabet 259, 266–69; *171*
Alta Verapaz 23, 30, 171,
 232, 299
Altar de Sacrificios 57, 168; *105*
Altar Q (Copan) 118; *74*
Altar of Zoomorph O
 (Quirigua) *75*
altars 108, 124, 129, 132,
 139, 237, 276, 292, 297; *28,
 73, 75*
Altun Ha 108, 141, 146, 160,
 277, 305; *178*
Alvarado, Jorge de 227, 289
Alvarado, Pedro de 224,
 227, 289
Amatitlan, Lake 54, 103; *16*
Andrews, Anthony 23, 213
Antigua Basin 196
apron moldings 81, 90, 120, 123
Archaic period 26, 46–49,
 58, 61; *12*
Argentina 13
arithmetic 259
Armijo, Ricardo 160, 243
Arroyo de Piedra 95, 150
Arroyo, Barbara 57
Asia 164, 247
Asselbergs, Florine 227
astrology 263

astronomy 61, 82, 193, 243,
 262, 263, 265, 270; *see also*
 Milky Way; stars and named
 constellations
Atitlan, Lake 28, 101, 291,
 304; *2*
Atlantic 15, 201
atlatl 99, 201, 231; *56*
Avendaño, Father 139
Aveni, Anthony 193, 263
avocado 18, 22, 56, 231
Awe, Jaime 8
axes 131, 230, 253, 290
Aztecs 9, 11, 20, 31, 48, 70,
 83, 100–1, 126, 129, 136,
 156, 178, 196, 206, 210, 215,
 218, 224, 227, 232, 233, 235,
 239, 241, 249, 250, 255, 266

Baaknal Chahk 161
Bacabs, Ritual of the 252
bajos 17, 20–21, 32, 49, 85,
 87, 139
bakab 248
Balankanche 212; *133*
balche' 232, 290, 297
ball court 70, 72, 132, 136,
 161, 196, 206, 209, 210, 216,
 224, 226, 304; *49, 70, 119,
 129, 130*
ball game 71, 196, 198, 258
ball players 70, 198, 210; *120*
Balsas River 46
baptism 233, 289, 296, 300
bar-and-dot numeration 67,
 99, 198, 259, 265
Barnhart, Edwin 151
Barra phase 50; *13*
Barrientos, Tomás 276
Barrios, President Rufino 280
basalt 45, 52; *27*
Bat God *101*
Beach, Sheryl 8
Beach, Timothy 8, 20
beans 13, 16, 46, 48, 230, 297
Becan 122, 125, 244, 304; *157*
Belize 7, 8, 11, 16, 17, 20–24,
 30, 45, 47, 48, 57, 59, 69, 84,
 85, 108, 116, 120, 124, 146,
 160, 171, 216, 223, 227, 231,

277, 279, 295, 296, 298, 299,
 302, 305; *5, 12, 19, 59, 62,
 140, 147–49, 178*
Belize City 302, 305
Belize River 17, 177
Benque Viejo 305
Bering Strait 41
Berlin, Heinrich 271, 274
Bernal Romero, Guillermo 160
Bey, George 194
Bilbao 196
Bird Jaguar 97, 273–74; *156,
 168, 175, 176*; XI
Black God *see* Ek' Chuwah
Black Jaguar *see* Ek' Balam
blades 23, 45, 48, 113, 123,
 171, 257; *27*
Blake, Michael 49–50
bloodletting 13, 89, 129, 150,
 184, 242, 274; *84, 156, 157*;
 XII, XXV
Blue Creek *5*
Bolontewitz 23
Bonampak 9, 126, 146–50, 156,
 164, 263, 304; *98*; XV, XVII
Bonampak murals 87, 149,
 150, 168, 174, 178, 274; XV,
 XVI, XVII
bone 43, 140; *27*
books 30, 116, 175, 219, 234,
 237, 239, 243, 250, 258; *155*;
 screenfold 13, 177; *153;*
 XII; *see also* named books
 and codices
Borhegyi, Stephan de 76
Bourbourg, Abbé Brasseur
 de 265
bow-and-arrow 231, 236
Brady, James 245
Brainerd, George 179
Braswell, Geoffrey 206, 215
Bravo, General Ignacio 296
breadnut tree 18, 231
Bronson, Bennett 22
Bronze Age 51, 54
Brown, Clifford 217
Bryan, Alan 45
burials 51, 59, 83, 86, 103,
 104, 106, 107, 111, 120, 160,
 168, 232, 234, 237, 253,

256, 274; *27, 32, 34, 50,
 51, 55, 66, 151;* XIV, XXI,
 XXII, XXIII, XXIV; *see also*
 funerals; mummification;
 offerings; tombs
Butterfly Goddess 106
Butz' Chan 121

cacao 50, 54, 70, 101, 112,
 196, 198, 230, 231, 232,
 290; *53*
Cacaxtla 178; XX
Cahal Pech 57
Calakmul 7, 81, 93, 95, 116,
 126, 144–46, 150, 160, 233,
 275, 276, 303, 304; *82, 83,
 151, 177*
calendar 9, 25, 31, 54, 60,
 61, 63–68, 72, 80, 89, 91,
 98, 107, 129, 198, 212, 219,
 237, 243, 249, 259–62, 265,
 289, 296; *21; see also* Long
 Count; Short Count
Calendar Round 25, 63, 65,
 66, 67, 73, 168, 260, 261,
 274, 292; *23, 105*
Callaghan, Michael 84
Campeche 16, 18, 20, 21, 24,
 31, 81, 90, 161, 162, 164,
 168, 171, 178, 202, 216, 231,
 232, 279, 295, 303; *109, 115,
 135, 136, 152*; XXVI
Cancuen 144, 171, 276
Cancun 296, 303
canoes 71, 146, 202, 231, 233,
 303; *81, 122*
Cantón Corralito 54
Canuto, Marcelo 8, 276
captives 41, 80, 99, 103, 124,
 129, 131, 150, 151, 161, 164,
 175, 219, 225, 236, 242, 272,
 275; *42, 151, 176*; XV
Caracol, Belize 21, 108, 116,
 120, 124, 146, 276, 305; *62*
Caracol, the (Chichen Itza)
 193, 263; *125*; VIII
Caribbean 13, 15, 16, 17,
 23, 98, 179, 220, 246, 304,
 305; *142*
Carmack, Robert 224